# ICSE 10

## CHEMISTRY

## 12 + 1 SAMPLE PAPERS

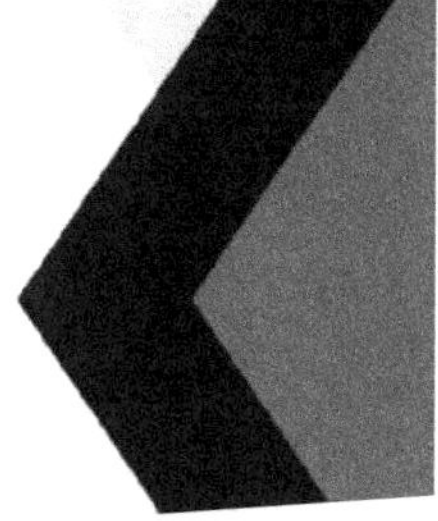

## KAUSHLESH DWIVEDI

### EDUCATOR

M.Sc. (Chemistry), B.Ed. (Science)

**BOARD SAMPLE PAPER WITH SOLUTION & ANALYSIS BASED ON LATEST CIRCULAR ISSUED IN JULY FOR 2022-23 EXAM**

| Title | : ICSE Class 10 Chemistry |
| --- | --- |
| **Author Name** | : Mr. Kaushlesh Dwivedi |
| **Published By** | : EduGorilla Community Pvt. Ltd. |
| **Publishers Address** | : Sector-12/651, First Floor Opp. Arvindo Park, Near Jama Masjid, Indira Nagar, Lucknow, Uttar Pradesh-226016, India |

## Copyright



- +91-63932 16806, +91-78000 04200
- book@edugorilla.com
- www.edugorilla.com

## Disclaimer

Although the author and publisher have made every effort to ensure the accuracy of information in this book, we do not assume any responsibility to errors and hereby disclaim any liability to any party for any loss, damage, or disruption caused by errors or omissions, whether such errors or omissions result from negligence, accident, or any other cause.

Created & Compiled by EduGorilla Publication

**Printed by EduGorilla Community Pvt. Ltd.**

# INDEX

## ICSE X CHEMISTRY



## TO GET FREE ACCESS SCAN THE QR CODE

* PREVIOUS YEAR PAPERS
* TOPPERS ANSWER SHEET
* STUDY NOTES & VIDEO LECTURES
* VIDEO SOLUTION OF SELF-ASSESSMENT PAPERS
* LIVE DISCUSSION ON MEQ (MOST EXPECTED QUESTIONS)

**SCIENCE (52)**
**CHEMISTRY**
**SCIENCE Paper - 2**
**CLASS X**

There will be one written paper of **two hours** duration of **80 marks** and Internal Assessment of practical work carrying **20 marks**.

**Note:** All chemical processes / reactions should be studied with reference to the reactants, products, conditions, observation, the (balanced) equations and diagrams.

**1 Periodic Properties and variations of Properties – Physical and Chemical**

(i) Periodic properties and their variations in groups and periods.

Definitions and trends of the following periodic properties in groups and periods should be studied: • atomic size

- Metallic character
- Non-metallic character
- Ionisation potential
- Electron affinity
- Electronegativity

(ii) Periodicity on the basis of atomic number for elements.

- The study of modern periodic table up to period 4(students to be exposed to the complete modern periodic table but no questions will be asked on elements beyond period 4 - Calcium).
- Periodicity and other related properties to be explained on the basis of nuclear charge and shells (not orbitals).

  **(Special reference to the alkali metals, alkaline earth metals, halogens and inert gases).**

**2 Chemical Bonding**

**Electrovalent,** covalent and co-ordinate bonding, structures of various compounds, Electron dot structure.

**(a)** Electrovalent bonding:

- Electron dot structure of Electrovalent compounds NaCl, MgCl2, CaO.

- Characteristic properties of electrovalent compounds – state of existence, melting and boiling points, conductivity (heat and electricity), dissociation in Answer. and in molten state to be linked with electrolysis.

**(b)** Covalent Bonding:

- Electron dot structure of covalent molecules on the basis of duplet and octet of electrons (example: hydrogen, oxygen, chlorine, nitrogen, ammonia, carbon tetrachloride, methane.
- Polar Covalent compounds – based on difference in electronegativity:
- Examples – HCl, NH3 and H2O including structures.
- Characteristic properties of Covalent compounds – state of existence, melting and boiling points, conductivity (heat and electricity), ionisation in Answer..

  **Comparison of Electrovalent and Covalent compounds.**

**(c)** Coordinate Bonding:

- Definition

  The lone pair effect of the oxygen atom of the water molecule and the nitrogen atom of the ammonia molecule to explain the formation of $H_3O^+$ and $OH^-$ ions in water and $NH_4^+$ ion.

  **The meaning of lone pair; the formation of hydronium ion and ammonium ion must be explained with the help of electron dot diagrams.**

**3** Study of Acids, Bases and Salts

  (i) Simple definitions, classification and their characteristic properties.

  (ii) Ions present in mineral acids, alkalis and salts and their Answer.s; use of litmus and pH paper to test for acidity and alkalinity.

- Examples with equation for the ionisation/dissociation of acids, bases and salts.
- Acids form hydronium ions (only positive ions) which turn blue litmus red, alkalis form hydroxyl ions (only negative ions) with water which turns red litmus blue.
- Salts are formed by partial or complete replacement of the hydrogen ion of an acid by a metal or ionic definition of salt. (To be explained with suitable examples).
- Introduction to pH scale to test for acidity, neutrality and alkalinity by using pH paper or Universal indicator and common acid base indicators.

  (iii) Types of salts: normal salts, acid salt, basic salt, definition and examples.

  (iv) Action of dilute acids on salts. Decomposition of hydrogen carbonates, **carbonates**, sulphites and sulphides by appropriate acids with heating if necessary.
(Relevant laboratory work must be done).

**4** Analytical Chemistry

  (i) Action of Ammonium Hydroxide and Sodium Hydroxide on Answer. of salts: colour of salt and its Answer.; formation and colour of hydroxide precipitated for Answer.s of salts of Ca, Fe, Cu, Zn and Pb; special action of ammonium hydroxide on Answer.s of copper salt and sodium hydroxide on ammonium salts.
On Answer. of salts:

- Colour of salt and its Answer..
- Action on addition of Sodium Hydroxide to Answer. of Ca, Fe, Cu, Zn, and Pb salts drop by drop and in excess. Formation and colour of hydroxide precipitated to be highlighted with the help of equations.
- Action on addition of Ammonium Hydroxide to Answer. of Ca, Fe, Cu, Zn, and Pb salts drop by drop and in excess. Formation and colour of hydroxide precipitated to be highlighted with the help of equations.
- Special action of Ammonium
- Hydroxide on Answer.s of copper salts and sodium hydroxide on ammonium salts.

  (ii) Action of alkalis (NaOH, KOH) on certain metals, their oxides and hydroxides. The metals must include aluminium, zinc and lead, their oxides and hydroxides, which react with caustic alkalis (NaOH, KOH), showing the amphoteric nature of these substances.

**5** Mole Concept and Stoichiometry

  (i) Gay Lussac's Law of Combining Volumes Statement and explanation with numerical problems.

  (ii) Vapour Density and its relation to relative molecular mass:

- Molecular mass = 2×vapour density (formal proof not required)
- Deduction of simple (empirical) and molecular formula from:
  **(a)** the percentage composition of a compound.

**(b)** the masses of combining elements.

6  Electrolysis

(i)  Electrolytes and non-electrolytes. Definitions and examples.

(ii)  Substances containing molecules only, ions only, both molecules and ions.
- Substances containing molecules only  ions only, both molecules and ions.
- Examples: relating their composition with their behaviour as **strong and weak electrolytes as well as non-electrolytes.**

(iii)  Definition and explanation of electrolysis, electrolyte, electrode, anode, cathode, anion, cation, oxidation and reduction (on the basis of loss and gain of electrons).

(iv)  An elementary study of the migration of ions, with reference to the factors influencing selective discharge of ions (reference should be made to the activity series as indicating the tendency of metals, e.g., Na, Mg, Fe, Cu, to form ions) illustrated by the electrolysis of:
- Molten lead bromide
- acidified water with platinum electrodes
- Aqueous copper (II) sulphate with inert electrode, copper electrodes; electron transfer at the electrodes. **The above electrolytic processes can be studied in terms of electrolyte used, electrodes used, ionization reaction, anode reaction, cathode reaction, use of selective discharge theory, wherever applicable.**

(v)  Applications of electrolysis.
- Electroplating with nickel and silver, choice of electrolyte for electroplating.
- Electro refining of copper.
**Reasons and conditions for electroplating; names of the electrolytes and the electrodes used should be given. Equations for the reactions at the electrodes should be given for electroplating, refining of copper.**

7  Metallurgy

(i)  Occurrence of metals in nature:
- Mineral and ore - Meaning only.
- Common ores of iron, aluminium and  zinc.

(ii)  Extraction of Aluminium.
  **(a)** Chemical method for purifying bauxite by using  NaOH – Baeyer's Process.
  **(b)** Electrolytic extraction  –  Hall Heroult's process:
  Structure of electrolytic cell -  the various components as part of the electrolyte, electrodes and electrode reactions.
  **Description of the changes occurring, purpose of the substances used and the main reactions with their equations.**

(iii)  Alloys – composition and uses. Stainless steel, duralumin, magnalium, brass, bronze, fuse metal / solder.

8  Study of Compounds        A. Hydrogen Chloride

**A.** Hydrogen chloride: preparation of hydrogen chloride from sodium chloride; refer to the density and solubility of hydrogen chloride (fountain experiment); reaction with ammonia; acidic properties of its Answer..
- Preparation of hydrogen chloride from sodium chloride; the laboratory method of preparation can be learnt in terms of reactants, product, condition, equation, diagram or setting of the apparatus, proce-

dure, observation, precaution, collection of the gas and identification/tests.

- Simple experiment to show the density of the gas (Hydrogen Chloride) –heavier than air.
- Solubility of hydrogen chloride (fountain experiment); setting of the apparatus, procedure, observation, inference.
- Method of preparation of hydrochloric acid by dissolving the gas in water- the special funnel arrangement and the mechanism by which the back suction is avoided should be learnt.
- Reaction with ammonia
- Acidic properties of its Answer. - reaction with metals, their oxides, hydroxides and carbonates to give their chlorides; decomposition of carbonates, hydrogen carbonates, sulphides, sulphites.
- Reaction of Manganese dioxide with concentrated HCl.
- Precipitation reactions with silver nitrate Answer. and lead nitrate Answer..

**B. Ammonia**

Ammonia: its laboratory preparation from ammonium chloride and collection; ammonia from nitrides like $Mg_3N_2$ and AlN and ammonium salts. Manufacture by Haber's Process; density and solubility of ammonia (fountain experiment); aqueous Answer. of ammonia; its reactions with hydrogen chloride and with hot copper (II) oxide and lead monoxide and chlorine; the burning of ammonia in oxygen.

Laboratory preparation from ammonium chloride and collection; (the preparation to be studied in terms of, setting of the apparatus and diagram, procedure, observation, collection and identification/tests.)

- Ammonia from nitrides like $Mg_3N_2$ and AlN using warm water. Ammonia from ammonium salts using alkalies.

**The reactions to be studied in terms of reactants, products, conditions and equations.**

- Manufacture by Haber's Process.
- Density and solubility of ammonia (fountain experiment).
- The burning of ammonia in oxygen.
- The catalytic oxidation of ammonia (with conditions and reaction)
- Its reactions with hydrogen chloride and with hot copper (II) oxide, lead monoxide and chlorine (both chlorine in excess and ammonia in excess).

**All these reactions may be studied in terms of reactants, products, conditions, equations and observations.**

- Aqueous Answer. of ammonia - reaction with sulphuric acid, nitric acid, hydrochloric acid and Answer.s of iron(III) chloride, iron(II) sulphate, lead nitrate, zinc nitrate and copper sulphate.

**C. Nitric Acid**

Nitric Acid: one laboratory method of preparation of nitric acid from potassium nitrate or sodium nitrate. Large scale preparation. Nitric acid as an oxidizing agent.

- Laboratory preparation of nitric acid from potassium nitrate or sodium nitrate; the laboratory method to be studied in terms of reactants, products, conditions,

- equations, setting up of apparatus,
- diagram, precautions, collection and identification/tests.
- Manufacture of Nitric acid by Ostwald's process (Only equations with conditions where applicable).
- As an oxidising agent: its reaction with copper, carbon, sulphur.
- Thermal decomposition of nitrates.

**D. Sulphuric Acid**

Large scale preparation, its behaviour as an acid when dilute, as an oxidizing agent when concentrated - oxidation of carbon, sulphur and copper; as a dehydrating agent - dehydration of sugar (cane sugar/glucose) and copper (II) sulphate crystals; its non-volatile nature.

- Manufacture by Contact Process Equations with conditions where applicable).
- Its behaviour as an acid when dilute -reaction with metal, metal oxide, metal hydroxide, metal carbonate, metal bicarbonate, metal sulphite, metal sulphide.
- Concentrated sulphuric acid as an oxidizing agent - the oxidation of carbon sulphur and copper.
- Concentrated sulphuric acid as a dehydrating agent- (a) the dehydration of sugar (b) Copper (II) sulphate crystals.
- Non-volatile nature of sulphuric acid - reaction with sodium or potassium chloride and sodium or potassium nitrate.
- Tests for dilute and concentrated sulphuric acid.

**9  Organic Chemistry**

(i) Introduction to Organic compounds.

- Unique nature of Carbon atom – tetra valency, catenation.
- Formation of single, double and triple bonds, straight chain, branched chain, cyclic compounds (only benzene).

(ii) Structure and Isomerism.

- Structure of compounds with single, double and triple bonds.
- Structural formulae of hydrocarbons. Structural formula must be given for: alkanes, alkenes, alkynes, alcohols, aldehydes and carboxylic acid up to 5 carbon atoms.
- Isomerism – structural (chain, position)

(iii) Homologous series – characteristics with examples.

Alkane, alkene, alkyne series and their gradation in properties and the relationship with the molecular mass or molecular formula.

(iv)       Simple nomenclature.

Simple nomenclature of the hydrocarbons with simple functional groups – (double bond, triple bond, alcoholic, aldehydic, carboxylic group) longest chain rule and smallest number for functional groups rule – trivial and IUPAC names (compounds with only one functional group).

(v) Hydrocarbons: alkanes, alkenes, alkynes.

- Alkanes - general formula; methane (greenhouse gas) and ethane - methods of preparation from sodium ethanoate (sodium acetate), sodium propanoate (sodium propionate), from iodomethane (methyl iodide) and bromoethane (ethyl bromide). Complete combustion of methane and ethane, reaction of methane and ethane with chlorine through substitution.

- Alkenes – (unsaturated hydrocarbons with a double bond); ethene as an example. Methods of preparation of ethene by dehydro halogenation reaction and dehydration reactions.

- Alkynes - (unsaturated hydrocarbons with a triple bond); ethyne as an example of alkyne; Methods of preparation from calcium carbide and 1,2 dibromoethane ethylene dibromide).

  **Only main properties, particularly addition products with hydrogen and halogen namely $Cl_2$, $Br_2$ and $I_2$ pertaining to alkenes and alkynes.**

## INTERNAL ASSESSMENT OF PRACTICAL WORK

Candidates will be asked to observe the effect of reagents on substances supplied to them. The exercises will be simple and may include the recognition and identification of certain gases and ions listed below. The examiners will not, however, be restricted in their choice to substances containing the listed ions.

**Gases**: Hydrogen, Oxygen, Carbon dioxide, Chlorine, Hydrogen chloride, Sulphur dioxide, Hydrogen sulphide, Ammonia, Water vapour, Nitrogen dioxide.

**Ions**: Calcium, Copper, Iron, Lead, Zinc and Ammonium, Carbonate, Chloride, Nitrate, Sulphide, Sulphite and Sulphate.

Knowledge of a formal scheme of analysis is not required. Semi-micro techniques are acceptable but candidates using such techniques may need to adapt the instructions given to suit the size of the apparatus being used.

Candidates are expected to have completed the following minimum practical work:

1 Make a Answer. of the unknown substance: add sodium hydroxide Answer. or ammonium hydroxide Answer., make observations and give your deduction. Warming the mixture may be needed. Choose from substances containing $Ca^{2+}$, $Cu^{2+}$, $Fe^{2+}$, $Fe^{3+}$, $Pb^{2+}$, $Zn^{2+}$, $NH_4^+$.

2 Determine which of the given Answer.s is acidic and which is basic, giving two tests for each.

3 Add concentrated hydrochloric acid to each of the given substances, warm, make observations, identify any product and make deductions: (a) copper oxide (b) manganese dioxide

## EVALUATION

The assignments/project work are to be evaluated by the subject teacher and by an External Examiner. (The External Examiner may be a teacher nominated by the Head of the school, who could be from the faculty, **but not teaching the subject in the section/class.** For example, a teacher of Chemistry of Class VIII may be deputed to be an External Examiner for Class X Chemistry projects.)

The Internal Examiner and the External Examiner will assess the assignments independently.

**Award of Marks**          (20 Marks)

Subject Teacher (Internal Examiner)          10
marks

External Examiner          10 marks

The total marks obtained out of 20 are to be sent to the Council by the Head of the school. The Head of the school will be responsible for the online entry of marks on the Council's CAREERS portal by the due date.

**NOTE:** According to the recommendation of International Union of Pure and Applied Chemistry (IUPAC), the groups are numbered from 1 to 18 replacing the older notation of groups IA .... VIIA, VIII, IB ...... VIIB and 0. However, for the examination both notations will be accepted.

| Old notation | IA | IIA | IIIB | IVB | VB | VIB | VIIB | VIII | | | IB | IIB | IIIA | IVA | VA | VIA | VIIA | 0 |
|---|---|---|---|---|---|---|---|---|---|---|---|---|---|---|---|---|---|---|
| New notation | 1 | 2 | 3 | 4 | 5 | 6 | 7 | 8 | 9 | 10 | 11 | 12 | 13 | 14 | 15 | 16 | 17 | 18 |

# Mind Map : Periodic Properties

**Periodic Properties and Variations of Properties**

## Periodic Table

### Groups (columns): 18 vertical columns

| Group 1 | Alkali Metals (Li, Na, K, Rb, Cs, Fr) (Form strongest alkalis with water) |
| Group 2 | Alkaline earth Metals (Be, Mg, Ca, Sr, Ba, Ra) (Form weak alkalis with water) |
| Group 3-12 | (Transition Metals) (Have their two outermost shells incomplete (Sc, Ti, V) Group 3 and sixth period elements are called lanthanides). (e.g., La, Ce, Pr, Nd, etc.) Group 3 and seventh period elements are called actinides. (E.g., Ac, Th, Pa, U, Np, etc.) Group 11 – Coinage metals(Cu,Ag,Au) |
| Group 13 | B, Al, Ga, In, Tl, Nh are called Boron family because first member is boron. |
| Group 14 | C, Si, Ge, Sn, Pb, are called Carbon family because first member is carbon. |
| Group 15 | N, P, As, Sb, Bi are called Nitrogen family because first member is nitrogen. |
| Group 16 | O, S, Se, Te, Po, are called Oxygen family because first member is oxygen. They are also called chalcogens. |
| Group 17 | F, Cl, Br, I, At, Ts are salt-formingknown as halogens. |
| Group 18 | He, Ne Ar, Kr, Xe, Rn are known as Zero group or noble gases. |

### Periods (Rows): Seven horizontal rows in periodic table are known as periods.

Classification of periods

| | Length of period | No. of elements | Atomic no. of elements |
|---|---|---|---|
| 1 | Shortest period | 2 | 1 - 2 |
| 2 | Short period | 8 | 3 - 10 |
| 3 | Short period | 8 | 11 - 18 |
| 4 | Long period | 18 | 19 - 36 |
| 5 | Long period | 18 | 37 - 54 |
| 6 | Longest period | 32 | 55 - 86 |
| 7 | Longest period | 32 | 87 - 118 |

Modern Periodic Table (Mosley's) : Periodic properties of elements are the periodic function of their atomic number.

## Periodicity

The recurrence of elements with similar properties after certain regular intervals when these are arranged in the increasing order of their atomic number is called periodicity.

Due to similar electronic configuration.

## Historical development

The physical and chemical properties of elements are the periodic functions of their atomic mass.

**Periodic law**

Drawbacks: Position of certain elements could not be explained.

Drawbacks:
- Position of hydrogen.
- Position of isotopes.
- Position of lanthanides and actinides.

Mendeleev's Periodic Table

**Dobereiner Triads**

The atomic weight approximately the middle element was the arithmetic mean of the other two.

| | Ca, | Sr, | Ba |
|---|---|---|---|
| Atomic Mass | 40 | 88 | 137 |

Mean of Sr $= \dfrac{40+137}{2} = 88.5$

**Newland's Law of Octaves**

The periodicity (repetion of elements with similar properties) as the property of elements was recognised for the first time.

The elements when arranged in the increasing order of their atomic weights, the eight succeeding element was the repetition of the first one like the 8th note of the musical scale, i.e. the first and eight element were found to have similar properties.

**Limitations.**

with discover of rare gases, it was the ninth element and not the eighth having similar chemical properties.

## Atomic Number

Atomic number of an element is equal to the number of protons in nucleus.

## Number Mass

- It is the sum of the number of protons and neutrons present in the nucleus of an atom.
- $A = Z + {}_0n^1$
  where A is atomic mass, Z is number of protons and ${}_0n^1$ is number of neutrons.

## Periodic Properties

### Across a period (Decrease)

- Atomic size - Most probable distance between the centre of the nucleus to the outermost shell of electrons.
  e.g., F < Cl < Br < I < At
- Metallic character - Tendency of an element to loose an electron and form a positive ion.
  e.g., - In 2nd Period
  $$\underbrace{\text{Li} \quad \text{Be}}_{\text{Metals}} \quad \underbrace{\text{B}}_{\text{Metalloid}} \quad \underbrace{\text{C} \quad \text{N} \quad \text{O} \quad \text{F}}_{\text{Non-Metals}}$$

Down a group (Increase)

### Across a period [Increase]

- Non Metallic character - Tendency of an element to gain electrons. E.g., In 3rd period
  $$\underbrace{\text{Na} < \text{Mg}}_{\text{Metals}} < \underbrace{\text{Al} < \text{Si}}_{\text{Metalloid}} < \underbrace{\text{P} < \text{S} < \text{Cl}}_{\text{Non-Metals}}$$
- Ionisation Enthalpy -
  (First) Ionisation enthalpy is the amount of energy required to remove one valency electron from an isolated neutral gaseous atom.
  e.g., - $M(g) + I.E \longrightarrow M^+(g) - e^-$
- Electron affinity - The amount of energy released when one electron is added to a neutral gaseous atom to form a mono valent negative ion.
- Relative Electronegativity -
  Tendency of an atom in a molecule to attract the shared pair of electrons towards itself.
  e.g., In group-2 Be > Mg > Ca, Sr > Ba

Down a group (Decrease)

## Shells (orbits) and valency

Electrons revolve around the nucleus in a certain circular path.

**Trends in Number of shells** — Shells(orbit)

| Across a period | Remain same |
| Down a group | It increase |

### Trends in valency

**Valency**

Valency is the combining power (capacity) of an element

- Across period number of electrons in valence shell increases. But the valency increases then decreases.
- Down a group it remains same.

# Mind Map : Chemical Bonding

**Chemical Bonding**

**Statement:** The force of attraction between any two atoms in molecule to maintain stability

## Electrovalent or ionic bond

### Statement
Bond formed by the transfer of one or more atom to other to get a stable configuration called ionic or electrovalent bond.

### Justification
- A metallic atom which loses electron become a positively charged ion known as cation.
- A non-metallic atom, which gains electron becomes a negatively charged ion and is known as an anion.
- Metallic element in which one atom readily lose an electron to from a positive ion, known as electropositive element. $Na - e^- \rightarrow Na^+$ (cation)
- Non-metallic element in which atoms readily accepts electron(s) to form a negatively charge ion is known as electronegative element. $Cl + e^- \rightarrow Cl^-$ (anion)

### Conditions
1. Low ionisation potential of a particular atom.
2. High electron affinity.
3. Large electronegative difference between two elements.

### Reason of stability of ion compounds
The electrostatic force of attraction between opposite charge is much higher.

### Electron dot symbol
$Na + Cl \rightarrow Na^+ + Cl^-$ or $NaCl$

### Redox process
- The electropositive atom undergoes oxidation and electronegative atom undergoes reduction. When process occur simultaneously, this known as redox reaction. e.g.
$2Na \rightarrow 2Na^+ + 2e^-$ (oxidation)
can be written as
$Cl_2 + 2e^- \rightarrow 2Cl^-$ (reduction)
$$2Na + Cl_2 \xrightarrow{\text{Oxidation / Reduction}} 2Na^+ + 2Cl^-$$
- Oxidation and reduction occur simultaneously because the electrons lost by the reducing agent must be gained by oxidising agent.

### Properties
**Nature of particles:**
- Constituent particles are ions.
- Hard solid consisting of ions.

**B.P. or M.P.:** Non-volatile with high boiling or melting point.

**Electrical conducting nature:**
- Do not conduct electricity in solid state.
- Conduct electricity in liquid or in aqueous state.

**Solubility:** These are soluble in water but insoluble in organic solvent.

**Dissociation:** Ions dissociates and migrates when electric current passes.

**Rate of reaction:** Rapid speed in aqueous solution. $NaCl \rightarrow Na^+ + Cl^-$

## Coordinate Bond

### Conditions
Bond formed between two atoms by sharing a pair of electron provided by one of the combining atoms but shared by both.
- One pair of the two atoms must have atleast one lone pair of electron, E.g., $NH_3$, $H_2O$
- Another atoms should be short of atleast a lone pair of electron E.g., $H^+$ (ions)

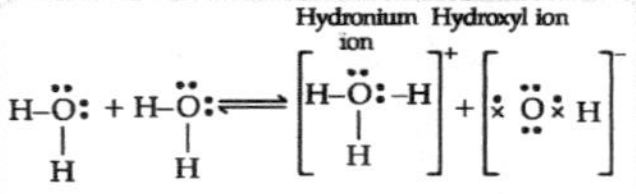

### Formation of Hydroxyl ion
- Water molecule contains two H-atoms and one O-atom.
- When water ionises, a positive $[H^+]$ ion is formed. $H_2O \rightarrow H^+ + OH^-$

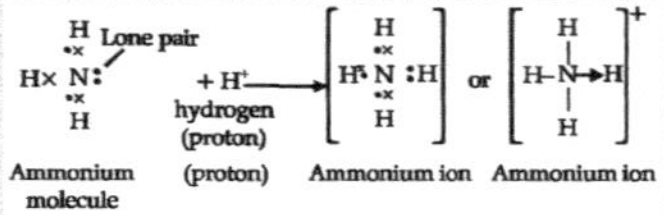

### Self ionisation of water
- $H^+$ ion transfers to another water molecule to form $H_3O^+$ ion. $H^+ + H_2O \rightarrow H_3O^+ + OH^-$

### Formation of Ammonium ion

Hydronium ion / Hydroxyl ion

## Covalent Bond

### Conditions for formation
- Both atoms should have four or more electrons in their outermost shell i.e., non-metals. Exception are (H, Be, B, Al, etc).
- Both atoms should have high electronegativity.
- Both atoms should have high ionisation potential.
- Both atoms should have high electron affinity.
- Electronegativity difference between combining atoms should be negligible or zero.

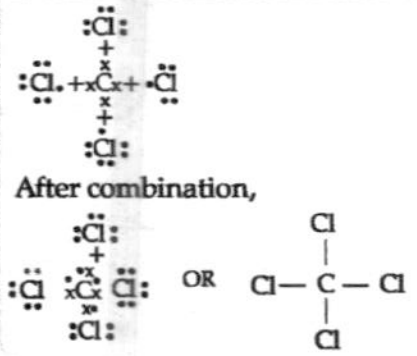

### Polar covalent
The pairs of electrons are not at equal distance between the two atoms. This causes in the development of partial positive and partial negative charge on atoms.
$HCl \rightarrow H^+ + Cl^- \rightarrow H^{\delta+} Cl^{\delta-} \rightarrow C l^-$
$HF \rightarrow H^+ + F^-$
Other examples : Water molecule, Ammonia molecule.

- Coordinate bond has properties of both covalent and ionic bonds. So it is also called co-ionic bond.
- Atom which provides the electron pair for the formation of coordinate bond is known as donor and the atoms or ion sharing the donated electron pair is known as acceptor.

Ammonium molecule — Ammonium ion

- Hydroxide ion is formed when one hydrogen ion ($H^+$) is removed from water molecule. $H_2O \rightarrow H^+ + OH^-$
- When $H^+$ is removed from water molecule, the shared pair of electrons remain with oxygen because it is more electronegative than hydrogen.
$H{:}\ddot{O}{:}H \rightarrow H^+ + [{:}\ddot{O}{:}H]^-$

### Properties
**Nature:**
- Constituent particles are molecule.
- These are gases, liquid or soft solids.

**Boiling and Melting point:** Volatile with low melting and boiling point.

**Electrical conducting nature:** Non-conductors of electricity in solid, molten or aqueous state.

**Solubility:** These are insoluble in water but dissolve in organic solvents.

**Rate of Reaction:** Slow speed chemical reaction takes place.

**Ionisation in solution:**
- Non-polar compound do not ionise.
- Polar compound ionizes in their solution. eq: $HCl + H_2O = H_3O^+ + Cl^-$ (polar)

### Statement
The chemical bond that is formed between two combining atoms by mutual sharing of one or more pair of electron is called covalent bond.

### Single covalent bond
A single covalent bond is formed by the sharing of one pair of electron (s) between the atoms, where each atom contribute one electron. It is denoted as (–) (short line between atoms.)
E.g. H–H, Cl–Cl, H–O–H
(Hydrogen) (Chlorine) (Water)

### Double covalent bond
A double bond is formed by the sharing of two pair of electrons between two atoms.
E.g- $O_2 \rightarrow O{=}O$, $CO_2 \rightarrow O{=}C{=}O$.

### Triple covalent bond
A triple bond is formed by sharing of three pair of electrons between two atoms.
E.g., $N_2 \rightarrow N{\equiv}N$

### Polar & Non-polar covalent bond
When shared pair of electrons are equally distributed between the atoms, no charge distribution takes place and the molecule is symmetrical and neutral.
Examples-
- $H_2$, $Cl_2$, $O_2$ (Similar atoms)
- $CCl_4$, $CH_4$ (Dissimilar atoms)
- Because of least difference in electronegatively different atoms show non-polarity.

### Non-polar (Formation of non-polar molecule, Similar atoms)
Electron dot structure before combination,
$:\!\ddot{C}l\!: + :\!\ddot{C}l\!:$
After combination,
$:\!\ddot{C}l\!:\!\ddot{C}l\!:$ or [Cl–Cl], ($Cl_2$)
one shared pair of electron

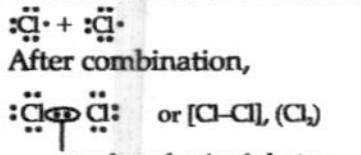

### Dissimilar atoms
Formation of carbon tetrachloride molecule, Electron dot structure before combination,
After combination,
Cl–C–Cl (with Cl above and below the central C)

# Mind Map : Acids, Base

## Acids, Bases

### Acids and Bases

#### Classification of Acids

**General uses of some acids**
- Boric acid - Antiseptic for eye wash
- Oxalic acid - Ink stain remover
- Tartaric acid - Baking powder
- Citric acid - Food preservative
- Carbonic acid - Flavoured drink
- Phosphoric acid - Fertilizer

**Concentration of an acid**

Concentration of acid means the amount of acid present in a definite amount of its aqueous solution.

**Statement**

Compounds which contain one or more hydrogen atoms and when dissolved in water, produces hydronium $(H_3O)^+$ ions as positively charged ions.

$HCl \xrightarrow{H_2O} H^+ + Cl^-$

$H^+ + H_2O \longrightarrow H_3O^+$

**Strength an acid**

- The strength of an acid depends of the degree of ionisation (∝) and concentration of hydronium ions $[H_3O^+]$ produced by that acid in aqueous solution.

Degree of ionisation (∝) = $\frac{\text{No. of acid molecules ionised}}{\text{(Total no. of acid molecules present in aq. solution)}}$

- If (∝) for an acid or alkali in aq. solution is greater than 30%, it is strong and if it is less then 30%, it is weak.

**Depending on their sources**

- Organic acid → Usually obtained from plants. e.g., Oxalic acid $(COOH)_2$, acetic acid $(CH_3COOH)$, formic acid (HCOOH).
- Inorganic acid → Usually obtained from minerals. e.g., Sulphuric acid $(H_2SO_4)$, Nitric acid $(HNO_3)$.
- They are strong acids. They ionise completely in solution.
- Acids which contain oxygen along with hydrogen and some other element are known as oxy acids e.g. Nitric acid $(HNO_3)$, sulphuric acid $(H_2SO_4)$
- Hydracids contain hydrogen and a non - metallic element. Do not contain oxygen. e.g., HCl, HBr.
- Carbonic acid $(H_2CO_3)$ is a weak mineral acid.

**Depending on their basicity**

*Statement*

The basicity of an acid is defined as the number of $H_3O^+$ ion produced by the ionisation of one molecule of acid in aqueous solution.

*Types*

(i) Monobasic → Acids which on ionisation in water produce $H_3O^+$ ion per atom.
e.g., $HCl + H_2O \rightarrow H_3O^+ + Cl^-$

(ii) Dibasic acid → Acids which on ionisation in water produce two hydronium $(H_3O^+)$ ions per molecule.
e.g., $H_2SO_4 + H_2O \rightleftharpoons H_3O^+ + HSO_4^-$
$HSO_4^- + H_2O \rightleftharpoons H_3O^+ + SO_4^{2-}$

- Dibasic acids have two replaceable hydrogen ions, therefore they form one acid salt or one normal salt.

e.g., $NaOH + H_2SO_4 \rightarrow NaHSO_4 + H_2O$ (Acid salt)

$2NaOH + H_2SO_4 \rightarrow Na_2SO_4 + 2H_2O$ (Normal salt)

- $H_3PO_3$ is a dibasic acid because in oxyacids of phosphorus, hydrogen atoms are attached to oxygen atoms which are not replaceable.

HO-P(=O)(H)-OH → Not replaceable.

(iii) Tribasic acid → Acids which on ionisation in water produce three hydronium ion per molecule.
e.g., $H_3PO_4 + H_2O \rightleftharpoons H_3O^+ + H_2PO_4^-$
$H_2PO_4^- + H_2O \rightleftharpoons H_3O^+ + HPO_4^{2-}$
$HPO_4^{2-} + H_2O \rightleftharpoons H_3O^+ + PO_4^{3-}$

#### Preparation of Acids

(i) By synthesis.
Binary acids are prepared by this method.
e.g., $H_2 + Cl_2 \rightarrow 2HCl$ (acid)
$H_2 + S \rightarrow H_2S$ (acid)

(ii) By action of water on non-metallic oxides.
$SO_3 + H_2O \rightarrow H_2SO_4$ (Sulphuric acid)
$SO_2 + H_2O \rightarrow H_2SO_3$ (Sulphurous acid)

(iii) By displacement.
$NaCl + H_2SO_4 \rightarrow NaHSO_4 + HCl$ (acid)
$NaNO_3 + H_2SO_4 \rightarrow NaHSO_4 + HNO_3$ (acid)

#### Properties of Acids

**Physical Properties**

- Acids have sour taste.
- Some acids are solids and some are liquids at room temp.
  - e.g., $H_3BO_3$ (Boric acid), $(COOH)_2$ (Oxalic acid)] } Solid
  - $CH_3COOH$) (Acetic acid), $(HNO_3)$ (Nitric acid)] } Volatile liquid
  - $(H_2SO_4)$ (Sulphuric acid) } Non -volatile liquid
- All mineral acids have corrosive action on skin and caused painful burns but carbonic acid (mineral acid) and organic acid are not corrosive in nature.
- They change the colour of indicators.

| | |
|---|---|
| Litmus | Blue to red |
| Methyl orange | Orange to pink |
| Phenolphthalein | Remain colourless |

- They conduct electricity in the aqueous state.
- Reaction with active metals liberate hydrogen.
  $Mg + 2HCl \rightarrow MgCl_2 + H_2\uparrow$

**Chemical Properties of Acids**

- Note → Nitric acid is very strong oxidising agent and does not liberate hydrogen. Only Mn and Mg ion produce hydrogen with nitric acid.
  $Mn + 2HNO_3 \rightarrow Mn(NO_3)_2 + H_2\uparrow$
- It reacts with base to form salt and water.
  $CuO + H_2SO_4 \rightarrow CuSO_4 + H_2O$

### Bases

A base is either a metallic oxide or a metallic hydroxide or ammonium hydroxide which reacts with hydronium ions of an acid to form salt and water only. e.g., CuO (Metallic acid), $Mg(OH)_2$ (Metallic hydroxides)

**Basic Hydroxide**

It is a metallic hydroxide which contains $OH^-$ ions and will react with an acid to give salt and water only.
e.g., $NaOH + HCl \rightarrow NaCl + H_2O$

**Basic Oxide**

A basic oxide is a metallic oxide which contains the ion $O_2^-$ and reacts with an acid to form salt and water only.

**Alkalis**

An alkali is a basic hydroxide which when dissolved in water produces hydroxyl $(OH)^-$ ions only negative ions. They turn red litmus blue.
e.g., $NaOH \rightleftharpoons Na^+ + OH^-$

#### Classification of Bases (Alkali)

**On the basis of their strength**

- A strong alkali: It undergoes almost complete dissociation in aqueous solution to produce $OH^-$ ion.
  $KOH(aq) \rightleftharpoons K^+(aq) + OH^-(aq)$
- A weak alkali: It undergoes only partial dissociation or ionisation in aqueous solution to produce a low concentration of $OH^-$ in solution.
  e.g., $NH_4OH \rightleftharpoons NH_4^+(aq) + OH^-(aq)$

**On the basis of their acidity**

- Mono - acidic base: Produce one $OH^-$ ion per molecule. $NaOH \rightarrow Na^+ + OH^-$
- Di - acidic base: Produce two $OH^-$ ions per molecule. $Ca(OH)_2\ (aq) \rightleftharpoons Ca^{2+} + 2OH^-$
- Tri - acidic base: Produce three $OH^-$ ions per molecule $Al(OH)_3\ (aq) \rightleftharpoons Al^+ + 3OH^-$

#### Preparation of bases

- From metals: Metals react with oxygen give base $4Na + O_2 \rightarrow 2Na_2O$
- Action of water or metals: $2Na + H_2O \rightarrow 2NaOH + H_2\uparrow$; $2K + 2H_2O \rightarrow 2KOH + H_2\uparrow$
- By double decomposition: $FeCl_3 + 3NaOH \rightarrow Fe(OH)_3\downarrow + NaCl$
- By decomposition of salt: $CaCO_3 \rightarrow CaO + CO_2\uparrow$

#### Properties

**Physical Properties**

- They have a sharp and bitter taste.
- They change colour of indicators:

| | |
|---|---|
| Litmus | Red to blue |
| Methyl orange | Orange to yellow |
| Phenolphthalein | Colourless to pink |

- They are soapy substance i.e they are slippery to touch.
- Strong electrolyte.
- Mild corrosive on skin.

**Chemical Properties**

- Strong alkali absorb carbon dioxide from the air to from carbonates.
  $2NaOH + CO_2 \rightarrow Na_2CO_3 + H_2O$
- Neutralise acids to form salt and water.
  $Ca(OH)_2 + 2HCl \rightarrow CaCl_2 + 2H_2O$
- They precipitate as insoluble metallic hydroxides when added to the salt solutions of the salts of the heavy metals.
  $CuSO_4 + 2NH_4OH \rightarrow (NH_4)_2SO_4 + Cu(OH)_2\downarrow$
  (aq.) (aq.) (aq.) (Pale Blue)
- Ammonia gases evolved when alkalis warmed with an ammonium salt.
  $NH_4Cl + NaOH \xrightarrow{\Delta} NaCl + H_2O + NH_3\uparrow$
  $2NH_4Cl + Ca(OH)_2 \xrightarrow{\Delta} CaCl_2 + 2H_2O + 2NH_3\uparrow$

#### Uses of bases and test for Acidity and Alkalinity

**Uses of Bases**

- Sodium hydroxide is used in manufacture of soap.
- Potassium hydroxide manufacture of salts and soaps and used in batteries.
- Ammonium hydroxide remove grease stains from clothes.
- Magnesia (MgO) used in making refractory bricks.
- Magnesium hydroxide used as an antacid.

**Test for Acidity and Alkanility**

It can be measured by pH scale

0 1 2 3 4 5 6 7 8 9 10 11 12 13 14

Increasing Acidic Nature ← Neutral → Increasing Alkaline Nature

Trace the Mind Map: First Level, Second Level, Third Level

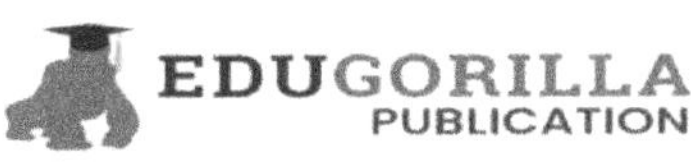

# Mind Map : Salts

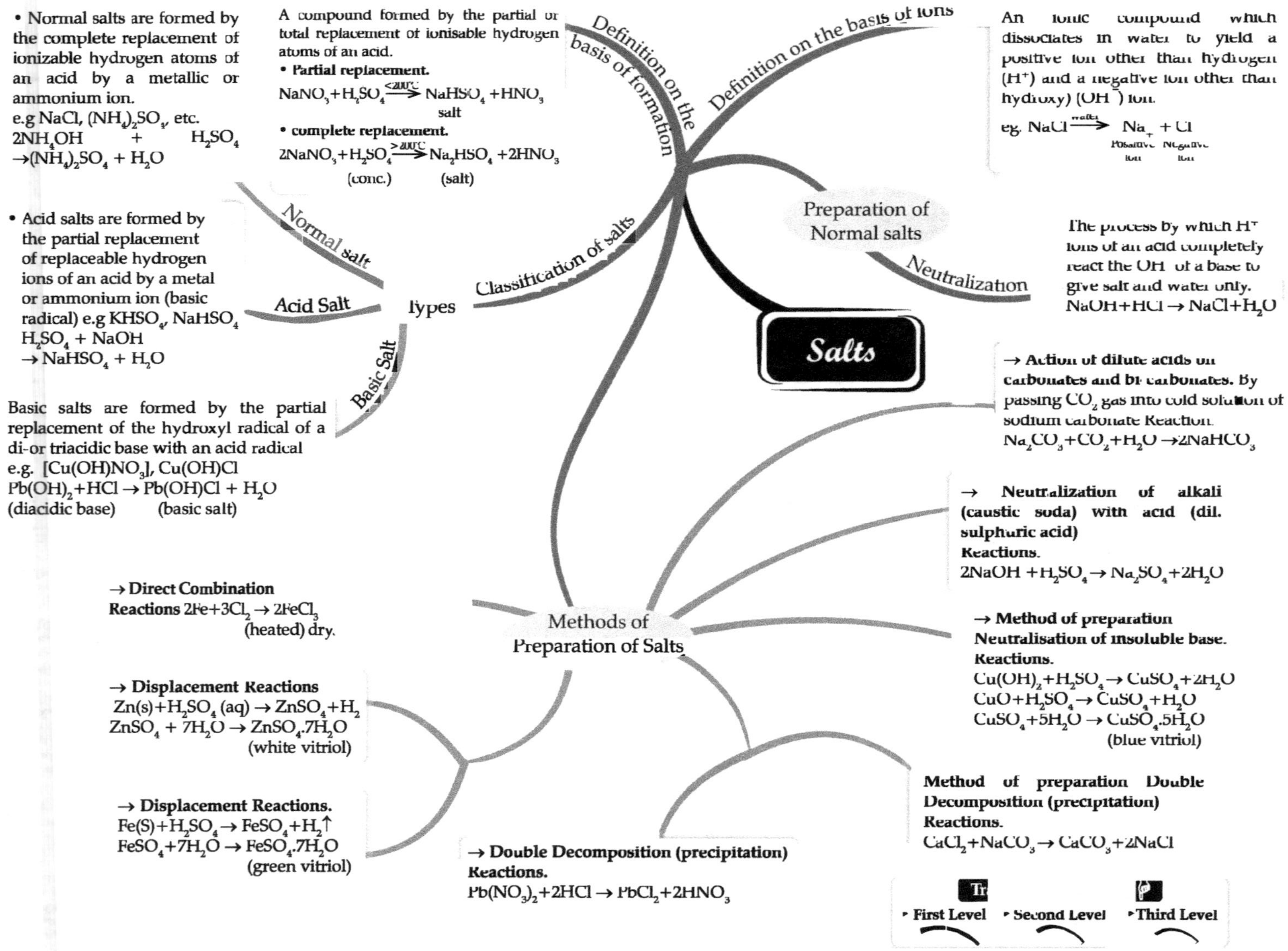

## Salts

### Definition on the basis of formation

**Normal salt**
- Normal salts are formed by the complete replacement of ionizable hydrogen atoms of an acid by a metallic or ammonium ion.
  e.g NaCl, $(NH_4)_2SO_4$, etc.
  $$2NH_4OH + H_2SO_4 \rightarrow (NH_4)_2SO_4 + H_2O$$

**Acid Salt**
- Acid salts are formed by the partial replacement of replaceable hydrogen ions of an acid by a metal or ammonium ion (basic radical) e.g $KHSO_4$, $NaHSO_4$
  $$H_2SO_4 + NaOH \rightarrow NaHSO_4 + H_2O$$

**Basic Salt**
Basic salts are formed by the partial replacement of the hydroxyl radical of a di-or triacidic base with an acid radical
e.g. $[Cu(OH)NO_3]$, $Cu(OH)Cl$
$$Pb(OH)_2 + HCl \rightarrow Pb(OH)Cl + H_2O$$
(diacidic base)          (basic salt)

### Definition on the basis of formation / Classification of salts — Types

A compound formed by the partial or total replacement of ionisable hydrogen atoms of an acid.
- **Partial replacement.**
  $$NaNO_3 + H_2SO_4 \xrightarrow{<200°C} NaHSO_4 + HNO_3$$
  salt
- **complete replacement.**
  $$2NaNO_3 + H_2SO_4 \xrightarrow{>200°C} Na_2HSO_4 + 2HNO_3$$
  (conc.)          (salt)

### Definition on the basis of ions

An ionic compound which dissociates in water to yield a positive ion other than hydrogen ($H^+$) and a negative ion other than hydroxy) ($OH^-$) ion.
e.g. $NaCl \xrightarrow{melt} Na^+ + Cl^-$
Positive   Negative
ion          ion

### Preparation of Normal salts

**Neutralization**

The process by which $H^+$ ions of an acid completely react the $OH^-$ of a base to give salt and water only.
$$NaOH + HCl \rightarrow NaCl + H_2O$$

→ **Action of dilute acids on carbonates and bi-carbonates.** By passing $CO_2$ gas into cold solution of sodium carbonate Reaction.
$$Na_2CO_3 + CO_2 + H_2O \rightarrow 2NaHCO_3$$

→ **Neutralization of alkali (caustic soda) with acid (dil. sulphuric acid)** Reactions.
$$2NaOH + H_2SO_4 \rightarrow Na_2SO_4 + 2H_2O$$

→ **Method of preparation Neutralisation of insoluble base.** Reactions.
$$Cu(OH)_2 + H_2SO_4 \rightarrow CuSO_4 + 2H_2O$$
$$CuO + H_2SO_4 \rightarrow CuSO_4 + H_2O$$
$$CuSO_4 + 5H_2O \rightarrow CuSO_4.5H_2O$$
(blue vitriol)

**Method of preparation Double Decomposition (precipitation)** Reactions.
$$CaCl_2 + NaCO_3 \rightarrow CaCO_3 + 2NaCl$$

### Methods of Preparation of Salts

→ **Direct Combination** Reactions $2Fe + 3Cl_2 \rightarrow 2FeCl_3$ (heated) dry.

→ **Displacement Reactions**
$$Zn(s) + H_2SO_4 (aq) \rightarrow ZnSO_4 + H_2$$
$$ZnSO_4 + 7H_2O \rightarrow ZnSO_4.7H_2O$$
(white vitriol)

→ **Displacement Reactions.**
$$Fe(S) + H_2SO_4 \rightarrow FeSO_4 + H_2\uparrow$$
$$FeSO_4 + 7H_2O \rightarrow FeSO_4.7H_2O$$
(green vitriol)

→ **Double Decomposition (precipitation)** Reactions.
$$Pb(NO_3)_2 + 2HCl \rightarrow PbCl_2 + 2HNO_3$$

**Tr** ▸ First Level   ▸ Second Level   ▸ Third Level

# Mind Map : Analytical Chemistry

## Examples of coloured ions

| Cation | Symbol | Colour | Anion | Symbol | Colour |
|---|---|---|---|---|---|
| Copper ion | $Cu^{2+}$ | Blue | Permanganate ion | $MnO_4^-$ | Pink/purple |
| Ferrous ion | $Fe^{2+}$ | Light green | Dichromate ion | $Cr_2O_7^{2-}$ | Orange |
| Ferric ion | $Fe^{3+}$ | Brown | Chromate ion | $CrO_4^{2-}$ | Yellow |
| Nickel ion | $Ni^{2+}$ | Green | | | |

## Examples of colourless ions

| Cation | Symbol | Anion | Symbol |
|---|---|---|---|
| Ammonium ion | $NH_4^+$ | Chloride ion | $Cl^-$ |
| Sodium ion | $Na^+$ | Sulphate ion | $SO_4^{2-}$ |
| Potassium ion | $K^+$ | Carbonate ion | $CO_3^{2-}$ |
| Calcium ion | $Ca^{2+}$ | Hydrogen carbonate ion | $HCO_3^-$ |

## Analytical Chemistry

### Analysis

**Qualitative**
- It is done by carrying out chemical tests with the help of reagents.
- It involves the identification of the unknown substances.

**Quantitative**
- Determination of chemical components in a given sample.
- It involves the determination of composition of a mixture.

### Precipitation

The process of formation of an insoluble solid when solutions are mixed. The solid formed is called precipitate.

### Colour of the salts & their solution

- Salt of transition elements — Salts of Group 3 to 12 are generally coloured.
- Salt of representative elements — Salts of Group 1, 2 and 13 to 17 are generally colourless.

### Action of alkalis on Metals

(1) **Zinc:**
$$Zn + 2NaOH \rightarrow Na_2ZnO_2 + H_2 \quad \text{Sodium zincate}$$
(Hot & conc.) (Colourless)
$$Zn + 2KOH \rightarrow K_2ZnO_2 + H_2 \quad \text{Potassium zincate}$$
(Hot & conc.) (Colourless)

(2) **Aluminium:**
Aluminium reacts with boiling caustic alkali sol.
$$2Al + NaOH + 2H_2O \rightarrow 2NaAlO_2 + 3H_2 \quad \text{Sodium aluminate (Colourless)}$$
Aluminium reacts with faded alkali to produce sodium aluminate.
$$2Al + 6NaOH \rightarrow 2Na_3AlO_3 + 3H_2$$

(3) **Lead:**
$$Pb + 2NaOH \rightarrow Na_2PbO_2 + H_2 \quad \text{Sodium plumbite (Colourless)}$$
$$Pb + 2KOH \rightarrow K_2PbO_2 + H_2 \quad \text{Potassium plumbite (Colourless)}$$

### Action of alkalis on metal oxides and hydroxides

Oxide/hydroxide + acid $\rightarrow$ salt + water
Oxide/hydroxide + alkali $\rightarrow$ salt + water

Some metal oxides and hydroxides exhibit dual character i.e. they show acidic as well as basic character, they are said to be amphoteric in nature. Examples:

(1) $ZnO + 2NaOH \rightarrow Na_2ZnO_2 + H_2O$ Sodium zincate
$Zn(OH)_2 + 2NaOH \rightarrow Na_2ZnO_2 + H_2O$ Sodium zincate

(2) $Al_2O_3 + 2NaOH \rightarrow 2NaAlO_2 + H_2O$ sodium aluminate
$Al(OH)_3 + NaOH \rightarrow NaAlO_2 + 2H_2O$

### Action of sodium hydroxide on solution of salts

Salt + Alkali $\rightarrow$ Metal hydroxide + Salt formed in solution

**1. Calcium salts ($Ca^{2+}$ ion)**
$$Ca(NO_3)_2 + 2NaOH \rightarrow Ca(OH)_2 + 2NaNO_3$$
Calcium nitrate (Colourless) — Caustic soda — Calcium hydroxide (White ppt) — Sodium nitrate (Colourless)
White, Sparingly soluble

**2. Iron:**

a) Ferrous Salts ($Fe^{2+}$ ion)
$$FeSO_4 + 2NaOH \rightarrow Fe(OH)_2 + Na_2SO_4$$
Ferrous sulpate (Green) — Caustic soda (Colourless) — Ferrous hydroxide (Dirty green gelatinous ppt) — Sodium sulphate (Colourless)
Dirty green

b) Ferric Salts ($Fe^{3+}$ ion)
$$FeCl_3 + 3NaOH \rightarrow Fe(OH)_3 + 3NaCl$$
Ferric chloride (Yellow) — Caustic soda (Colourless) — Ferric hydroxide (Reddish Brown ppt) — Sodium chloride (Colourless)
Reddish brown, Insoluble

**3. Copper Salts ($Cu^{2+}$ ion)**
$$CuSO_4 + 2NaOH \rightarrow Cu(OH)_2 + Na_2SO_4$$
Copper sulphate (Blue) — Caustic soda (Colourless) — Copper hydroxide (Pale blue ppt) (Colourless) — Sodium sulphate (Colourless)
Pale blue, Insoluble

**4. Copper (II) Salts ($Cu^{2+}$ ion)**
$$CuSO_4 + 2NH_4OH \rightarrow Cu(OH)_2 + (NH_4)_2SO_4$$
(Blue) — (Pale blue ppt) (Colourless it sol.)
With excess of $NH_4OH$ ppt dissolves.

$Cu(OH)_2 + (NH_4)_2SO_4 + 2NH_4OH \rightarrow (Cu(NH_3)_4) SO_4 + 4H_2O$

$Cu(OH)_2 + 4NH_4OH(excess) \rightarrow (Cu(NH_3)_4)(OH)_2 + 4H_2O$ Soluble in excess of $NH_4OH$ and forms blue solution
Tetraammine copper hydroxide

- This reaction is a characteristic property of $Cu^{2+}$ ion and is used for its detection in qualitative analysis.
- Potassium hydroxide (Caustic potash) solution also shows similar behaviour.

### Action of ammonium hydroxide on solution of salts

- Potassium hydroxide (Caustic potash) solution also shows similar behaviour.

**Zinc Salts ($Zn^{2+}$ ion)**
$$ZnSO_4 + 2NaOH \rightarrow Zn(OH)_2 + Na_2SO_4$$
(Colourless) (Colourless) — (White, gelatinous ppt) (Colourless) — Gelatinous white, soluble.
(with ecess of NaOH ppt dissolves)
$$Zn(OH)_2 + 2NaOH \rightarrow Na_2ZnO_2 + H_2O$$
(excess) — (Sodium zincate, colourless)

**Lead Salts ($Pb^{2+}$ ion)**
$$Pb(NO_3)_2 + 2NaOH \rightarrow Pb(OH)_2 + 2NaNO_3$$
(Colourless) (Colourless) — (White ppt) (Colourless)
Chalky white, soluble.

(with excess of NaOH ppt dissolves)
$$Pb(OH)_2 + 2NaOH \rightarrow Na_2PbO_2 + 2H_2O$$
(excess) — (Sodium plumbite, colourless)

Salt + Ammonium hydroxide $\rightarrow$ Metal + salt formed solution hydroxide in solution

**1. Calcium salts:**
No precipitation even on addition of excess of $NH_4OH$. This is because, the concentration of $OH^-$ ions from ionisation of $NH_4OH$ is low such that it cannot precipitate the hydroxide of calcium.

**2. Zinc Salts ($Zn^{2+}$ ion):**
$$ZnSO_4 + 2NH_4OH \rightarrow Zn(OH)_2 + (NH_4)_2SO_4$$
(colourless solution) — (White gelatinous) — (colour in solution)
Gelatinous white ppt

With excess of $NH_4OH$ ppt dissolves
$$Zn(OH)_2 + (NH_4)_2SO_4 + 2NH_4OH \rightarrow Zn(NH_3)_4 SO4 + 4H_2O$$
Zinc hydroxide (excess) — tetraamminezinc sulphate (colourless sol)
$$Zn(OH)_2 + NH_4OH \rightarrow Zn(NH_3)_4 (OH)_2 + 4H_2O$$
Tetrammine zinc hydroxide

## Trace the Mind Map

▸ First Level  ▸ Second Level  ▸ Third Level

# Mind Map : Mole Concept and Stoichiometry

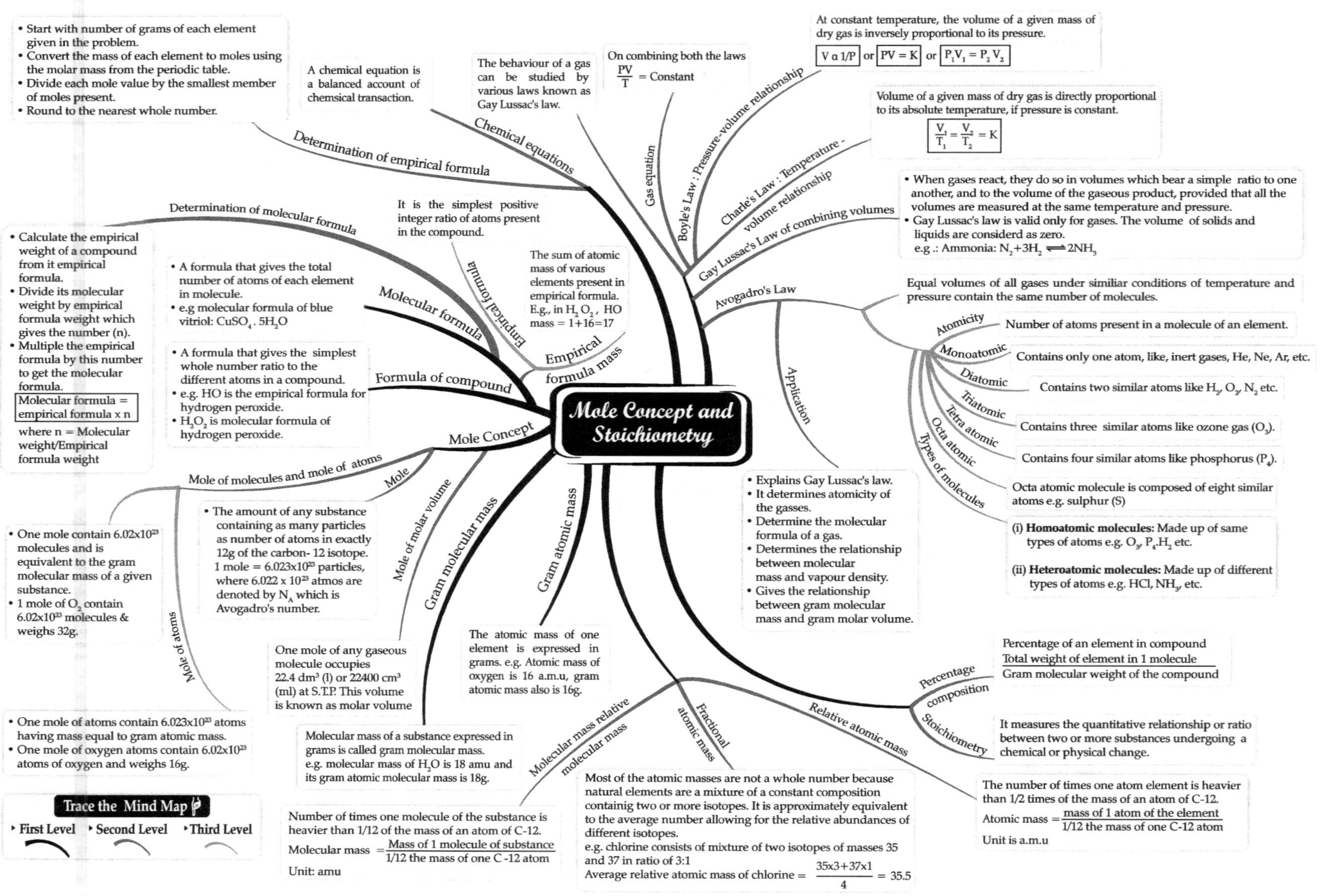

**Central topic:** Mole Concept and Stoichiometry

## Gas equation / Gas laws

- The behaviour of a gas can be studied by various laws known as Gay Lussac's law.

**Boyle's Law : Pressure-volume relationship**
- At constant temperature, the volume of a given mass of dry gas is inversely proportional to its pressure.
- $V \alpha 1/P$ or $PV = K$

**Charle's Law : Volume-Temperature relationship**
- Volume of a given mass of dry gas is directly proportional to its absolute temperature, if pressure is constant.
- $\dfrac{V}{T} = \dfrac{V_1}{T_1} = \dfrac{V}{T_2} = K$

**Gay Lussac's Law of combining volumes**
- When gases react, they do so in volumes which bear a simple ratio to one another, and to the volume of the gaseous product, provided that all the volumes are measured at the same temperature and pressure.
- Gay Lussac's law is valid only for gases. The volume of solids and liquids are considered as zero.
- e.g.: Ammonia: $N_2 + 3H_2 \rightleftharpoons 2NH_3$

**On combining both the laws**
- $\dfrac{PV}{T} = \text{Constant}$

## Avogadro's Law
- Equal volumes of all gases under similar conditions of temperature and pressure contain the same number of molecules.

**Atomicity** — Number of atoms present in a molecule of an element.
- Monoatomic: Contains only one atom, like, like, inert gases, He, Ne, Ar, etc.
- Diatomic: Contains two similar atoms like $H_2$, $O_2$, $N_2$, etc.
- Triatomic: Contains three similar atoms like ozone gas $(O_3)$.
- Tetra atomic: Contains four similar atoms like phosphorus $(P_4)$.
- Octa atomic: Octa atomic molecule is composed of eight similar atoms e.g. sulphur (S)

**Types of molecules**
- (i) **Homoatomic molecules:** Made up of same types of atoms e.g. $O_2$, $P_4$, $H_2$ etc.
- (ii) **Heteroatomic molecules:** Made up of different types of atoms e.g. HCl, $NH_3$, etc.

**Application**
- Explains Gay Lussac's law.
- It determines atomicity of the gases.
- Determine the molecular formula of a gas.
- Determines the relationship between molecular mass and vapour density.
- Gives the relationship between gram molecular mass and gram molar volume.

## Percentage composition
- Percentage of an element in compound
- $\dfrac{\text{Total weight of element in 1 compound}}{\text{Gram molecular weight of the compound}}$

## Stoichiometry
- It measures the quantitative relationship or ratio between two or more substances undergoing a chemical or physical change.

## Relative atomic mass
- The number of times one atom element is heavier than 1/2 times of the mass of an atom of C-12.
- Atomic mass $= \dfrac{\text{mass of 1 atom of the element}}{1/12 \text{ the mass of one C-12 atom}}$
- Unit is a.m.u

## Fractional atomic mass
- Most of the atomic masses are not a whole number because natural elements are a mixture of a constant composition containing two or more isotopes. It is approximately equivalent to the average number allowing for the relative abundances of different isotopes.
- e.g. chlorine consists of mixture of two isotopes of masses 35 and 37 in ratio of 3:1
- Average relative atomic mass of chlorine $= \dfrac{35 \times 3 + 37 \times 1}{4} = \dfrac{35.5}{}$ = 35.5

## Molecular mass relative
- Number of times one molecule of the substance is heavier than 1/12 of the mass of an atom of C-12.
- Molecular mass $= \dfrac{\text{Mass of 1 molecule of substance}}{1/12 \text{ the mass of one C-12 atom}}$
- Unit: amu

## Gram molecular mass
- Molecular mass of a substance expressed in grams is called gram molecular mass.
- e.g. molecular mass of $H_2O$ is 18 amu and its gram molecular mass is 18g.

## Gram atomic mass
- The atomic mass of one element is expressed in grams. e.g. Atomic mass of oxygen is 16 a.m.u, gram atomic mass also is 16g.

## Mole of molar volume
- One mole of any gaseous molecule occupies 22.4 dm³ (l) or 22400 cm³ (ml) at S.T.P. This volume is known as molar volume

## Mole
- The amount of any substance containing as many particles as number of atoms in exactly 12g of the carbon- 12 isotope.
- 1 mole = $6.023 \times 10^{23}$ particles, where $6.022 \times 10^{23}$ atmos are denoted by $N_A$ which is Avogadro's number.

## Mole of atoms
- One mole contain $6.02 \times 10^{23}$ molecules and is equivalent to the gram molecular mass of a given substance.
- 1 mole of $O_2$ contain $6.02 \times 10^{23}$ molecules & weighs 32g.

## Mole of atoms
- One mole of atoms contain $6.023 \times 10^{23}$ atoms having mass equal to gram atomic mass.
- One mole of oxygen atoms contain $6.02 \times 10^{23}$ atoms of oxygen and weighs 16g.

## Formula of compound

**Molecular formula**
- A formula that gives the total number of atoms of each element in molecule.
- e.g molecular formula of blue vitriol: $CuSO_4 \cdot 5H_2O$

**Empirical formula**
- It is the simplest positive integer ratio of atoms present in the compound.
- The sum of atomic mass of various elements present in empirical formula. E.g. in $H_2O_2$, HO mass = 1+16=17

**Determination of empirical formula**
- Start with number of grams of each element given in the problem.
- Convert the mass of each element to moles using the molar mass from the periodic table.
- Divide each mole value by the smallest member of moles present.
- Round to the nearest whole number.

**Determination of molecular formula**
- Calculate the empirical weight of a compound from it empirical formula.
- Divide its molecular weight by empirical formula weight which gives the number (n).
- Multiple the empirical formula by this number to get the molecular formula.
- Molecular formula = empirical formula × n where n = Molecular weight/Empirical formula weight

**Empirical formula**
- A formula that gives the simplest whole number ratio to the different atoms in a compound.
- e.g. HO is the empirical formula for hydrogen peroxide.
- $H_2O_2$ is molecular formula of hydrogen peroxide.

## Chemical equations
- A chemical equation is a balanced account of chemical transaction.

**Trace the Mind Map**
- First Level
- Second Level
- Third Level

# Mind Map : Electrolysis

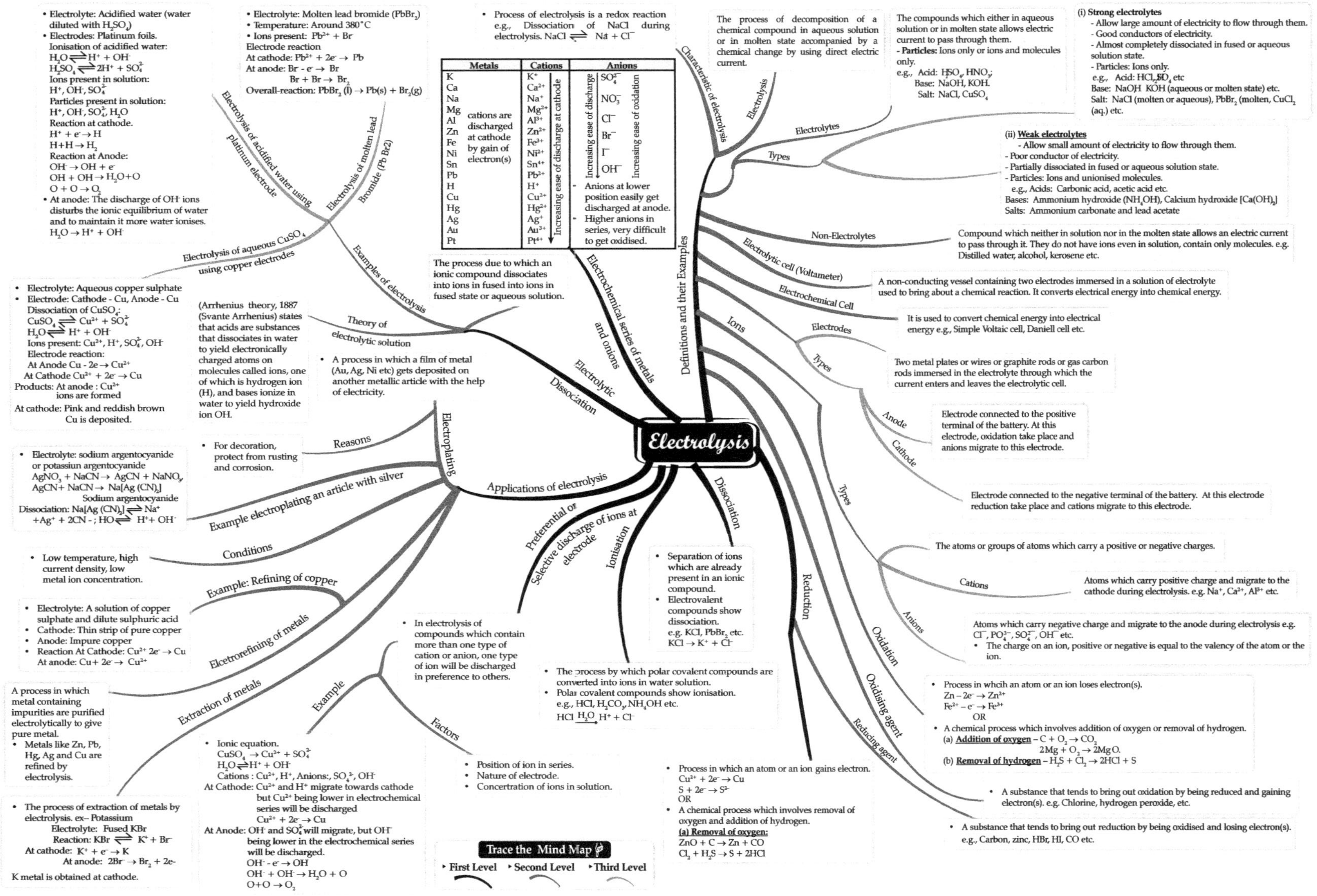

**Electrolysis**

## Definitions and their Examples

**Electrolysis**
The process of decomposition of a chemical compound in aqueous solution or in molten state accompanied by a chemical change by using direct electric current.

**Characteristic of electrolysis**
- Process of electrolysis is a redox reaction during electrolysis. e.g., Dissociation of $NaCl$ during electrolysis. $NaCl \rightleftharpoons Na^+ + Cl^-$

### Electrolytes
The compounds which either in aqueous solution or in molten state allows electric current to pass through them.
- Particles: Ions only or ions and molecules only.
e.g., Acid: $H_2SO_4$, $HNO_3$;
Base: NaOH, KOH
Salt: $NaCl$, $CuSO_4$

**Types**

**(i) Strong electrolytes**
- Allow large amount of electricity to flow through them.
- Good conductors of electricity.
- Almost completely dissociated in fused or aqueous solution state.
- Particles: Ions only.
e.g., Acid: HCl, $H_2SO_4$ etc
Base: NaOH, KOH (aqueous or molten state) etc.
Salt: NaCl (molten or aqueous), $PbBr_2$ (molten, $CuCl_2$ (aq.) etc.

**(ii) Weak electrolytes**
- Allow small amount of electricity to flow through them.
- Poor conductor of electricity.
- Partially dissociated in fused or aqueous solution state.
- Particles: Ions and unionised molecules.
e.g. Acids: Carbonic acid, acetic acid etc.
Bases: Ammonium hydroxide $(NH_4OH)$, Calcium hydroxide $[Ca(OH)_2]$
Salts: Ammonium carbonate and lead acetate

### Non-Electrolytes
Compound which neither in solution nor in the molten state allows an electric current to pass through it. They do not have ions even in solution, contain only molecules. e.g. Distilled water, alcohol, kerosene etc.

### Electrolytic cell (Voltameter)
A non-conducting vessel containing two electrodes immersed in a solution of electrolyte used to bring about a chemical reaction. It converts electrical energy into chemical energy.

### Electrochemical Cell
It is used to convert chemical energy into electrical energy e.g., Simple Voltaic cell, Daniell cell etc.

### Electrodes
Two metal plates or wires or graphite rods or gas carbon rods immersed in the electrolyte through which the current enters and leaves the electrolytic cell.

**Types**

**Anode**
Electrode connected to the positive terminal of the battery. At this electrode, oxidation take place and anions migrate to this electrode.

**Cathode**
Electrode connected to the negative terminal of the battery. At this electrode, reduction take place and cations migrate to this electrode.

### Ions
The atoms or groups of atoms which carry a positive or negative charges.

**Types**

**Cations**
Atoms which carry positive charge and migrate to the cathode during electrolysis. e.g. $Na^+$, $Ca^{2+}$, $Al^{3+}$ etc.

**Anions**
Atoms which carry negative charge and migrate to the anode during electrolysis e.g. $Cl^-$, $PO_4^{3-}$, $SO_4^{2-}$, $OH^-$ etc.
- The charge on an ion, positive or negative is equal to the valency of the atom or the ion.

### Oxidation
- Process in which an atom or an ion loses electron(s).
$Zn - 2e^- \rightarrow Zn^{2+}$
$Fe^{2+} - e^- \rightarrow Fe^{3+}$
OR
(a) **Addition of oxygen** $\rightarrow C + O_2 \rightarrow CO_2$
$2Mg + O_2 \rightarrow 2MgO$
(b) **Removal of hydrogen** : $H_2S + Cl_2 \rightarrow 2HCl + S$

**Oxidising agent**
A substance that tends to bring out oxidation by being reduced and gaining electron(s). e.g. Chlorine, hydrogen peroxide, etc.

**Reducing agent**
A substance that tends to bring out reduction by being oxidised and losing electron(s). e.g. Carbon, zinc, HBr, $H_2$, CO etc.

### Reduction
- Process in which an atom or an ion gains electron.
$Cu^{2+} + 2e^- \rightarrow Cu$
$S + 2e^- \rightarrow S^{2-}$
OR
(a) **Removal of oxygen:**
$ZnO + C \rightarrow Zn + CO$
$Cl_2 + H_2S \rightarrow S + 2HCl$
- A chemical process which involves removal of oxygen and addition of hydrogen.

### Dissociation
Separation of ions which are already present in an ionic compound. Electrovalent compounds show dissociation. e.g. KCl, $PbBr_2$ etc. $KCl \rightarrow K^+ + Cl^-$

### Ionisation
- The process by which polar covalent compounds are converted into ions in water solution. Polar covalent compounds show ionisation. e.g. HCl, $H_2CO_3$, $NH_4OH$ etc. $HCl \rightleftharpoons H^+ + Cl^-$

## Electrochemical series of metals and anions

| Metals | Cations |
|--------|---------|
| K | $K^+$ |
| Ca | $Ca^{2+}$ |
| Na | $Na^+$ |
| Mg | $Mg^{2+}$ |
| Al | $Al^{3+}$ |
| Zn | $Zn^{2+}$ |
| Fe | $Fe^{2+}$ |
| Ni | $Ni^{2+}$ |
| Sn | $Sn^{2+}$ |
| Pb | $Pb^{2+}$ |
| H | $H^+$ |
| Cu | $Cu^{2+}$ |
| Hg | $Hg^{2+}$ |
| Ag | $Ag^+$ |
| Au | $Au^{3+}$ |
| Pt | $Pt^{4+}$ |

Increasing ease of discharge at cathode. Cations are discharged at cathode by gain of electron(s).

| Anions |
|--------|
| $SO_4^{2-}$ |
| $NO_3^-$ |
| $Cl^-$ |
| $Br^-$ |
| $I^-$ |
| $OH^-$ |

Increasing ease of oxidation. Anions at lower position easily get discharged at anode. Higher anions in series, very difficult to get oxidised.

### Electrolytic Dissociation
The process due to which an ionic compound dissociates into ions in fused state or aqueous solution.

## Applications of electrolysis

### Selective discharge of ions at electrode
In electrolysis of compounds which contain more than one type of cation or anion, one type of ion will be discharged in preference to others.

**Preferential or Selective discharge — Factors:**
- Position of ion in series.
- Nature of electrode.
- Concentration of ions in solution.

### Electroplating
A process in which a film of metal (Au, Ag, Ni etc) gets deposited on another metallic article with the help of electricity.

**Reasons**
- For decoration, protect from rusting and corrosion.

**Example: electroplating an article with silver**
- Electrolyte: sodium argentocyanide or potassium argentocyanide
$AgNO_3 + NaCN \rightarrow AgCN + NaNO_3$
$AgCN + NaCN \rightarrow Na[Ag(CN)_2]$
Sodium argentocyanide
Dissociation: $Na[Ag(CN)_2] \rightleftharpoons Na^+ + [Ag(CN)_2]^-; \rightleftharpoons Ag^+ + 2CN^-$; $H_2O \rightleftharpoons H^+ + OH^-$

**Conditions**
- Low temperature, high current density, low metal ion concentration.

### Electrorefining of metals
A process in which metal containing impurities are purified electrolytically to give pure metal.
- Metals like Zn, Pb, Hg, Ag and Cu are refined by electrolysis.

**Example: Refining of copper**
- Electrolyte: A solution of copper sulphate and dilute sulphuric acid
- Cathode: Thin strip of pure copper
- Anode: Impure copper
- Reaction At Cathode: $Cu^{2+} + 2e^- \rightarrow Cu$
At anode: $Cu - 2e^- \rightarrow Cu^{2+}$

**Example**
- Ionic equation.
$CuSO_4 \rightarrow Cu^{2+} + SO_4^{2-}$
$H_2O \rightleftharpoons H^+ + OH^-$
Cations: $Cu^{2+}$, $H^+$, Anions: $SO_4^{2-}$, $OH^-$
At Cathode: $Cu^{2+}$ and $H^+$ migrate towards cathode but $Cu^{2+}$ being lower in electrochemical series will be discharged
$Cu^{2+} + 2e^- \rightarrow Cu$
At Anode: $OH^-$ and $SO_4^{2-}$ will migrate, but $OH^-$ being lower in the electrochemical series will be discharged.
$OH^- - e^- \rightarrow OH$
$OH^- + OH \rightarrow H_2O + O$
$O + O \rightarrow O_2$

### Extraction of metals
The process of extraction of metals by electrolysis. ex– Potassium
Electrolyte: Fused KBr
Reaction: $KBr \rightleftharpoons K^+ + Br^-$
At cathode: $K^+ + e^- \rightarrow K$
At anode: $2Br^- \rightarrow Br_2 + 2e^-$
K metal is obtained at cathode.

## Examples of electrolysis

### Electrolysis of molten lead bromide (PbBr₂)
- Electrolyte: Molten lead bromide $(PbBr_2)$
- Temperature: Around 380°C
- Ions present: $Pb^{2+} + Br^-$
Electrode reaction
At cathode: $Pb^{2+} + 2e^- \rightarrow Pb$
At anode: $Br - e \rightarrow Br$
$Br + Br \rightarrow Br_2$
Overall-reaction: $PbBr_2 (l) \rightarrow Pb(s) + Br_2(g)$

### Theory of electrolytic solution
(Arrhenius theory, 1887 (Svante Arrhenius) states that acids are substances that dissociates in water to yield electronically charged atoms on molecules called ions, one of which is hydrogen ion (H), and bases ionize in water to yield hydroxide ion OH.

### Electrolysis of acidified water using platinum electrode
- Electrolyte: Acidified water (water diluted with $H_2SO_4$)
- Electrodes: Platinum foils.
Ionisation of acidified water:
$H_2O \rightleftharpoons H^+ + OH^-$
$H_2SO_4 \rightleftharpoons 2H^+ + SO_4^{2-}$
Ions present in solution:
$H^+, OH^-, SO_4^{2-}$
Reaction at cathode.
$H^+ + e^- \rightarrow H$
$H + H \rightarrow H_2$
Reaction at Anode:
$OH^- \rightarrow OH + e^-$
$OH + OH \rightarrow H_2O + O$
$O + O \rightarrow O_2$
- At anode: The discharge of $OH^-$ ions disturbe the ionic equilibrium of water and to maintain it more water ionises.
$H_2O \rightarrow H^+ + OH^-$

### Electrolysis of aqueous copper sulphate using copper electrodes
- Electrolyte: Aqueous copper sulphate
- Electrode: Cathode – Cu, Anode – Cu
Dissociation of $CuSO_4$:
$CuSO_4 \rightleftharpoons Cu^{2+} + SO_4^{2-}$
$H_2O \rightleftharpoons H^+ + OH^-$
Ions present: $Cu^{2+}, H^+, SO_4^{2-}, OH^-$
Electrode reaction:
At Anode $Cu - 2e \rightarrow Cu^{2+}$
At Cathode $Cu^{2+} + 2e^- \rightarrow Cu$
Products: At anode : $Cu^{2+}$ ions are formed
At cathode: Pink and reddish brown Cu is deposited.

**Trace the Mind Map**
→ First Level  → Second Level  → Third Level

# Mind Map : Metallurgy

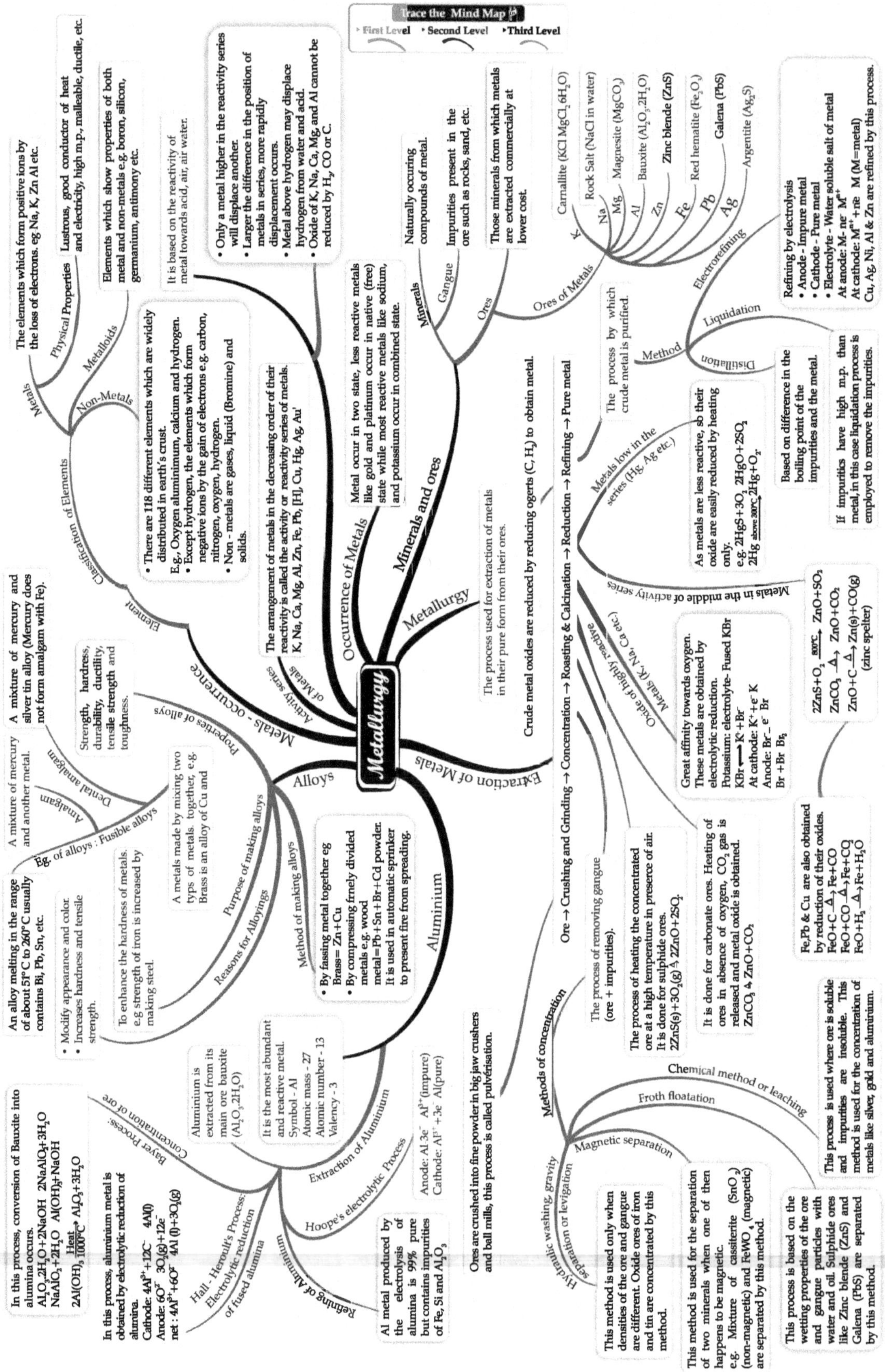

**Metallurgy** (central node)

## Metals - occurrence

**Physical Properties**
- Metals: The elements which form positive ions by the loss of electrons. eg Na, K, Zn Al etc.
- Lustrous, good conductor of heat and electricity, high m.p., malleable, ductile, etc.
- Metalloids: Elements which show properties of both metal and non-metals e.g. boron, silicon, germanium, antimony etc.

**Activity series of Metals**
- It is based on the reactivity of metal towards acid, air, air water.
- Only a metal higher in the reactivity series will displace another.
- Larger the difference in the position of metals in series, more rapidly displacement occurs.
- Metal above hydrogen may displace hydrogen from water and acid.
- Oxide of K, Na, Ca, Mg, and Al cannot be reduced by $H_2$, CO or C.
- The arrangement of metals in the decreasing order of their reactivity is called the activity or reactivity series of metals. K, Na, Ca, Mg, Al, Zn, Fe, Pb, [H], Cu, Hg, Ag, Au'

## Classification of Elements

**Element**
- There are 118 different elements which are widely distributed in earth's crust. E.g., Oxygen aluminium, calcium and hydrogen.

**Non-Metals**
- Except hydrogen, the elements which form negative ions by the gain of electrons e.g. carbon, nitrogen, oxygen, hydrogen.
- Non - metals are gases, liquid (Bromine) and solids.

## Occurrence of Metals
- Metal occur in two state, less reactive metals like gold and platinum occur in native (free) state while most reactive metals like sodium, and potassium occur in combined state.

## Minerals and ores

**Minerals** – Naturally occuring compounds of metal.

**Gangue** – Impurities present in the ore such as rocks, sand, etc.

**Ores** – Those minerals from which metals are extracted commercially at lower cost.

**Ores of Metals**
- K – Carnallite ($KCl\ MgCl_2\ 6H_2O$)
- Na – Rock Salt (NaCl in water)
- Mg – Magnesite ($MgCO_3$)
- Al – Bauxite ($Al_2O_3.2H_2O$)
- Zn – Zinc blende (ZnS)
- Fe – Red hematite ($Fe_2O_3$)
- Pb – Galena (PbS)
- Ag – Argentite ($Ag_2S$)

## Metallurgy
- The process used for extraction of metals in their pure form from their ores.
- Crude metal oxides are reduced by reducing ogents (C, $H_2$) to obtain metal.

## Extraction of Metals

**Method** – The process by which crude metal is purified.

**Electrorefining / Refining by electrolysis**
- Anode - Impure metal
- Cathode - Pure metal
- Electrolyte - Water soluble salt of metal
- At anode: $M - ne^- \rightarrow M^{n+}$
- At cathode: $M^{n+} + ne^- \rightarrow M$ (M=metal)
- Cu, Ag, Ni, Al & Zn are refined by this process.

**Distillation** – Metals low in the series (Hg, Ag etc.)
- As metals are less reactive, so their oxide are easily reduced by heating only.
- e.g. $2HgS + 3O_2 \rightarrow 2HgO + 2SO_2$; $2HgO \xrightarrow{above\ 300°C} 2Hg + O_2$

**Liquidation** – Based on difference in the boiling point of the impurities and the metal.
- If impurities have high m.p. than metal, in this case liquidation process is employed to remove the impurities.

**Oxide of highly reactive metals (K, Na, etc.)** – Metals of highly reactive (K, Na, Ca etc.)
- Great affinity towards oxygen. These metals are obtained by electrolytic reduction.
- Potassium: electrolyte- Fused KBr
- $KBr \rightarrow K^+ + Br^-$
- At cathode: $K^+ + e^- \rightarrow K$
- Anode: $Br^- - e^- \rightarrow Br$
- $Br + Br \rightarrow Br_2$

**Metals in the middle of activity series**
- $2ZnS + O_2 \xrightarrow{50°C} ZnO + SO_2$
- $ZnCO_3 \xrightarrow{\Delta} ZnO + CO_2$
- $ZnO + C \xrightarrow{\Delta} Zn(s) + CO(g)$ (zinc spelter)
- Fe, Pb & Cu are also obtained by reduction of their oxides.
- $FeO + C \xrightarrow{\Delta} Fe + CO$
- $FeO + CO \xrightarrow{\Delta} Fe + CO_2$
- $FeO + H_2 \xrightarrow{\Delta} Fe + H_2O$

**Process**
- Ore → Crushing and Grinding → Concentration → Roasting & Calcination → Reduction → Refining → Pure metal
- The process of removing gangue (ore + impurities).
- The process of heating the concentrated ore at a high temperature in presence of air. It is done for sulphide ores. $2ZnS(s) + 3O_2(g) \xrightarrow{\Delta} 2ZnO + 2SO_2$
- It is done for carbonate ores. Heating of ores in absence of oxygen, $CO_2$ gas is released and metal oxide is obtained. $ZnCO_3 \xrightarrow{\Delta} ZnO + CO_2$

## Methods of concentration

**Methods**
- Ores are crushed into fine powder in big jaw crushers and ball mills, this process is called pulverisation.

**Chemical method or leaching** – This process is used where ore is soluble and impurities are insoluble. This method is used for the concentration of metals like silver, gold and aluminium.

**Froth floatation** – This process is based on the wetting properties of the ore and gangue particles with water and oil. Sulphide ores like Zinc blende (ZnS) and Galena (PbS) are separated by this method.

**Magnetic separation** – This method is used for the separation of two minerals when one of then happens to be magnetic. e.g. Mixture of cassiterite ($SnO_2$) and $FeWO_4$ (magnetic) are separated by this method.

**Hydraulic washing, gravity separation or levigation** – This method is used only when densities of the ore and gangue are different. Oxide ores of iron and tin are concentrated by this method.

## Alloys

**Properties of alloys** – Strength, hardness, ductility, tensile strength and toughness.

**Amalgam** – A mixture of mercury and another metal.
- Dental amalgam: A mixture of mercury and silver tin alloy (Mercury does not form amalgam with Fe).

**Eg. of alloys : Fusible alloys** – An alloy melting in the range of about 51°C to 260°C usually contains Bi, Pb, Sn, etc.

**Purpose of making alloys**
- Modify appearance and color.
- Increases hardness and strength.

**Reasons for Alloying** – To enhance the hardness of metals. e.g strength of iron is increased by making steel.

**Method of making alloys** – A metals made by mixing two typs of metals. together, e.g. Brass is an alloy of Cu and
- By fassing metal together eg Brass = Zn+Cu
- By compressing frmely divided metals e.g. wood metal = Pb+Sn+Br+Cd powder. It is used in automatic sprinker to present fire from spreading.

## Aluminium
- Aluminium is extracted from its main ore bauxite ($Al_2O_3.2H_2O$)
- It is the most abundant and reactive metal. Symbol - Al; Atomic mass - 27; Atomic number - 13; Valency - 3

**Extraction of Aluminium**

**Concentration of ore / Bayer Process:**
- In this process, conversion of Bauxite into alumina occurs.
- $Al_2O_3.2H_2O + 2NaOH \rightarrow 2NaAlO_2 + 3H_2O$
- $NaAlO_2 + 2H_2O \rightarrow Al(OH)_3 + NaOH$
- $2Al(OH)_3 \xrightarrow[1000°C]{Heat} Al_2O_3 + 3H_2O$

**Hall - Heroult's Process: Electrolytic reduction of fused alumina**
- In this process, aluminium metal is obtained by electrolytic reduction of alumina.
- Cathode: $4Al^{3+} + 12e^- \rightarrow 4Al(l)$
- Anode: $6O^{2-} \rightarrow 3O_2(g) + 12e^-$
- net : $4Al^{3+} + 6O^{2-} \rightarrow 4Al(l) + 3O_2(g)$

**Hoope's electrolytic Process / Refining of Aluminium**
- Anode: $Al - 3e^- \rightarrow Al^{3+}$ (impure)
- Cathode: $Al^{3+} + 3e^- \rightarrow Al$ (pure)

# Mind Map : Hydrogen chloride Gas and Hydrochloric Acid

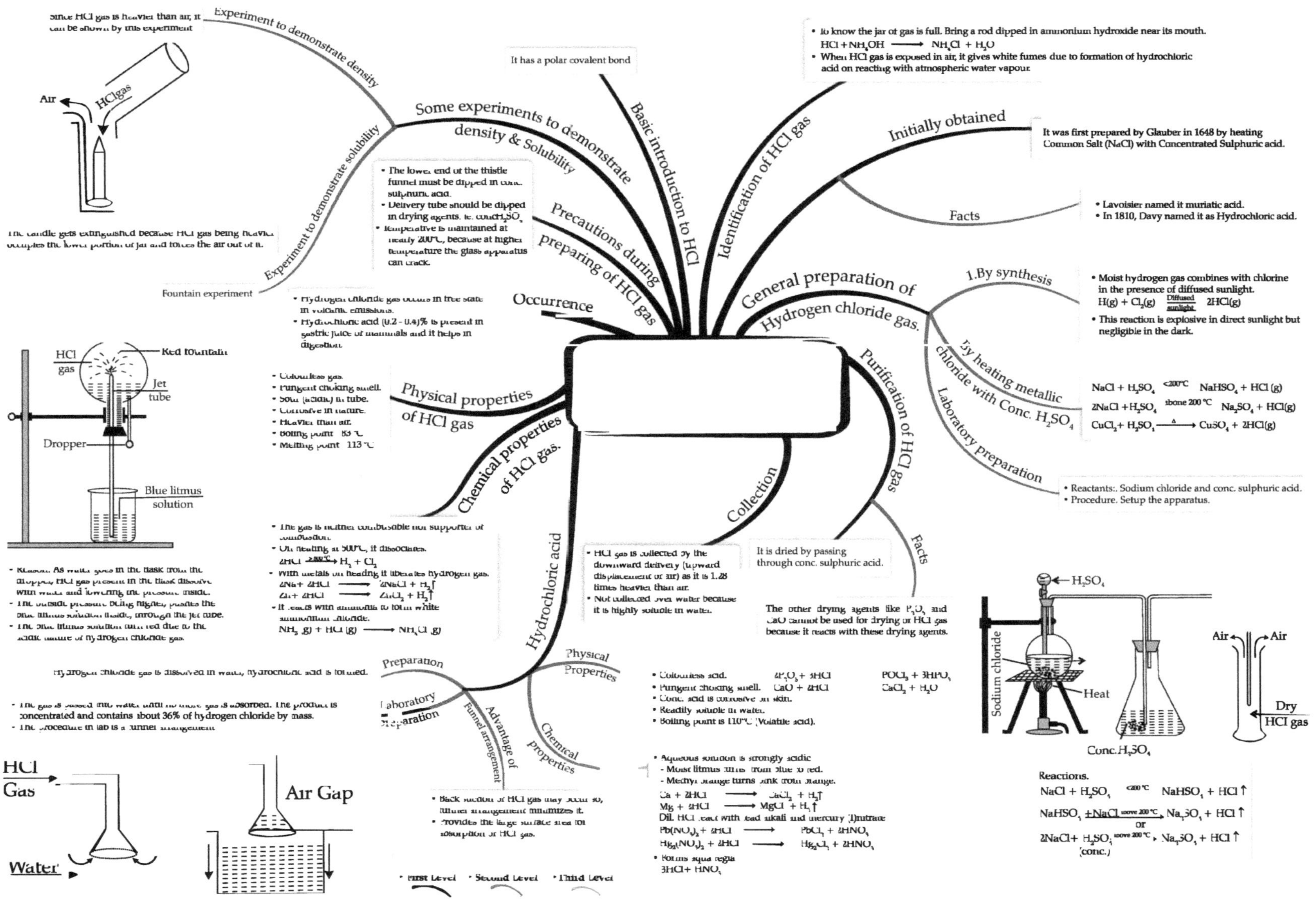

**General preparation of Hydrogen chloride gas.**

## Initially obtained
It was first prepared by Glauber in 1648 by heating Common Salt (NaCl) with Concentrated Sulphuric acid.

## Facts
- Lavoisier named it muriatic acid.
- In 1810, Davy named it as Hydrochloric acid.

## 1. By synthesis
- Moist hydrogen gas combines with chlorine in the presence of diffused sunlight.

$$H_2(g) + Cl_2(g) \xrightarrow[sunlight]{Diffused} 2HCl(g)$$

- This reaction is explosive in direct sunlight but negligible in the dark.

## By heating metallic chloride with Conc. $H_2SO_4$

$$NaCl + H_2SO_4 \xrightarrow{<200\,°C} NaHSO_4 + HCl\,(g)$$
$$2NaCl + H_2SO_4 \xrightarrow{above\ 200\,°C} Na_2SO_4 + 2HCl(g)$$
$$CuCl_2 + H_2SO_4 \xrightarrow{\Delta} CuSO_4 + 2HCl(g)$$

## Laboratory preparation
- Reactants:- Sodium chloride and conc. sulphuric acid.
- Procedure:- Setup the apparatus.



**Reactions.**

$$NaCl + H_2SO_4 \xrightarrow{<200\,°C} NaHSO_4 + HCl\uparrow$$
$$NaHSO_4 + NaCl \xrightarrow{above\ 200\,°C} Na_2SO_4 + HCl\uparrow$$
$$or$$
$$2NaCl + H_2SO_4 \xrightarrow{above\ 200\,°C} Na_2SO_4 + HCl\uparrow \ (conc.)$$

## Identification of HCl gas
- To know the jar of gas is full. Bring a rod dipped in ammonium hydroxide near its mouth.

$$HCl + NH_4OH \longrightarrow NH_4Cl + H_2O$$

- When HCl gas is exposed in air, it gives white fumes due to formation of hydrochloric acid on reacting with atmospheric water vapour

## Basic introduction to HCl
It has a polar covalent bond

## Purification of HCl gas

### Facts
It is dried by passing through conc. sulphuric acid.

The other drying agents like $P_2O_5$ and CaO cannot be used for drying or HCl gas because it reacts with these drying agents.

$$P_2O_5 + 3H_2O$$
$$CaO + 2HCl \longrightarrow CaCl_2 + H_2O$$

### Collection
- HCl gas is collected by the downward delivery (upward displacement of air) as it is 1.28 times heavier than air.
- Not collected over water because it is highly soluble in water.

## Occurrence
- Hydrogen chloride gas occurs in free state in volcanic emissions.
- Hydrochloric acid (0.2 – 0.4)% is present in gastric juice of mammals and it helps in digestion.

## Precautions during Preparing of HCl gas
- The lower end of the thistle funnel must be dipped in conc. sulphuric acid.
- Delivery tube should be dipped in drying agents i.e. conc.$H_2SO_4$
- Temperature is maintained at nearly 200°C, because at higher temperature the glass apparatus can crack

## Physical properties of HCl gas
- Colourless gas.
- Pungent choking smell.
- Corrosive in nature.
- Fuming fluid air.
- Boiling point 85°C
- Melting point 113°C

## Chemical properties of HCl gas
- The gas is neither combustible nor supporter of combustion.
- On heating at 500°C, it dissociates.

$$2HCl \xrightarrow{500\,°C} H_2 + Cl_2$$

- With metals on heating it liberates hydrogen gas.

$$2Na + 2HCl \longrightarrow 2NaCl + H_2\uparrow$$
$$Zn + 2HCl \longrightarrow ZnCl_2 + H_2\uparrow$$

- It combines with ammonia to form white ammonium chloride.

$$NH_3(g) + HCl(g) \longrightarrow NH_4Cl(g)$$

## Some experiments to demonstrate density & Solubility

### Experiment to demonstrate density
Since HCl gas is heavier than air, it can be shown by this experiment



### Experiment to demonstrate solubility — Fountain experiment
Reason:- As water goes in the flask from the dropper, HCl gas present in the flask dissolves with water and lowering the pressure inside. Due to this reason, during lowering pressure, pushes the blue litmus solution itself, through the jet tube. The blue litmus solution turned due to the acidic nature of hydrogen chloride gas.



## Hydrochloric acid

### Physical Properties
- Colourless acid.
- Pungent choking smell.
- Sour (acidic) in taste.
- Conc. acid is corrosive to skin.
- Readily soluble in water.
- Boiling point is 110°C (Volatile acid).

### Chemical properties
- Aqueous solution is strongly acidic
  - Moist litmus turns from blue to red.
  - Methyl orange turns red from orange.

$$Ca + 2HCl \longrightarrow CaCl_2 + H_2\uparrow$$
$$Mg + 2HCl \longrightarrow MgCl_2 + H_2\uparrow$$

Dil. HCl conc with red alkali and mercury ]]nitrate

$$Pb(NO_3)_2 + 2HCl \longrightarrow PbCl_2 + 2HNO_3$$
$$Hg_2(NO_3)_2 + 2HCl \longrightarrow Hg_2Cl_2 + 2HNO_3$$

Forms aqua regia
$$3HCl + HNO_3$$

### Advantage of Funnel arrangement
- Back suction of HCl gas may occur so, it funnel arrangement minimizes it.
- Provides the large surface area for absorption of HCl gas.

### Laboratory Preparation
Hydrogen chloride gas is dissolved in water, hydrochloric acid is formed.
- The gas is passed till water, until no more gas is absorbed. The product is concentrated and contains about 36% of hydrogen chloride by mass.
- The absorbance in air is a funnel arrangement.

# Mind Map : Organic Chemistry

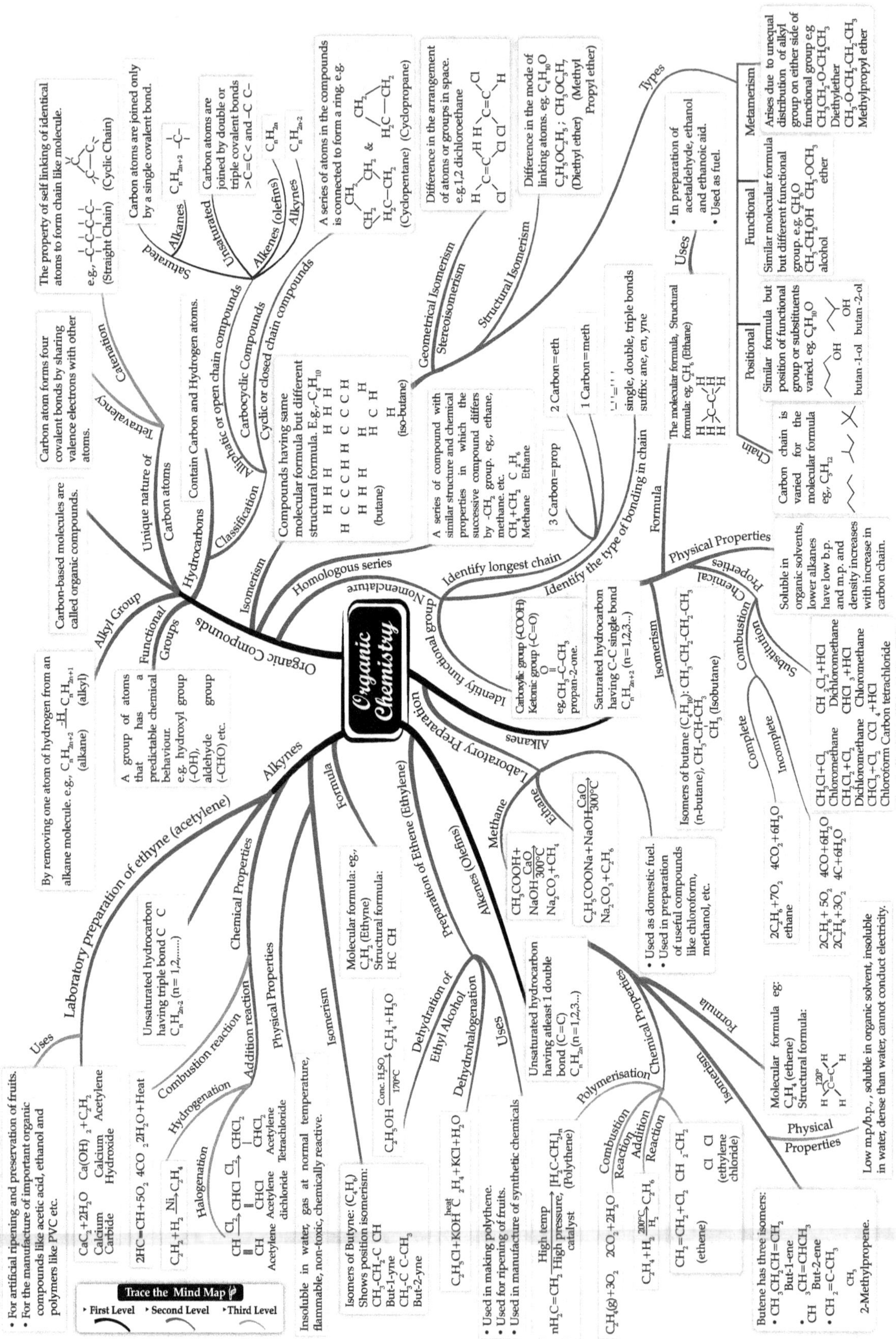

**Organic Chemistry**

## Organic Compounds

### Unique nature of Carbon atoms

- **Catenation** — The property of self linking of identical atoms to form chain like molecule. e.g., $-C-C-C-C-$ (Straight Chain); (Cyclic Chain)
- **Tetravalency** — Carbon atom forms four covalent bonds by sharing valence electrons with other atoms.
- Carbon-based molecules are called organic compounds.

### Hydrocarbons
Contain Carbon and Hydrogen atoms.

#### Classification
- **Aliphatic** or open chain compounds
  - **Saturated**
    - **Alkanes** $C_nH_{2n+2}$ — Carbon atoms are joined only by a single covalent bond.
  - **Unsaturated** — Carbon atoms are joined by double or triple covalent bonds $>C=C<$ and $-C\equiv C-$
    - **Alkenes (olefins)** $C_nH_{2n}$
    - **Alkynes** $C_nH_{2n-2}$
- **Carbocyclic Compounds** / Cyclic or closed chain compounds — A series of atoms in the compounds is connected to form a ring. e.g. (Cyclopropane), (Cyclopentane)

### Functional Groups
A group of atoms that has a predictable chemical behaviour. e.g. hydroxyl group (-OH), aldehyde (-CHO) etc.

### Alkyl Group
By removing one atom of hydrogen from an alkane molecule. e.g., $C_nH_{2n+2} \xrightarrow{-H} C_nH_{2n+1}$ (alkane) → (alkyl)

## Isomerism

Compounds having same molecular formula but different structural formula. E.g. $-C_4H_{10}$ (butane), (iso-butane)

### Structural Isomerism
- **Chain** — The molecular formula, Structural formula: e.g. $C_2H_6$ (Ethane). Carbon chain is varied for the molecular formula. e.g., $C_5H_{12}$
- **Positional** — Similar formula but position of functional group or substituents varied. e.g. $C_4H_{10}O$; butan-1-ol, butan-2-ol
- **Functional** — Similar molecular formula but different functional group. e.g. $C_2H_6O$; $CH_3-CH_2OH$ alcohol, $CH_3-O-CH_3$ ether
- **Metamerism** — Arises due to unequal distribution of alkyl group on either side of functional group e.g. $CH_3CH_2-O-CH_2CH_3$ Diethylether, $CH_3-O-CH_2-CH_2-CH_3$ Methylpropyl ether

### Stereoisomerism
- **Geometrical Isomerism**
- Difference in the mode of linking atoms. e.g. $C_4H_{10}$; $C_2H_5OC_2H_5$ (Diethyl ether), $CH_3OC_3H_7$ (Methyl Propyl ether)

#### Types
- **Uses**
  - In preparation of acetaldehyde, ethanol and ethanoic aid.
  - Used as fuel.
- Difference in the arrangement of atoms or groups in space. e.g.1,2 dichloroethane

## Homologous series
A series of compound with similar structure and chemical properties in which the successive compound differs by -CH₂ group. e.g., ethane, methane etc. $CH_4+CH_2$, $C_2H_6$; Methane, Ethane

## Nomenclature
- Identify longest chain
- Identify the type of bonding in chain
- Identify functional group

### Formula
- 1 Carbon = meth
- 2 Carbon = eth
- 3 Carbon = prop
- single, double, triple bonds suffix: ane, en, yne

### Physical Properties
Soluble in organic solvents, lower alkanes have low b.p. and m.p. and density increases with increase in carbon chain.

## Alkanes
Saturated hydrocarbon having C-C single bond $C_nH_{2n+2}$ (n=1,2,3...)

### Isomerism
Isomers of butane ($C_4H_{10}$): $CH_3-CH_2-CH_2-CH_3$ (n-butane), $CH_3-CH-CH_3$ with $CH_3$ (Isobutane)

### Chemical Properties
- **Combustion**
  - Complete: $2CH_4+7O_2 \rightarrow 4CO_2+6H_2O$
  - Incomplete
  - $2C_2H_6+5O_2 \rightarrow 4CO+6H_2O$; $2C_2H_6+3O_2 \rightarrow 4C+6H_2O$
- **Substitution**
  - $CH_4+Cl_2 \rightarrow CH_3Cl+HCl$ Chloromethane
  - $CH_3Cl+Cl_2 \rightarrow CH_2Cl_2+HCl$ Dichloromethane
  - $CH_2Cl_2+Cl_2 \rightarrow CHCl_3+HCl$ Chloroform
  - $CHCl_3+Cl_2 \rightarrow CCl_4+HCl$ Carbon tetrachloride

## Laboratory Preparation

### Methane
$CH_3COOH + NaOH \xrightarrow{CaO, 300°C} Na_2CO_3 + CH_4$

### Ethane
$C_2H_5COONa + NaOH \xrightarrow{CaO, 300°C} Na_2CO_3 + C_2H_6$

- Used as domestic fuel.
- Used in preparation of useful compounds like chloroform, methanol, etc.

## Alkenes (Olefins)
Unsaturated hydrocarbon having atleast 1 double bond (C=C) $C_nH_{2n}$ (n=1,2,3...)

### Formula
Molecular formula e.g. $C_2H_4$ (ethene). Structural formula: $H_2C=CH_2$

### Chemical Properties
- **Polymerisation**
  $nH_2C=CH_2 \xrightarrow[\text{catalyst}]{\text{High temp, High pressure}} [H_2C-CH_2]_n$ (Polythene)
- **Combustion Reaction**: $C_2H_4+H_2 \xrightarrow{200°C} C_2H_6$
- **Addition Reaction**: $CH_2=CH_2+Cl_2 \rightarrow CH_2Cl-CH_2Cl$ (ethylene chloride)

### Physical Properties
Low m.p./b.p., soluble in organic solvent, insoluble in water, dense than water, cannot conduct electricity.

### Preparation of Ethene (Ethylene)
- **Dehydration of Ethyl Alcohol**: $C_2H_5OH \xrightarrow[170°C]{\text{Conc. }H_2SO_4} C_2H_4+H_2O$
- **Dehydrohalogenation**: $C_2H_5Cl+KOH \xrightarrow{heat} C_2H_4+KCl+H_2O$

### Uses
- Used in making polythene.
- Used for ripening of fruits.
- Used in manufacture of synthetic chemicals

## Alkynes
Unsaturated hydrocarbon having triple bond $C\equiv C$ $C_nH_{2n-2}$ (n=1,2,......)

### Physical Properties
Insoluble in water, gas at normal temperature, flammable, non-toxic, chemically reactive.

### Isomerism
Isomers of Butyne: ($C_4H_6$); Shows position isomerism: $CH_3-CH_2-C\equiv CH$ But-1-yne; $CH_3-C\equiv C-CH_3$ But-2-yne

### Chemical Properties
- **Addition reaction**
- **Hydrogenation**: $C_2H_2+H_2 \xrightarrow{Ni} C_2H_4$
- **Combustion reaction**
- **Halogenation**: $CH\equiv CH \xrightarrow{Cl_2} CHCl=CHCl \xrightarrow{Cl_2} CHCl_2-CHCl_2$; Acetylene, Acetylene dichloride, Acetylene Tetrachloride

### Laboratory preparation of ethyne (acetylene)
$CaC_2+2H_2O \rightarrow Ca(OH)_2+C_2H_2$; Calcium Carbide, Calcium Hydroxide, Acetylene
$2HC\equiv CH+5O_2 \rightarrow 4CO_2+2H_2O+Heat$

### Uses
- For artificial ripening and preservation of fruits.
- For the manufacture of important organic compounds like acetic acid, ethanol and polymers like PVC etc.

**Functional groups:** Carboxylic group (-COOH); Ketonic group (-C=O), O=; e.g. $CH_3-C-CH_3$, propan-2-one.

**Butene has three isomers:** $CH_3\,CH_2\,CH=CH_2$ But-1-ene; $CH_3\,CH=CHCH_3$ But-2-ene; $CH_2=C-CH_3$ with $CH_3$, 2-Methylpropene.

$C_4H_6(g)+3O_2 \rightarrow 2CO_2+2H_2O$

---

**Trace the Mind Map**
- First Level
- Second Level
- Third Level

# Mind Map : Organic Chemistry

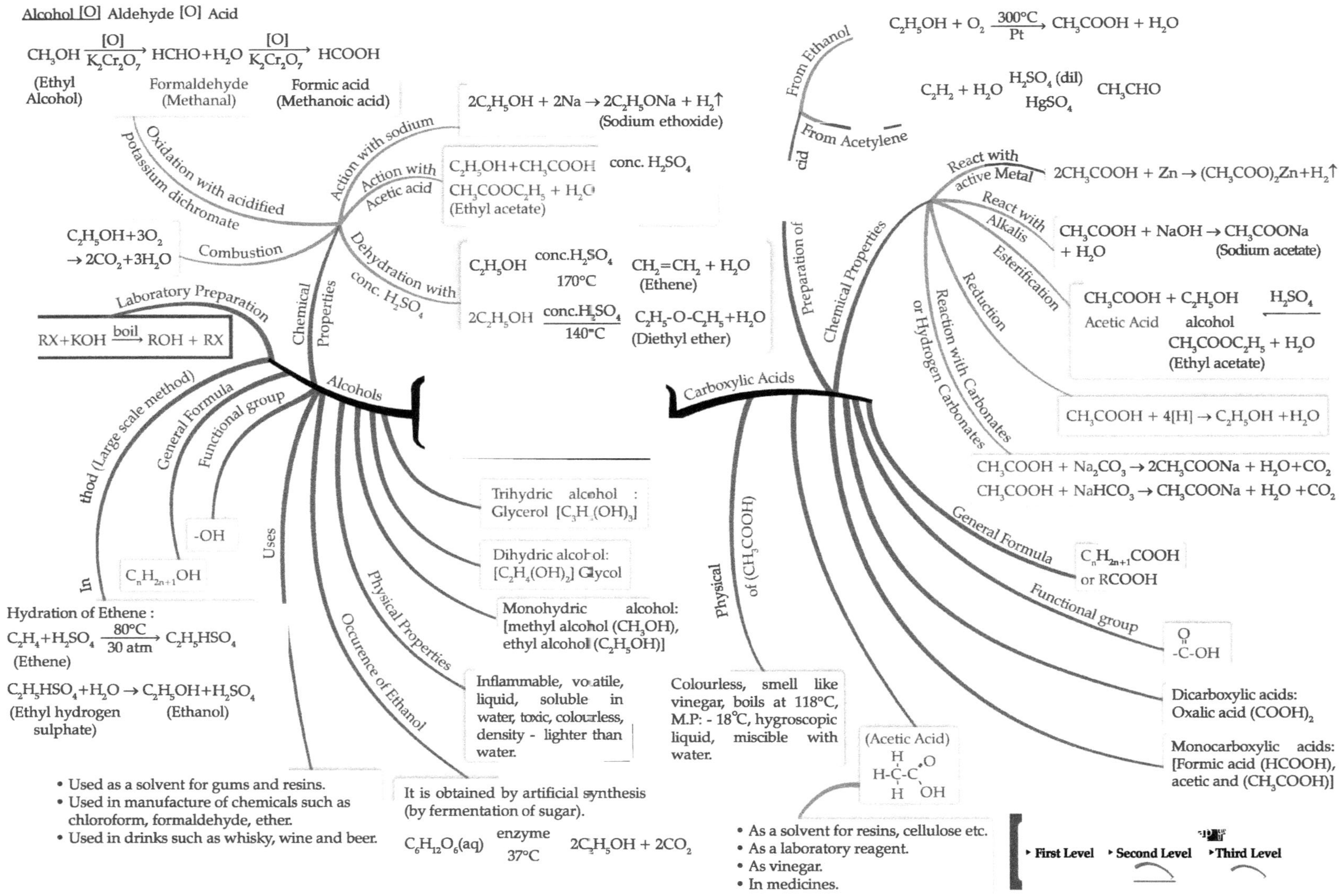

## Carboxylic Acids

**Chemical Properties**

- React with active Metal: $2CH_3COOH + Zn \rightarrow (CH_3COO)_2Zn + H_2\uparrow$
- React with Alkalis: $CH_3COOH + NaOH \rightarrow CH_3COONa + H_2O$ (Sodium acetate)
- Esterification: $CH_3COOH + C_2H_5OH \xrightarrow{H_2SO_4} CH_3COOC_2H_5 + H_2O$ (Ethyl acetate) — Acetic Acid, alcohol
- Reduction: $CH_3COOH + 4[H] \rightarrow C_2H_5OH + H_2O$
- Reaction with Carbonates or Hydrogen Carbonates: $CH_3COOH + Na_2CO_3 \rightarrow 2CH_3COONa + H_2O + CO_2$; $CH_3COOH + NaHCO_3 \rightarrow CH_3COONa + H_2O + CO_2$

**Preparation of Carboxylic Acids**

- From Ethanol: $C_2H_5OH + O_2 \xrightarrow[Pt]{300°C} CH_3COOH + H_2O$
- From Acetylene: $C_2H_2 + H_2O \xrightarrow[HgSO_4]{H_2SO_4\ (dil)} CH_3CHO$

**General Formula:** $C_nH_{2n+1}COOH$ or $RCOOH$

**Functional group:** $-\overset{O}{\underset{}{C}}-OH$

- Dicarboxylic acids: Oxalic acid $(COOH)_2$
- Monocarboxylic acids: [Formic acid (HCOOH), acetic acid and ($CH_3COOH$)]

**Physical** of ($CH_3COOH$): Colourless, smell like vinegar, boils at 118°C, M.P.:- 18°C, hygroscopic liquid, miscible with water.

(Acetic Acid)

**Uses**

- As a solvent for resins, cellulose etc.
- As a laboratory reagent.
- As vinegar.
- In medicines.

Legend: ▸ First Level    ▸ Second Level    ▸ Third Level

## Alcohols

**Chemical Properties**

- Action with sodium: $2C_2H_5OH + 2Na \rightarrow 2C_2H_5ONa + H_2\uparrow$ (Sodium ethoxide)
- Action with Acetic acid: $C_2H_5OH + CH_3COOH \xrightarrow{conc.\ H_2SO_4} CH_3COOC_2H_5 + H_2O$ (Ethyl acetate)
- Dehydration with conc. $H_2SO_4$: $C_2H_5OH \xrightarrow[170°C]{conc.\ H_2SO_4} CH_2=CH_2 + H_2O$ (Ethene); $2C_2H_5OH \xrightarrow[140°C]{conc.\ H_2SO_4} C_2H_5-O-C_2H_5 + H_2O$ (Diethyl ether)
- Oxidation with acidified Potassium dichromate: Alcohol [O] → Aldehyde [O] → Acid; $CH_3OH \xrightarrow{[O]\ K_2Cr_2O_7} HCHO + H_2O \xrightarrow{[O]\ K_2Cr_2O_7} HCOOH$ (Ethyl Alcohol) — Formaldehyde (Methanal), Formic acid (Methanoic acid)
- Combustion: $C_2H_5OH + 3O_2 \rightarrow 2CO_2 + 3H_2O$

**Types**

- Trihydric alcohol: Glycerol $[C_3H_5(OH)_3]$
- Dihydric alcohol: $[C_2H_4(OH)_2]$ Glycol
- Monohydric alcohol: [methyl alcohol ($CH_3OH$), ethyl alcohol ($C_2H_5OH$)]

**Physical Properties:** Inflammable, volatile, liquid, soluble in water, toxic, colourless, density - lighter than water.

**Occurence of Ethanol:** It is obtained by artificial synthesis (by fermentation of sugar). $C_6H_{12}O_6(aq) \xrightarrow[37°C]{enzyme} 2C_2H_5OH + 2CO_2$

**Uses**

- Used as a solvent for gums and resins.
- Used in manufacture of chemicals such as chloroform, formaldehyde, ether.
- Used in drinks such as whisky, wine and beer.

**Laboratory Preparation** (Large scale method): $RX + KOH \xrightarrow{boil} ROH + RX$

**Functional group:** -OH

**General Formula:** $C_nH_{2n+1}OH$

**Hydration of Ethene:** $C_2H_4 + H_2SO_4 \xrightarrow[30\ atm]{80°C} C_2H_5HSO_4$ (Ethene); $C_2H_5HSO_4 + H_2O \rightarrow C_2H_5OH + H_2SO_4$ (Ethyl hydrogen sulphate) (Ethanol)

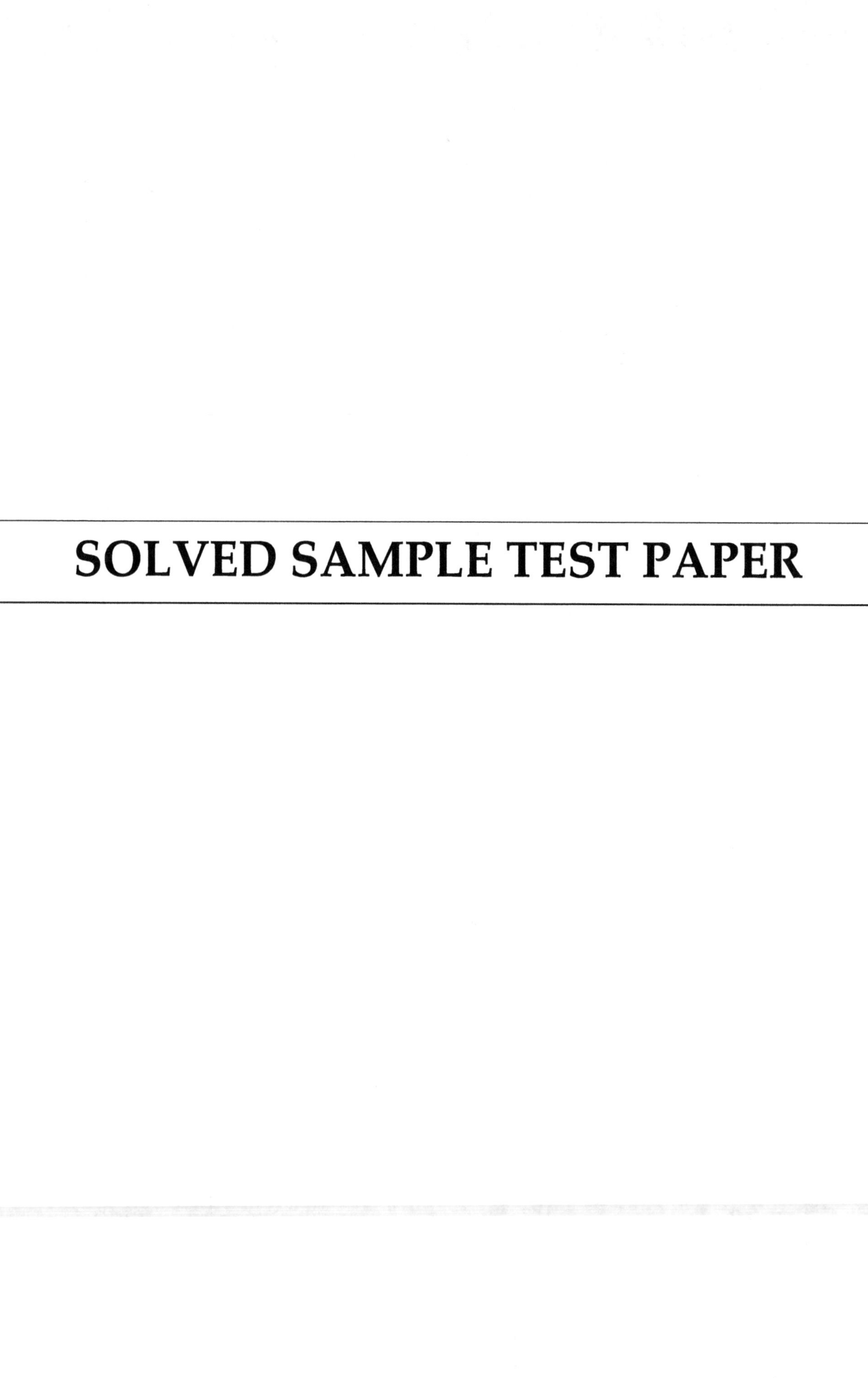
SOLVED SAMPLE TEST PAPER

**ICSE 2023 EXAMINATION**

SPECIMEN QUESTION PAPER

**CHEMISTRY**

(SCIENCE PAPER-2)

**Maximum Marks: 80**

Time allowed: Two hours

Answers to this Paper must be written on the paper provided separately.

You will not be allowed to write during first 15 minutes.

This time is to be spent in reading the question paper.

The time given at the head of this Paper is the time allowed for writing the answers.

**(Section A is compulsory. Attempt any four questions from Section B.**

**The intended marks for questions or parts of questions are given in brackets [ ].**

## SECTION A

**Answer all the questions from this section**

**Question 1.**

Choose one correct answer to the questions from the given options:　　　　　　　　　　　**[15]**

(i)　A weak electrolyte is:

  **(a)** Alcohol

  **(b)** Potassium hydroxide

  **(c)** Ammonium hydroxide

  **(d)** Glucose

  **Answer.** (c) Ammonium hydroxide

(ii)　An electron of unity is maximum in:

  **(a)** Alkaline earth metals

  **(b)** Halogens

  **(c)** Inert gases

  **(d)** Alkali metals

  **Answer.** (b) Halogens

(iii)　The main components of bronze are:

  **(a)** Copper and tin

  **(b)** Copper and iron

  **(c)** Copper and lead

  **(d)** Copper and zinc

  **Answer.** (a) Copper and tin

(iv)　A polar covalent compound is:

  **(a)** Methane

  **(b)** Ammonia

  **(c)** Nitrogen

**(d)** Chlorine
**Answer.** (b) Ammonia

(v)   An acid that has two replaceable hydrogen ions:
     **(a)** Acetic acid
     **(b)** Hydrochloric acid
     **(c)** Phosphoric acid
     **(d)** Carbonic acid
     **Answer.** (d) Carbonic acid

(vi)   The hydroxide which is soluble in excess of NaOH is:
     **(a)** Ferric hydroxide
     **(b)** Lead hydroxide
     **(c)** Copper hydroxide
     **(d)** Calcium hydroxide
     **Answer.** (b) Lead hydroxide

(vii)   If the RMM of carbon dioxide is 44, then its vapor density is:
     **(a)** 22
     **(b)** 32
     **(c)** 44
     **(d)** 88
     **Answer. (a)** 22

(viii)   Drying agent used to dry Hydrogen chloride gas:
     **(a)** Concentrated Sulphury acid
     **(b)** Calcium oxide
     **(c)** Sulfurous acid
     **(d)** Calcium hydroxide
     **Answer.** (a) Concentrated Sulphury acid

(ix)   The catalyst used in Haber's Process is:
     **(a)** Molybdenum
     **(b)** Platinum
     **(c)** Nickel
     **(d)** Finely divided Iron
     **Answer.** (d) Finely divided Iron

(x)   An aqueous compound that turns colorless phenolphthalein to pink:
     **(a)** Ammonium hydroxide
     **(b)** Nitric acid
     **(c)** Anhydrous calcium chloride
     **(d)** Sulphury acid

**Answer.** (a) Ammonium hydroxide

(xi) The gas is formed when carbon reacts with concentrated sulphury acid:
    **(a)** Hydrogen
    **(b)** Sulfur trioxide
    **(c)** Sulfur dioxide
    **(d)** Oxygen
    **Answer.** (c) Sulfur dioxide

(xii) The organic compound prepared when Ethanol undergoes dehydration:
    **(a)** Methane
    **(b)** Ethane
    **(c)** Acetylene
    **(d)** Ethene
    **Answer.** (d) Ethene

(xiii) The IUPAC name of methyl acetylene is:
    **(a)** Propyne
    **(b)** Ethene
    **(c)** Propane
    **(d)** Ethyne
    **Answer.** (a) Propyne

(xiv) The product formed at the cathode in electroplating of an article with Nickel is:
    **(a)** Hydrogen gas
    **(b)** Nickel ions
    **(c)** Nickel atoms
    **(d)** Oxygen gas
    **Answer.** (c) Nickel atoms

(xv) An alkali metal found in period 3 and group 1 is:
    **(a)** Magnesium
    **(b)** Lithium
    **(c)** Sodium
    **(d)** Potassium
    **Answer.** (c) Sodium

## Question 2.

(i) The diagram shows an experiment set up for the laboratory preparation of a pungent smelling gas. The gas is alkaline.     **[5]**

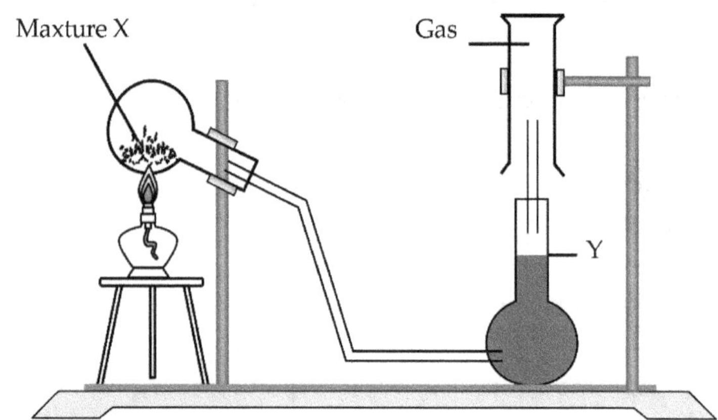


(a) Name the gas collected in the gas jar.
(b) Write a balanced chemical equation for the above preparation.
(c) How is the gas being collected?
(d) What is the purpose of using Y?
(e) How will you and that the jar is full of gas?

**Answer.**

(a) Ammonia

(b) $2NH_4Cl + Ca(OH)_2 \xrightarrow{\text{Heat}} CaCl_2 + 2H_2O + 2NH_{3(g)}$

(c) Downward Displacement of air

(d) To get dry ammonia from moist ammonia.

(e) Moist Red litmus Turn to Blue

(ii) Match the following Column A with Column B.                    [5]

| Column I | Column II |
|---|---|
| (a) Acid Salt | i. Black in color |
| (b) Copper Oxide | ii. Reddish brown |
| (c) Zine hydroxide | iii. Hydrogen chloride |
| (d) Copper Metal | iv. Sodium Hydrogen Carbonate |
| (e) Polar compound | v. Copper Metal |

**Answer.**

(a) Sodium Hydrogen Carbonate

(b) Black in color

(c) Soluble in excess sodium hydroxide

(d) Reddish brown

(e) Hydrogen chloride

(iii) Complete the following by choosing the correct answers from the bracket:                    [5]

(a) Ammonia in the liquefied form is ________ [neutral/basic]

(b) Organic compounds are generally insoluble in ________ [Water / Organic solvents]

(c) An inert electrode used in the electrolysis of acidified water is________ [iron/platinum]

(d) Hydrocarbons having a double bond is ________ [alkenes/alkynes]

(e) Alkaline gas gives dense white fumes of _______ [$NH_4OH$ / $NH_4Cl$] with hydrogen chloride gas.

**Answer.**

(a) Neutral

(b) Water

(c) Platinum

(d) Alkenes

(e) $NH_4Cl$

(iv) Identify the following: [5]

(a) The property by which carbon bonds with itself to form a long chain.

(b) A substance that conducts electricity in a molten or aqueous state.

(c) The energy required to remove an electron from the valence shell of a neutral isolated gaseous atom.

(d) The name of the process by which the Bauxite ore is concentrated.

(e) The bond is formed by a shared pair of electrons with both electrons coming from the same atom.

**Answer.**

(a) Catenation

(b) Electrolyte

(c) Ionization Energy or enthalpy

(d) Bayer's Process

(e) Co-Ordinate Bond or dative bond,

(v) (a) Draw the structural formula for the following: [5]

   i. 2-pentanol

   ii. Ethanal

   iii. 1-butene

**Answer.**

   i.

$$CH_3-CH_2-CH_2-\overset{\displaystyle OH}{\overset{|}{CH}}-CH_3$$

   ii.

$$H-\overset{\overset{\displaystyle H}{|}}{\underset{\underset{\displaystyle H}{|}}{C}}-\overset{\displaystyle O}{C}$$

   iii. $CH_3-CH_2-CH=CH_2$

(b) Name the following organic compounds in IUPAC system:

i.

$$H-\overset{\displaystyle H}{\underset{\displaystyle H}{C}}-\overset{\displaystyle H}{\underset{\displaystyle H}{C}}-\overset{\displaystyle H}{\underset{\displaystyle H}{C}}-\overset{\displaystyle H}{\underset{\displaystyle H}{C}}-O-H$$

ii.

$$H-C\equiv C-\overset{\displaystyle H}{\underset{\displaystyle H}{C}}-H$$

**Answer.**

i.   butan-1-ol

ii.  propyne

## SECTION B
### (Attempt any four questions.)

**Question 3.**

(i) Identify the Anion present in each of the following compounds.                [2]

   **(a)** When Barium Chloride Answer. is added to a Answer. of compound B, a white precipitate sulphate insoluble in dilute Hydrochloric acid is formed.

   **(b)** When dilute Sulphuric acid is added to compound D, a gas is produced which turns lime water milky but has no effect on acidified potassium dichromate Answer..

   **Answer.**

   **(a)** $SO_4^{--}$ (sulphate ion)

   **(b)** $CO_3^{--}$ (carbonate ion )

(ii) Write the products and balance the equation.                [5]

   **(a)** $S + Conc\ HNO_3 \rightarrow$

   **(b)** $ZnS + HCl \rightarrow$

   **Answer.**

   **(a)** $S + 6HNO_3 \rightarrow H_2SO_4 + 6NO_2 + 2H_2O$

   **(b)** $ZnS + 2\underset{\text{dil.}}{HCl} \rightarrow ZnCl_2 + H_2S$

(iii) Arrange the following as per the instruction given in the brackets:                [3]

   **(a)** Na, k, Cl, Si, S (increasing order of electro negativity)

   **(b)** Be, Li, F, C, B, N, O (increasing order of metallic character)

   **(c)** Br, F, I, CI (increasing order of atomic size)

   **Answer.**

   **(a)** $K < Na < Si < S < 0$

   **(b)** $F < 0 < N < C < B < Be < Li$

   **(c)** $F < C < Br < I$

(iv) Fill in the blanks selecting the appropriate word from the given choice:                [3]

**(a)** In a covalent compound, the bond is formed due to ________of electrons (sharing/transfer)

**(b)** A molecule that has a single lone pair of electrons ________ ($NH_3$/$H_2O$)

**(c)** Electrovalent compounds do not conduct electricity in their________ state. (molten / solid)

**Answer.**

**(a)** Sharing

**(b)** $NH_3$

**(c)** Solid

## Question 4.

(i) For each of the substances given below, what is the role played in the extraction of Aluminum? **[2]**

**(a)** Cryolite

**(b)** Graphite

**Answer.**

**(a)** Cryolite ($Na_3 AlF_6$) is used to lower the m.p. of alumina from 2050°C to nearly 950°C.

**(b)** Thick graphite rods are used as anode.

(ii) Calculate: **[2]**

**(a)** A gas cylinder is filled with hydrogen, and it holds 5 gms of gas. The same cylinder holds 85gms of gas X under the same temperature and pressure. Calculate the vapor density of gas X.

**(b)** Give the empirical formula of $CH_3COOH$.

**Answer.**

**(a)** $V \cdot D \cdot = \dfrac{\text{mass of certain vol. of a gas}}{\text{mass of same vol. of Hydrogen gas}}$

(vol. are at the same condition of temp. & pressure.)

$$\therefore V \cdot D \cdot = \frac{85}{5} = 17$$

**(b)** Empirical formula of $CH_3COOH$

condense mol. formula $= C_2H_4O_2$

$\therefore$ simplest whole no. the ratio of atoms of element (Empirical formula) will be-
$CH_2O$

(iii) The following questions are about the laboratory preparation of Hydrogen chloride gas. **[3]**

**(a)** Write a balanced chemical equation for its preparation mentioning the condition required.

**(b)** Why is concentrated Nitric Acid not used in the preparation of Hydrogen Chloride gas?

**(c)** How is Hydrogen Chloride gas collected?

**Answer.**

(a) $\underset{\text{1 mol}}{NaCl} + \underset{\text{1 mol}}{\overset{\text{Conc.}}{H_2SO_4}} \xrightarrow{<200°C} NaHSO_4 + HCl_{(g)}$ .

conditions: 1 → Temp. Should lie below 200°C.

2 → molar (molecular) ratio of reactant should be 1:1

(b) Conc. $HNO_3$ is volatile and decomposes on heating.

(c) Upward displacement of Air as HCl gas is heavier than air.

(iv) Explain the following: [3]

(a) Concentrated Nitric acid appears yellow when it is left standing in a glass bottle.

(b) An inverted Funnel is used to dissolve Hydrogen Chloride gas in water.

(c) All apparatus made of glass is used in the laboratory preparation of Nitric acid.

**Answer.**

(a) Because on standing in a glass bottle conc. $HNO_3$ decomposes as

$$4HNO_3 \rightarrow \underset{\text{reddish brown gas}}{4NO_2} + 2H_2O + O_2$$

due to the formation of $NO_2$ gas, which is found dissolved in the mixture, it appears yellow.

(b) Funnel arrangement is used to dissolve the HCl gas in water due to the following reasons:

i. To minimize the back suction.

ii. To increase the efficiency of disAnswer. of HCl gas in water.

(c) Because The vapors of nitric acid are highly corrosive and attack materials like rubber and cork.

## Question 5.

(i) (a) State one property of Ammonia demonstrated in the Fountain Experiment. [2]

(b) Give the ionic equation when Ammonium Hydroxide is dissolved in water.

**Answer.**

(a) The fountain Experiment demonstrate high Solubility of $NH_3$ gas in $H_2O$.

(b) $NH_4OH_{(aq.)} \underset{}{\overset{\text{Partial dissociation}}{\rightleftharpoons}} NH_{4(aq.)}^{+} + OH_{(aq.)}^{-}$

(ii) Name a probable Cation present based on the following Observations: [2]

(a) Reddish brown precipitate insoluble in Ammonium Hydroxide.

(b) Blue-colored sulfate Answer..

**Answer.**

(a) $Fe^{3+}$

(b) $Cu^{++}$

(iii) Give a balanced chemical equation for the following: [3]

(a) Laboratory Preparation of Methane from Sodium Acetate.

(b) Preparation of Ethyne from 1, 2 dibromoethane.

**(c)** Ethene reacting with Chlorine.

**Answer.**

$$\textbf{(a)} \quad CH_3 - \overset{\displaystyle O}{\underset{\displaystyle ||}{C}} - ONa + NaOH \xrightarrow[\text{Heat}]{\text{CaO}} CH_4 + Na_2CO_3$$

$$\textbf{(b)} \quad CH_2Br - CH_2Br + 2KOH_{(alc.)} \xrightarrow{\text{Heat}} H - C \equiv C - H + 2KBr + 2H_2O$$

$$\textbf{(c)} \quad H_2C = CH_2 + Cl_2 \xrightarrow{CCl_4} \quad \overset{\displaystyle Cl}{\underset{\displaystyle |}{H_2C}} - \overset{\displaystyle Cl}{\underset{\displaystyle |}{CH_2}}$$

(iv) State one relevant observation for each of the following reactions: **[3]**
   **(a)** When excess Ammonia is passed through an aqueous Answer. of Lead Nitrate.
   **(b)** Copper Sulphate Answer. is electrolyzed using Copper electrodes.
   **(c)** Ammonium hydroxide is added to the Ferrous Sulphate Answer..

**Answer.**
(a) A chalky white ppt of $Pb(OH)_2$ is obtained.
(b) Deposition of Reddish pink metal at cathode.
(c) A dirty green ppt. of $Fe(OH)_2$ is formed.

## Question 6.

(i) Define: **[2]**
   **(a)** Gay Loussac's law of combining volume.
   **(b)** Vapour Density

**Answer.**
(a) It states that the chemical reaction in which the gaseous reactants combine together to form one or more gaseous products, the ratio of the volumes of reactants and products will be in the whole number ratio.

   **Example:** $H_{2(g)} + Cl_{2(g)} \rightarrow 2HCl_{(g)}$

   1vol :1vol.        :2Vol

**(b)** V.D. of a gas is the ratio mass of a certain volume of a gas to that mass of the same vol. of Hydrogen gas at the same condition of temp. & pressure,

(ii) Solve: **[2]**
   1250cc of oxygen was burnt with 300cc of ethane ($C_2H_6$). Calculate the volume of the unused oxygen. and the volume of the carbon dioxide formed.
   $2C_2H_6 + 7O_2 \rightarrow 4CO_2 + 6H_2O$
   **Answer.** Given volumes= 300 cc.

   $2C_2H_6 + 7O_2 \rightarrow 4CO_2 + 6H_2O$
   2vol   7val.     4val.

In comparison, the limiting reagent is ethane, hence reaction will occur according to vol. of ethane.

2 vol. $C_2H_6 = 300$ C. C.

$\therefore$ 1 vol = 150 cc.

$2C_2H_6 + 7O_2 \rightarrow 4CO_2 + 6H_2O$

2val      7 vol    4Vol.

Hence      $\rightarrow$ ethane $\rightarrow$ Totally consumed

$\rightarrow$ unused oxygen = $(1250 - 10.50)$er = 200cc.

$\rightarrow CO_2$ produced =600 c.c.

(iii) State the conditions required for the following reactions: [3]

**(a)** Conversion of Sulphur dioxide to Sulphur trioxide.

**(b)** Conversion of Ammonia to Nitric acid

**(c)** Conversion of Nitrogen to Ammonia

**Answer.**

**(a)** Favorable conditions for the conversion of $SO_2$ to $SO_3$ are as follows: Exothermic reactions are favoured at low temperature, and the yield is maximum at about $410 - 450°C$. Pressure of about $1 - 2$ atmosphere is used. Excess of oxygen increases the production of sulfur dioxide.

**(b)** Catalytic oxidation of ammonia to nitric oxide. Conditions for catalytic oxidation of ammonia to nitric oxide: Platinum catalyst and $800°C$ temperature.

**(c)** Conversion of Nitrogen to Ammonia.

Required condition

$\rightarrow$ reactent $\rightarrow$ hydrogen gas

$\rightarrow$ Temp = $(450 - 500)°C$

$\rightarrow$ pressure = $200 - 900$ atm

$\rightarrow$catalyst =Finely divided iron

$\rightarrow$Promotor = Molybdenum

(iv) Choose the role played by concentrated Sulphuric acid as A, B, or C which is responsible for reactions 1 to 3. [3]

B Oxidizing agent

C Non-Volatile Acid

A Dehydrating agent

1 $NaNO_3 + H_2SO_4 \xrightarrow{<200°C} NaHSO_4 + HNO_3$

2 $S + 2H_2SO_4 \rightarrow 3SO_2 + 2H_2O.$

3 $S + 2H_2SO_4 \rightarrow 3SO_2 + 2H_2O$

**Answer.**

**(a)** B

**(b)** C

**(c)** A

**Question 7.**

(i) Find the empirical formula and molecular formula of an organic compound from the data given below: [2]

C = 75.92% H = 6.32%, N = 17.76% its vapour density is 39.5

(At.wt: C = 12, H = 1, N = 14 )

**Answer.**

| Element | Mass | At. Masses | At. Ratio | Simplest At. Ratios | Simplest role no at. Ration |
|---------|------|-----------|-----------|---------------------|------------------------------|
| C | 75.92 | 12 | $\dfrac{75.92}{12} = 6.66$ | $\dfrac{6.66}{1.26} = 5.285$ | 5 |
| H | 6.32 | 1 | $\dfrac{6.32}{1} = 6.32$ | $\dfrac{6.32}{1.26} = 5.015$ | 5 |
| N | 17.76 | 14 | $\dfrac{17.76}{14} = 1.26$ | $\dfrac{1.26}{1.26} = 1.0$ | 1 |

Empirical formula $= C_5H_5N$

Empirical formula ct $= (18 \times 5) + (1 \times 5) + 14 = 79$

$$\therefore n = \frac{2 \times V \cdot D \cdot}{Emp.\ for\ wt \cdot} = \frac{2 \times 39 \cdot 5}{79} = 1$$

$$\therefore \text{ molecular formula } = (C_5H_5\ N)_1$$
$$= C_5H_5\ N$$

(ii) Identify the functional group in the following organic compounds: **[2]**

    **(a)** HCHO

    **(b)** $C_2H_5COOH$

    **Answer.**

    **(a)** Aldehyde

    **(b)** The carboxylic acid of.

(iii) During the Electrolysis of Copper (II) Sulphate Answer. using platinum as cathode and graphite as an anode. **[3]**

    **(a)** State what you observe at the cathode.

    **(b)** State the change noticed in the electrolyte.

    **(c)** Write the reaction at the cathode.

    **Answer.**

    **(a)** Deposition of pink metal copper at cathode.

    **(b)** Blue Color electrolytes Answer. fades.

    **(c)** $Cu^{2+} + 2e^- \longrightarrow Cu_{(s)}$

(iv) Choose the answer from the list which fits the description. **[3]**

    [$CaO, CO_2, NaOH, Fe(OH)_3, CO$]

    **(a)** A basic oxide.

    **(b)** An acidic oxide.

    **(c)** An Alkali.

**Answer.**

**(a)** CaO

**(b)** $CO_2$

**(c)** NaOH

## Question 8.

(i) Draw the electron dot structure for the following. [2]

**(a)** $H_3O^+$

**(b)** $CH_4$

**Answer.**

**(a)** $\left[ H-\overset{..}{O}-H \right]^+$ with an H bonded below the O

**(b)**

$$\begin{array}{c} H \\ H:\overset{..}{\underset{..}{C}}:H \\ H \end{array}$$

(ii) Distinguish between the following as directed: [2]

**(a)** Sodium Carbonate and Sodium Sulphate by using dilute HCl

**(b)** Ammonium Sulphate and Sodium Sulphate by using Calcium hydroxide.

**Answer.**

**(a)** Sodium carbonate on treating with dil. HCl results in the formation of sodium chloride with the liberation of carbon dioxide gas. Sodium sulphatic on treating with dil. HCl results in the formation of sodium chloride with the liberation of sulfur dioxide gas

**(b)** Ammonium sulphate reacts with $Ca(OH)_2$ & produces pungent smelling $NH_3$ gas while sodium sulphate does not.
$$(NH_4)_2SO_4 + Ca(OH)_2 \longrightarrow CaSO_4 + 2H_2O + 2NH_3 \text{ (gas)}$$

(iii) Name the particles present in: [3]

**(a)** Strong Electrolyte

**(b)** Weak Electrolyte

**(c)** Non-Electrolyte

**Answer.**

**(a)** Ions

**(b)** Ions and molecules both

**(c)** Molecules

(iv) An element X has the atomic number 17. Answer the following questions. [3]

**(a)** State the period & group to which it belongs:

**(b)** Is it a Metal or Non-Metal?

**(c)** Write the formula between X and Hydrogen.

**Answer.**

**(a)** Period=3 group=17 (Halogen)

**(b)** Nonmetal

**(c)** HX

**Maximum Marks: 80**
Time allowed: Two hours
Answers to this Paper must be written on the paper provided separately.
You will not be allowed to write during first 15 minutes.
This time is to be spent in reading the question paper.
The time given at the head of this Paper is the time allowed for writing the answers.

**(Section A is compulsory. Attempt any four questions from Section B.**
**The intended marks for questions or parts of questions are given in brackets [ ].**

## SECTION A
### Answer all the questions from this section

**Question : 1** [15]

Choose one correct answer to the question from the given option:

(i) The alloy used for making surgical instruments:

**(a)** Brass

**(b)** Bronze

**(c)** Solder

**(d)** Stainless steel.

**Answer.** Stainless steel


(ii) From the given cations which one discharges preferentially at the cathode during electrolysis:

**(a)** $Al^{3+}$

**(b)** $Zn^{++}$

**(c)** $Pb^{2+}$

**(d)** $Cu^{2+}$

**Answer. (d)** $Cu^{2+}$


(iii) An element in period two have high electron affinity and high electronegativity it is likely to be a :

**(a)** Metal

**(b)** Non-metal

**(c)** Metalloid

**(d)** None

**Answer. (b)** Non-metal


(iv) Which of the following reaction shows the product of oxidation:

**(a)** $Sn^{4+} \rightarrow Sn^{2+} - 2e^-$

**(b)** $Cl + 1e^- \rightarrow Cl^{1-}$

**(c)** $O^{2-} \rightarrow O^{1-} + 1e^-$

**(d)** $N^- + 2e^- \rightarrow N^{3-}$

**Answer. (c)** $O^{2-} \rightarrow O^{1-} + 1e^-$

(v)  An aq. Answer.. of a chemical compound has a pH value 12 on the pH scale, which metal can react with the chemical compound

    **(a)** Mn

    **(b)** Mg

    **(c)** Zn

    **(d)** Cu

    **Answer. (c)** Zn

(vi)  From the following anions, which one is expected to be coloured

    **(a)** $SO_4^{2-}$

    **(b)** $Cl^{1-}$

    **(c)** $HSO_4^-$

    **(d)** $MnO_4^{1-}$

    **Answer. (d)** $MnO_4^{1-}$

(vii)  Which one is an Empirical formula of a compound?

    **(a)** $C_4H_8O_2$

    **(b)** $C_2H_4O_2$

    **(c)** $C_4H_6$

    **(d)** $H_2CO_2$

    **Answer. (d)** $H_2CO_2$

(viii) The element belonging to period three of the periodic table having atomicity one

    **(a)** chlorine

    **(b)** Sodium

    **(c)** Argon

    **(d)** Fluorine.

    **Answer. (c)** Argon

(ix)  A chemical substance which is used to prove that hydrochloric acid contains chlorine.

    **(a)** Al

    **(b)** NaOH

    **(c)** $MnO_2$

    **(d)** CuO

    **Answer. (c)** $MnO_2$

(x)  Calamine is an important ore of which metal:

    **(a)** Iron

    **(b)** Zinc

    **(c)** Aluminum

    **(d)** Copper

**Answer. (b)** Zinc

(xi) An Acid which converts blue-colored hydrated salt to white powder:
   **(a)** Conc. HCl
   **(b)** Conc. $HNO_3$
   **(c)** Conc. $H_2SO_4$
   **(d)** dil. $H_2SO_4$.
   **Answer. (c)** Conc. $H_2SO_4$

(xii) The metal which displaces Hydrogen from cold, dilute $HNO_3$ som,
   **(a)** Mn
   **(b)** Al
   **(c)** Zn
   **(d)** Fe
   **Answer. (b)** Al

(xiii) Compound lead chloride can be prepared by using dilute HCl and by reacting with:
   **(a)** PbO
   **(b)** $Pb(OH)_2$
   **(c)** $Pb(NO_3)_2$
   **(d)** Pd
   **Answer. (c)** $Pb(NO_3)_2$

(xiv) Calcium hydroxide is preferred alkali for preparation at Ammonia gas because:
   **(a)** It is deliquescent
   **(b)** It is not deliquescent
   **(c)** It has two hydroxyl group
   **(d)** none.
   **Answer. (b)** It is not deliquescent

(xv) Members of a Homologous series has:
   **(a)** Same physical properties and same chemical properties
   **(b)** Same physical properties but different chemical properties
   **(c)** Different physical properties but similar chemical properties
   **(d)** Different physical properties and different chemical properties
   **Answer. (c)** Different physical properties but similar chemical properties

## Question : 2

(i) Use the letter only written in the Periodic Table given below to answer the following questions: [5]

| Periods | Group 1 | Group 2 | Group 13 | Group 14 | Group 15 | Group 16 | Group 17 | Group 18 |
|---|---|---|---|---|---|---|---|---|
| P 2 | X | | E | G | J | Z | M | L |
| P 3 | Q | | | | | | | |
| P 4 | R | | | | | | | |
| P 5 | T | | | | | | | |

(a) State the number of valence electrons in J.
(b) Which element shows ions with a single negative charge?
(c) Which metallic element is more reactive than R?
(d) Which element has four shells?
(e) State the name assigned to the group of M.

**Answer.:**

(a) 5
(b) M
(c) T
(d) R
(e) Halogens

(ii) Match column A with column B: [5]

| **Column A** | **Column B** |
|---|---|
| (a) Acid Salt | i. Buff yellow. |
| (b) Lead Oxide | ii. Reddish brown |
| (c) Zinc hydroxide | iii. Ammonia |
| (d) Copper metal | iv. Sodium hydrogen carbonate |
| (e) Polar compound | v. Soluble in excess sodium hydroxide |

**Answer.:**

(a) iv
(b) i
(c) v
(d) ii
(e) iii

(iii) Arrange the following as per the instructions given in the brackets [5]

(a) $N_2, H_2, O_2$ (Increasing order of covalent bonds)
(b) F, Li, C, Be, N (Increasing order of atomic size)

(c) Mg, Cl, Na, S (Decreasing order of Ionization Potential)

(d) $(SO_4)^{2-}$, $OH^-$, $Cl^-$ (Increasing order of selective discharge at the anode)

(e) $H_3PO_2$, $H_3PO_4$, $H_3PO_3$ (Increasing order of basicity of oxyacids.)

**Answer.:**

(a) $H_2$, $O_2$, $N_2$

(b) F, N, C, Be, Li

(c) Cl > S > Mg > Na

(d) $SO_4^{--}$ < $Cl^-$ < $OH^-$

(e) $H_3PO_2$ < $H_3PO_3$ < $H_3PO_4$

(iv) Give reasons for the following : [5]

(a) A silica crucible is used for the electrolysis of molten lead bromide.

(b) Graphite anode is preferred to other inert electrodes in the electrolysis of molten lead bromide.

(c) Why Cryolite and Fluorspar are added in the extraction of aluminium?

(d) $H_2$ gas is liberated with the addition of aluminium to dilute Sulphuric acid.

(e) Powdered coke is sprinkled on the surface of electrolyte in the extraction of aluminium

**Answer.:**

(a) The crucible is made of silica since it is non-reacting, withstands high temperatures & is almost a non-conductor of electricity.

(b) A graphite anode is preferred - to other inert electrodes such as platinum since graphite is unaffected by the reactive bromine vapors.

(c) The addition of cryolite & fluorspar - enhances the mobility of the fused mixture by acting as a solvent for the electrolytic mixture. Thus cryolite in the molten state dissolves aluminum oxide.

(d) Metals react with acids to liberate hydrogen gas. Similarly aluminum also reacts with sulphury acid to liberate hydrogen gas.

(e) The layer of powdered coke prevents the - burning of the carbon electrodes in the air at the point where they emerge from the bath. It also prevents or minimizes - heat loss by radiation.

(v) Identify the cation present in each of the following compounds $-V, W, X, Y$ and Z. [5]

(a) To a salt **W**, a calcium hydroxide Answer. is added and then the mixture is heated. A pungent-smelling gas turning moist red litmus paper blue is obtained.

(b) To a Answer. **X**, ammonium hydroxide is added in a minimum amount first and then in excess. A reddish-brown precipitate is formed

(c) To a Answer. **Y**, ammonium hydroxide is added in a minimum amount first and then in excess. A white precipitate is formed which dissolves in excess to form a clear Answer..

(d) To a Answer. **Z**, ammonium hydroxide is added in a minimum amount first and then in excess. A pale blue precipitate is formed which dissolves in excess to form a deep blue Answer..

(e) To a Answer. V, Sodium hydroxide is added in a minimum amount first and then in excess. A white precipitate is formed which doesn't dissolve in excess.

**Answer.:**
(a) $NH_4^+$
(b) $Fe^{3+}$
(c) $Zn^{2+}$
(d) $Cu^{2+}$
(e) $Ca^{2+}$

**SECTION-B**

**Question : 3**

(i) Define the following: [2]
    **(a)** Electronegativity
    **(b)** Gay Loussac law

    **Answer.:**

    **Ans:**

    **(a)** The tendency of an atom in a molecule to attract the shared pair of electrons towards itself is known as **electronegativity**.

    **(b)** when gases react, they do so in volumes which bear a simple ratio to one another, and to the volume of the gaseous product, provided that all volumes are measured at the same temperature and pressure.

(ii) Nitrogen dioxide is called 'mixed acid anhydride'. Give reason. [2]

    **Answer.:**

    Nitrogen dioxide dissolves in water to yield a mixture of nitric acid and nitrous acid. Hence, nitrogen dioxide is called 'mixed acid anhydride'

$$2NO_2 + H_2O \longrightarrow HNO_3 + HNO_2$$

(iii) Some properties of sulphuric acid are listed below. Choose the property $A, B, C,$ or $D$ which is responsible for the reactions (a) to (c). Some properties may be repeated. [3]

    A : Acid

    B : Dehydrating agent

    C: Non-volatile acid

    D : Oxidising agent

    **(a)** $S + 2H_2SO_4 \longrightarrow 3SO_2 + 2H_2O$

    **(b)** $NaCl + H_2SO_4 \longrightarrow NaHSO_4 + HCl$

    **(c)** $CuO + H_2SO_4 \longrightarrow CuSO_4 + H_2O$

    **Answer.:**

    **(a)** D: Oxidizing agent

    **(b)** C: Non-volatile acid

    **(c)** A: Acid

(iv) **(a)** Name the acid formed when sulfur dioxide dissolves in water. [3]

    **(b)** Name the gas released when sodium carbonate is added to a dil. Answer. of $H_2SO_4$.

    **(c)** What are the two necessary conditions for the direct combination of sulphur dioxide and chlorine gases forming sulphuryl chloride?

    **Answer.:**

    **(a)** Sulfurous acid is formed when sulfur dioxide dissolves in water.

{41}

**(b)** Carbon dioxide gas is released when sodium carbonate is added to a dil. Answer. of $H_2SO_4$.

**(c)** i   Dry sulphur dioxide and chlorine gases.

ii.  Presence of sunlight.

## Question : 4

(i) Following questions based on the electrolysis of Acidified Water: [2]

   **(a)** i  Why is an acid used in the process?

     ii. Why is only sulphury acid preferred?

   **(b)** i  Why the ratio of the two gases evolved at the cathode and anode is 2:1? [2]

     ii. Why is this electrolysis an example of catalysis?

**Answer.:**

   **(a)** i  Acid causes ionization of water.

     ii  Because, $H_2SO_4$ is non-volatile and does not decompose on heating.

   **Answer.**

     i  $4H_2O \longrightarrow 4H^+ + 4\,H^-$

     Electrode reaction

     Anode          $4OH^- - 4e^- \longrightarrow 4OH$

                     $4OH \longrightarrow 2H_2O + O_2$

     Cathode        $4H^+ + 4\bar{e} \longrightarrow 4H$

                     $4H \longrightarrow 2H_2(g)$

     The Gases that evolve from cathode and anode are Hydrogen and oxygen respectively in the volume ratio of 2: 1 (Hydrogen: oxygen)

     ii  Because dil. $H_2SO_4$ added to water for electrolysis remains unaltered.


(ii) Select the process of oxidation and reduction in the following [3]

   **(a)** $Fe^{3+} \rightarrow Fe^{2+}$

   **(b)** $Cl^- \rightarrow Cl$

   **(c)** $Sn^{4+} \rightarrow Sn^{2+}$

**Answer.:**

**(a)** Reduction

**(b)** Oxidation

**(c)** Reduction

(iii) Differentiate between ionic and covalent compounds on the basis of the following properties [3]

**(a)** Solubility

**(b)** Melting and Boiling Points

**(c)** Physical State

**Answer.:**

**(a)**

| Ionic | Covalent |
| --- | --- |
| SOLUBILITY | SOLUBILITY |
| Soluble - in water | Soluble - in organic solvents [non-polar] |
| Insoluble  -  in  organic  solvents. | Insoluble  -  in  water  [polar] |
| REASON: Water [polar solvent] has a high | REASON: Organic solvents [non-polar] |

| dielectric constant i.e. capacity to weaken the force of attraction, thus resulting in free ions. Organic solvents [non-polar] have low dielectric constants and do not cause disAnswer.. | e.g. benzene, alcohol, dissolve non-polar covalent compounds [like dissolves like]. Water [polar solvent] cannot dissolve non-polar covalent compounds but dissolves polar. |

**(b)**

| MELTING & BOILING POINT | MELTING & BOILING POINT |
|---|---|
| High melting point and high boiling point. REASON: Strong electrostatic force of attraction between ions. A large amount of energy is required to break the force of attraction. | Low melting point and low boiling point. REASON: Weak Vander Waals force of attraction between molecules. Less amount of energy is required to break the force of attraction. |

**(c)**

| STATE-Bonding - electrovalent | COVALENT COMPOUNDS |
|---|---|
| Existence-Crystalline hard solids (room temp.] <br> Constituent Units - Ions [metallic nonmetallic] <br> Force of attraction-Strong Electrostatic forces exist between - ions. REASON: Ions [charged particles which attract one another to form electrovalent compounds] are closely packed with strong force of attraction, hence ionic compounds are - hard solids | STATE - BONDING - COVALENT <br> - EXISTENCE - GASES, LIQUIDS OR SOFT SOLIDS. <br> - CONSTITUENT UNITS - MOLECULES <br> - FORCE OF ATTRACTION - WEAK <br> Vander Wall forces exist between molecules. REASON: Molecules have weak forces of attraction between them and hence covalent compounds are gaseous [if molecules are less] \& liquid or soft solids [if molecules are more] |

## Question : 5

(i) Name: [2]

    **(a)** An inert Electrode

    **(b)** A positively charged Non-metallic ion

**Answer.**

    **(a)** Platinum

    **(b)** Ammonium Ion($NH_4^+$)

(ii) Differentiate between ionization & dissociation with examples. [2]

**Answer.**

**DISSOCIATION**

Undergoes electrolytic dissociation on passage of electric current.

The process involves - the separation of ions already presents in the ionic compound.

e.g. $NaCl \rightleftharpoons Na^{1+} + Cl^{1-}$ [in the molten state ]

IONiSATION
Undergoes ionisation in Answer. state on passage of electric current. The process involves - the formation of ions from molecules which are not in an ionic state. e.g. $HCl \rightarrow H^{1+} + Cl^{1-}$ [in Answer. state]

(iii) **(a)** Name the chief ore of aluminium and name the process of concentration of this ore. **[3]**

**(b)** Name the process of extraction of aluminium from alumina.

**(c)** Give one alloy of aluminium and its one use.

**Answer.:**

**(a)** Bauxite* $Al_2O_3 \cdot 2H_2O$ process of concentration baeyer's process.

**(b)** Electrometallurgy $\rightarrow$ Hall's Heroult's process.

**(c)** Magnalium $\rightarrow$ used for aircraft and beams of a balance.

(iv) Complete the following table: **[3]**

| Substance Heated | Product | Colour |
|---|---|---|
| $HNO_3$ | __________ | __________ |
| __________ | __________ | Black |
| $Zn(NO_3)_2$ | __________ | __________ |

**Answer.:**

| Substance Heated | Product | Colour |
|---|---|---|
| $HNO_3$ | $NO_2$ | Reddish brown |
| $Cu(NO_3)_2$ | $CuO$ | Black |
| $Zn(NO_3)_2$ | $ZnO$ | Yellow (when hot) |

## Question : 6

(i) Give one property of each (only Reaction) **[2]**

**(a)** Dilute Sulphuric acid

**(b)** Concentrate Sulphuricic Acid

**Answer.:**

**(a)** $ZnO + H_2SO_4 \xrightarrow{\text{dil.}} ZnSO_4 + H_2O$ (Typical acidic property)

**(b)** $C_2H_5OH \xrightarrow{\text{conc.}H_2SO_4} C_2H_4 + H_2O$ (Dehydrating agent)

(ii) Name the gas evolved when following are heated: **[2]**

**(a)** Sodium Nitrate

**(b)** Lead Nitrate

**Answer.:**

**(a)** $O_2$ gas

**(b)** $NO_2$ and $O_2$ both

(iii) A flow chart for manufacturing ammonia by Haber's process is given below: **[3]**

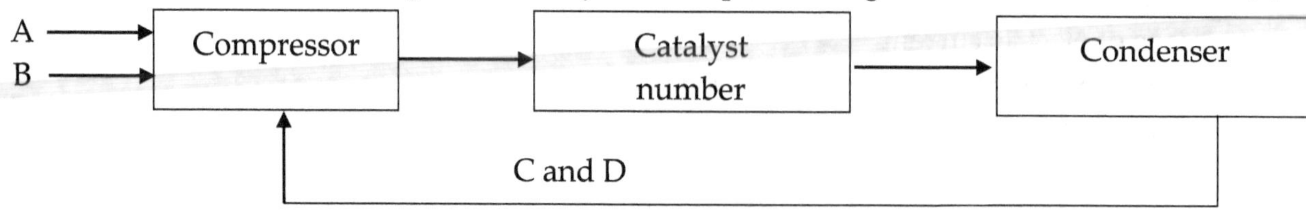

(a) State the pressure to which gases A and B are compressed in the compressor.

(b) Name the catalyst and the promoter of the catalyst.

(c) What do you obtain from the condenser?

**Answer.:**

(a) $200 - 300$ atm

(b) Catalyst: Iron (Fe).

The promoter of the catalyst: Molybdenum or a mixture of potassium and aluminium oxides.

(c) Liquid ammonia will be obtained from the condenser.

(iv) The following statements are incorrect but can be corrected by changing one word. Rewrite the statements and underline the one word that should be changed and give the correct word. [3]

(a) The best test for ammonia is to observe if it turns moist neutral litmus paper red.

(b) Sulphuric acid is used in industry to clean metals because it removes grease.

(c) Ammonia is prepared by heating ammonium chloride with sodium nitrate.

**Answer.:**

(a) The best test for ammonia is to see if it turns moist neutral litmus paper red. The correct Word is blue.

(b) Sulphuric acid is used in industry to clean metals because it removes grease. The correct Word is hydrochloric.

(c) Ammonia is prepared by heating ammonium chloride with sodium nitrate. The correct Word is slaked lime.

## Question : 7

(i) Define [2]

(a) Functional Group

(b) Empirical formula

**Answer.**

(a) Functional groups are groups of atoms or bonds that define the function of the hydrocarbon that they get attached to.

(b) The simplest formula for a compound which is defined as the ratio of subscripts of the smallest possible whole number of the elements present in the formula.

(ii) Find the percentage of chromium in Ammonium dichromate $(NH_4)_2Cr_2O_7$. [2]
$$[H = 1, N = 14, O = 16, Cr = 52]$$

**Answer.** Mass % of chromium $= \dfrac{\text{mass of chromium}}{\text{mass of molecule}} \times 100$

Molecular mass of $(NH_4)_2Cr_2O_7 = (18 \times 2) + (52 \times 2) + (16 \times 7)$
$$= 252$$

Mass % of chromium $= \dfrac{104}{252} \times 100 = 41.26$

Answer$= 41.26$

(iii) Select from the list (A to D) given below, the one substance in each case which matches the description given in parts (a) to (c) : [3]

A. Hydrogen sulphide

B. Hydrogen chloride

C. Ammonia

D. Copper sulphate

**(a)** This compound is not a metal hydroxide but its aqueous Answer. is alkaline in nature.

**(b)** It can be oxidised to chlorine.

**(c)** It has a rotten egg-like smell.

**Answer.:**

**(a)** C: Ammonia

**(b)** B: Hydrogen chloride

**(c)** A: Hydrogen sulphide

(iv) An organic compound with vapour density = 94 contains. [3]

$C = 12.67\%, H = 2.13\%$, and $Br=85.11\%$. Find the molecular formula.

[Atomic mass : $C = 12, H = 1, Br = 80$ ]

**Answer.:**

| Elements | % Ratio | Atomic mass | Relative no. of atoms | Simplest ratio |
|---|---|---|---|---|
| C | 12.67 | 12 | $12.67/12 = 1.055$ | $1.055/1.055 = 1$ |
| H | 2.13 | 1 | $2.13/1 = 2.13$ | $2.13/1.055 = 2$ |
| Br | 85.11 | 80 | $85.11/80 = 1.063$ | $1.063/1.055 = 1$ |

$\rightarrow$ empirical formula$= CH_2Br$

$\rightarrow$ empirical formula mass$=12 + 2 + 80 = 94$

$\rightarrow$ n$=\dfrac{\text{molecule mass}}{\text{emperical formula mass}} = \dfrac{2\times\text{Vapuor density}}{\text{empirical formula mass}} = \dfrac{2\times94}{94} = 2$

$\therefore$ molecular formula $=(CH_2Br)_2$

Simplest whole no. ratio $= C_2H_4Br_2$.

## Question : 8

(i) **(a)** Of the two gases, ammonia and HCl which is more dense? Name the method of collection of each gas. [2]

**(b)** Give one example of a reaction between the above two gases which produces a solid compound.

**Answer.**

**(a)**

| Gases | Molecular mass | Vapour density |
|---|---|---|
| $NH_3$ | 17 | 8.5 |

|              | HCl | 36.5 | 18.25 |

Hence HCl is more dense.

→ Method of collection of $NH_3$ & HCl gas

Both the gases are highly soluble in water and hence collected by displacement of Air, not by water.

→ $NH_3$ is lighter than air, hence collected by downward displacement of Air.

→ HCl is heavier than air, hence collected by upward displacement of Air.

**(b)** $NH_{3\,(g)} + HCl_{(g)} \longrightarrow NH_4Cl_{(g)}$

$$\text{dense white fumes}$$

(ii) Define with Examples [2]

**(a)** Chain isomerism

**(b)** Position isomerism

**Answer.**

**(a)** It is a type of structural isomerism in which molecular formula is the same but the arrangement of the carbon chain is different.

**(b)** Positional isomers are constitutional isomers with the same carbon skeleton and will have the same functional group.

(iii) Give Reaction only [3]

**(a)** Oxidation of Methane

**(b)** Chlorination of Ethylene

**(c)** Calcium carbide with water

**Answer.**

**(a)** $CH_4 + 2O_2 \rightarrow CO_2 + 2H_2O$

**(b)** $H_2C = CH_2 + Cl_2 \xrightarrow{CCl_4}$

$$\begin{array}{ccc} Cl & & Cl \\ | & & | \\ H_2C & - & CH \end{array}$$

**(c)** $CaC_2 + 2H_2O \xrightarrow{\text{Heat}} Ca(OH)_2 + C_2H_2$

(iv) Draw the structure of the following [3]

**(a)** Benzene

**(b)** Butanoic Acid

**(c)** Propanone

**Answer.**

**(a)**

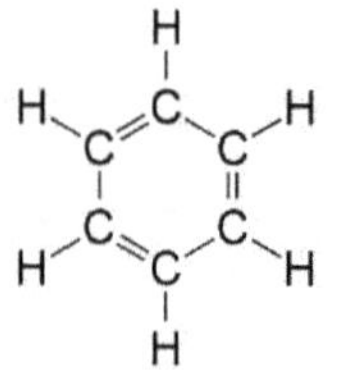

$$
\begin{array}{c}
\mathrm{C_6H_6} \text{ (benzene)}
\end{array}
$$

```
        H
        |
        C
      //  \
  H—C      C—H
     |      ‖
  H—C      C—H
      \   //
        C
        |
        H
```

**(b)**

```
    H   H   H    O
    |   |   |   //
 H—C — C — C — C
    |   |   |   \
    H   H   H    O—H
```

**(c)**

```
    H   O   H
    |   ‖   |
 H—C — C — C—H
    |       |
    H       H
```

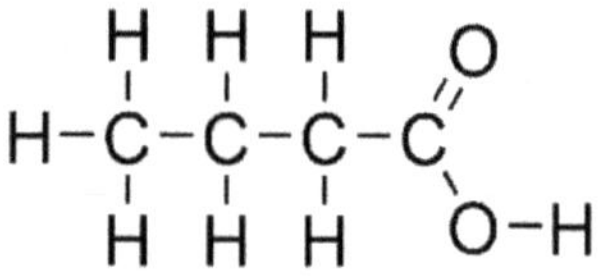

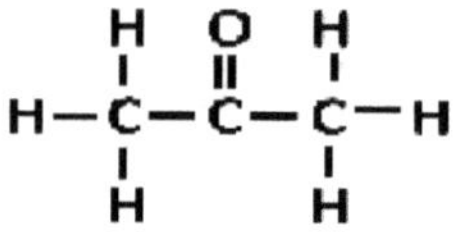

**ICSE 2023 EXAMINATION**
SAMPLE TEST PAPER-2
**CHEMISTRY**
(SCIENCE PAPER-2)

**Maximum Marks: 80**
Time allowed: Two hours
Answers to this Paper must be written on the paper provided separately.
You will not be allowed to write during first 15 minutes.
This time is to be spent in reading the question paper.
The time given at the head of this Paper is the time allowed for writing the answers.

**(Section A is compulsory. Attempt any four questions from Section B.**
**The intended marks for questions or parts of questions are given in brackets [ ].**

**SECTION A**
**Answer all the questions from this section**

**Question : 1** [15]

Choose one correct answer to the question from the given option:

(i) Isomers having same IUPAC names but has different Locants:

  **(a)** Chain isomers

  **(b)** Position isomers

  **(c)** Functional isomers

  **(d)** Geometrical

  **Answer.** (b) Position isomers

(ii) On adding conc $H_2SO_4$ And copper turns to salt followed by heating, a reddish-brown gas is evolved the anion present in salt is

  **(a)** $NO_3^-$

  **(b)** $SO_4^{--}$

  **(c)** $PO_4^{--}$

  **(d)** $S^-$

  **Answer.** (a) $NO_3^-$

(iii) General representation of the carboxylic acid series is:

**(a)**
$$R - \overset{\overset{\displaystyle O}{\displaystyle \|}}{C} - H$$

**(b)**
$$R - \overset{\overset{\displaystyle O}{\displaystyle \|}}{C} - R'$$

**(c)**
$$R - \overset{\overset{\displaystyle O}{\displaystyle \|}}{C} - OH$$

**(d)** $R - OH$

{49}

**Answer. (c)**

$$R - \overset{\overset{\textstyle O}{||}}{C} -OH$$

(iv) which of the following does not react with Hydrogen:

(a) $C_2H_4$

(b) $C_2H_6$

(c) $C_2H_2$

(d) None

**Answer.** (b) $C_2H_6$

(v) From the elements given below the element having least electronegativity value is:

(a) Li

(b) B

(c) F

(d) C

**Answer.** (a) Li

(vi) Which one is Expected to be most ionic compound of periodic table

(a) KCl

(b) CsCl

(c) NaCl

(d) LiCl

**Answer.** (b) CsCl

(vii) Which one of the following produces a mixture of acids when dissolved in water:

(a) $SO_2$

(b) $CO_2$

(c) $P_2O_5$

(d) $NO_2$

**Answer.** (d) $NO_2$

(viii) Name the reagent from the following which can be used to distinguish copper nitrate Answer. From Ferric nitrate Answer.

(a) NaOH

(b) $NH_4OH$

(c) Barium nitrate

(d) Both (a) and (b)

**Answer.** (d) Both (a) and (b)

(ix) The Empirical Formula of a compound is $CH_2O$ and its molecular formula has three carbon atoms, what will be the molecular formula of the compound:

(a) $C_6H_{12}O_6$

(b) $C_3H_6O_3$

(c) $C_3H_6O_6$

**(d)** $CH_2O$
**Answer.** (b) $C_3H_6O_3$

(x) During the electrolysis of alumina in the metallurgy of aluminum, the undesirable product produced at the anode is
**(a)** Oxygen
**(b)** Carbon monoxide
**(c)** Carbon dioxide
**(d)** Both (b) and (c)
**Answer.** (d) Both (b) and (c)

(xi) Which of the following is not present in stainless steel?
**(a)** Fe
**(b)** Cr
**(c)** C
**(d)** Al
**Answer.** (d) Al

(xii) A metal which reacts with dil HCl to evolve hydrogen?
**(a)** Pb
**(b)** Cu
**(c)** Ag
**(d)** Zn
**Answer. (a)** Pb

(xiii) Nitrogen gas can be obtained by heating:
**(a)** Aluminum nitride
**(b)** Ammonium chloride
**(c)** Ammonium nitrite
**(d)** Lead nitrate.
**Ans (c)** Ammonium chloride

(xiv) Magnesium and magnesium ions:
**(a)** Have same no of electrons
**(b)** Have same no of protons
**(c)** Have same no of neutrons
**(d)** Both (b) and (c)
**Ans(d)** Both (b) and (c)

(xv) Strong electrolytes contain:
**(a)** Molecules only
**(b)** Ions only
**(c)** Ions and molecules both

**(d)** None

**Answer. (c)** Ions and molecules both

## Question : 2

(i) **(a)** Give reasons - The oxidizing power of elements increases from left to right along a period.

[1]

> **Answer.** On moving from left to right along a period nuclear charge of elements increases, hence electron-accepting tendency increases due to which oxidizing power increases.
>
> $Na - e^- \rightarrow Na^+$ (Oxidation)
> $Cl + e^- \rightarrow Cl^-$ (Reduction)
> (oxidising agent)

**(b)** Select the correct answer - [2]
  - i. Across a period, the ionization potential [increases, decreases, remains the same]
  - ii. Down the group, electron affinity [increases, decreases, remains the same].

  **Answer.**
  - i. Increases
  - ii. Decreases

**(c)** Choose the correct answer from the choice given: [2]
  - i. In the periodic table alkali metals are placed in the group –
    - **(a)** A: 1
    - **(b)** B: 11
    - **(c)** C: 17
    - **(d)** D: 18

  **Answer.** (a)
  - ii. Which of the following properties do not match with elements of the halogen family?
    - **(a)** They have seven electrons in their valence shell.
    - **(b)** They are highly reactive chemically.
    - **(c)** They are metallic in nature.
    - **(d)** They are diatomic in their molecular form.

  **Answer.** (c)

(ii) Match the following: [5]

| Column A | | Column B |
|---|---|---|
| **(a)** Neon | i. | Insert gas |
| **(b)** NO | ii. | Amphoteric oxide |
| **(c)** NaCl | iii. | Normal Salt |
| **(d)** $CCl_4$ | iv. | Non-polar Solvent |
| **(e)** ZnO | v. | Neutral Oxides |

**Answer.**

**(a)** i.

**(b)** v.

**(c)** iii.

**(d)** Iv.

**(e)** ii.

(iii) Fill in the blanks: [5]

    **(a)** The modern periodic table has ______________period. [7/9]

    **(b)** A Answer. x turns blue litmus red, so it must contain ______________. [Hydronium / hydroxide]

    **(c)** Vinegar contains ______________ acid. [Acetic/Formic]

    **(d)** The ratio of certain mass of a gas or vapor to the mass of same volume of hydrogen is its ______________. [Vapor density / molecular density]

    **(e)** An electrically charged atom is called ______________. [ion/ molecule]

**Answer.**

**(a)** 7

**(b)** Hydronium

**(c)** Acetic

**(d)** Vapor density

**(e)** Ion

(iv) **(a)** Give two important characteristics of homologous series. [5]

    **Answer.** Consecutive members of homologous series differ by $-CH_2$ group and molecular mass 14.

        All the members have same elemental composition.

    **(b)** Give examples of each with IUPAC names.

       i.   Straight chain compound having 3 carbon atoms and 1 double bond

      ii.   Branched chain having 4 carbon atoms and 1 double bond.

     iii.   Cyclic compounds having alternate single and double bond

**Answer.**

    i.   $H_2C-CH{=}CH_2$

    ii.

$$\overset{\displaystyle CH_3}{\underset{\textstyle H_3C-C{=}CH_2}{|}}$$

    iii.

(v) Select one substance from the list given which matches the description given below: **[5]**
   A. Ammonia
   B. Sulphur
   C. Dilute nitric acid
   D. Sulphur dioxide
   E. Hydrogen chloride
   F. Nitroso-iron (II) sulphate
   G. Ammonium sulphate
   H. Chromium sulphate
   I. Platinum
   J. Hydrogen sulphide gas
   i. The compound is responsible for the brown ring during the ring test of nitrate ion.
   ii. The compound responsible for the green colorations when Sulphur dioxide it passed through acidified potassium dichromate Answer..
   iii. A non-metal which reacts with conc. nitric acid to form its own acid as one of the proudest.
   iv. An alkaline gas which gives dense white fumes with hydrogen chloride.
   v. A dilute acid which does not normally give hydrogen when reacted with metals but does give a gas when it reacts with copper.
   vi. The gas which has an offensive smell like rotten eggs.
   vii. A colorless gas which can be used as a bleaching agent.
   viii. A compound which can be oxidized to chlorine.
   ix. A compound which on heating with sodium hydroxide produces a gas which forms white fumes with hydrogen chloride.
   x. A catalyst used in the manufacture of nitric acid by Ostwald's Process.

   **Answer.**
   i. Nitroso-iron (II) sulphate
   ii. Chromium sulphate
   iii. Sulphur
   iv. Ammonia
   v. dil. nitric acid
   vi. Hydrogen sulphide
   vii. Sulphur dioxide
   viii. Hydrogen chloride
   ix. Ammonium sulphate
   x. Platinum

**SECTION-B**
**(Attempt any four questions.)**

**Question : 3**

(i) **(a)** Name the first and last element in period 3      [2]

**(b)** State why noble gases are considered unreactive elements

**Answer.**

**(a)** Sodium, Argon

**(b)** Noble gases are considered unreactive elements because they have filled octet/duplet.

(ii) Give a balanced equation to obtain      [2]

**(a)** $H_2S$

**(b)** $SO_2$

From dilute HCl.

**Answer.**

**(a)** $Na_2SO_3 + 2HCl \rightarrow 2NaCl + H_2O + SO_2 \uparrow$

**(b)** $Na_2S + 2HCl \rightarrow 2NaCl + H_2S \uparrow$

(iii) State one relevant observation for each of the following reactions:      [3]

**(a)** Addition of excess ammonium hydroxide into copper sulphate Answer..

**(b)** A piece of sodium metal is put into ethanol at room temperature.

**Answer:**

**(a)** Addition of excess ammonium hydroxide into copper sulphate Answer. leads to formation of a deep blue colored Answer..

When ammonium hydroxide is added in the Answer. of copper sulphate dropwise, a pale blue precipitate of copper hydroxide is obtained. The equation for this follows:

$$CuSO_4 + 2NH_4OH \rightarrow Cu(OH)_2 + (NH_4)_2SO_4 + 4H_2O$$

When ammonium hydroxide is added in excess, the precipitate dissolves and gives a deep blue Answer. of tetraamine copper (II) sulphate. The equation for this follows:

$$Cu(OH)_2 + (NH_4)_2SO_4 + 2NH_4OH \rightarrow [Cu(NH_3)_4]_2SO_4 + H_2O$$

Hence, the product formed is a complex named as tetraamine copper (II) sulphate.

**(b)** When a piece of sodium metal is put into ethanol at room temperature hydrogen gas is produced which can be identified by a pop sound and it extinguishes a burning splinter.

$$2Na(s) + 2C_2H_5OH(l) \rightarrow 2C_2H_5ONa(l) + H_2(g)$$

Sodium + Ethanol $\rightarrow$ Sodium ethoxide + Hydrogen

(iv) A compound has a formula $= $ " $H_2Y$ ". Y denotes a non-metal having atomic number 8. State the following:      [3]

**(a)** The electronic configuration of Y.

**(b)** The bonding present in " $H_2Y$ ".

**(c)** The formula of the compound formed between calcium [ $_{20}^{40}Ca$ ] and Y.

{55}

**Answer.**

(a) $_8Y=2,6$

(b) Covalent

(c) CaY

## Question : 4

(i) Find the percentage by mass of water of crystallization in green vitriol. $[FeSO_4 \cdot 7H_2O]$     **[2]**
Atomic masses (Fe=56, S=32, O=16, H=1)

**Answer.:**

$56 + 32 + (16 \times 4 = 64) + (7 \times 18 = 126)$

Total mass = 278

Percentage of water of crystallization $= \dfrac{126}{278} \times 100$

45.32%

(ii) **(a)** The acid which contains 4 Hydrogen Atoms is     **[2]**

  i. Formic acid

  ii. Sulphuric acid

  iii. Nitric acid

  iv. Acetic acid

**Answer. iv** Acetic acid

**(b)** Give a suitable chemical term for

  i. A definite number of water molecules bound to some salts.

  ii. A salt formed by incomplete neutralization of an acid by a base.

**Answer.**

  i. Water of crystallization

  ii. Acedic

(iii) Complete the table:     **[3]**

| Name of Process | Inputs | Equation | Output |
|---|---|---|---|
|  | Ammonia + Air |  | Nitric acid |

**Answer.**

| Name of Process | Inputs | Equation | Output |
|---|---|---|---|
| Ostwald's process | Ammonia + Air | $\rightarrow 4NH_3 + 5O_2 \xrightarrow[800°C]{Pt.} 4NO + 6H_2O + Heat$ <br> $\rightarrow 4NO + 2O_2 \xrightarrow{50°C} 4NO_2$ <br> $\rightarrow 4NO_2 + 2H_2O + O_2 \rightarrow 4NHO_3$ | Nitric acid |

(iv) **(a)** In the reaction of $Cl_2 + 2KI \rightarrow 2KCl + I_2$ the conversion of KI to $I_2$ is deemed as [oxidation/reduction].                                                                                                          [2]

**(b)** Explain the terms 'oxidation' and 'reduction' with reference to an atom or ion.

**Answer.**

  **(a)** Oxidation

  **(b)** Oxidation: In the electronic concept, oxidation is defined as a process in which an atom or an ion loses electron(s). Oxidation is also defined as a chemical process which involves addition of oxygen or removal of hydrogen.
  Reduction: In the electronic concept, reduction is defined as a process in which an atom or an ion gains electron(s). Reduction is also defined as a chemical process which involves removal of oxygen or addition of hydrogen.

## Question : 5

(i) **(a) Ionization** potential of element increases across a period                                                                          [2]

  **(b)** Which is greater in size and why cation or Anion.

  **Answer.**

  **(a)** The ionization energy tends to increase as one moves from left to right across a period (with exceptions), because the atomic size decreases due to an increase in the nuclear charge, and thus, more energy is required to remove the electron(s).

  **(b)** Cation is formed by the loss of electron(s), hence proton(s), are more than electron(s) in a cation. So, electrons are strongly attracted by the nucleus and are pulled inward. Hence the size decreases.

(ii) **(a)** Name a gas whose Answer. in water is alkaline.                                                                                      [2]

  **(b)** State the color of phenol phthalein Answer. after passage of ammonia through it.

  **Answer.**

  **(a)** Ammonia $(NH_3)$

  **(b)** Pink

(iii) In the extraction of aluminum: -                                                                                                          [3]

  **(c)** Which Answer. is used to react with bauxite as a first step in obtaining pure aluminum oxide.

  **(d)** The aluminum oxide for the electrolytic extraction of aluminum is obtained by heating aluminum hydroxide. Write the equation for this reaction.

  **(e)** Name the element which serves as the anode & cathode in the extraction of aluminum.

  **Answer.**

  **(a)** Caustic soda

  **(b)** $2Al(OH)_{3(s)} \xrightarrow{1300K} Al_2O_{3(s)} + 3H_2O_{(g)}$

  **(c)** Carbon

(iv) A compound gives following data $C = 57.82\%, O = 38.58\%$ & the rest hydrogen. Its vapors density is eighty-three. Find its empirical and molecular formula.                                                                              [3]

$$[C = 12, O = 16, H = 1]$$

**Answer.**

| % Of Element | Atomic Mass | Relative no. of atoms | Simplest Ratio |
|---|---|---|---|
| C = 57.82% | 12 | $\dfrac{57.82}{12} = 4.81$ | $\dfrac{4.81}{2.41} = 1.99 \cong 2$ |
| O = 38.58% | 16 | $\dfrac{38.58}{16} = 2.41$ | $\dfrac{2.41}{2.41} = 1$ |
| H = 3.6% | 1 | $\dfrac{3.6}{1} = 3.6$ | $\dfrac{3.6}{2.41} \cong 1.5$ |

Empirical Formula $= (C_2O_1H_{1.5}) \times 2$

$$C_4O_2H_3$$

Molecular mass $= 2 \times$ Vapour density

$$= 2 \times 83$$
$$= 166$$

$$n = \frac{\text{Molecular mass}}{\text{empirical formula mass}}$$

$$\frac{166}{83} = 2$$

Molecular Formula $= (C_4O_2H_3) \times 2$

$$= C_8H_6O_4$$

$C_4H_3O_2$ and $C_8H_6O_4$ **Answer.**

## Question : 6

(i) **(a)** What happens [state your observations] when dil. HCl is added to lead nitrate Answer.

  **(b)** Name the ions obtained when HCl dissociates in aqueous Answer..                [2]

  **Answer.**

  **(a)** It forms a white precipitate of lead chloride and nitric acid.

  **(b)** Hydronium Ion

(ii) **Define:**                [2]

  **(a)** Electrolytic cell

  **(b)** Alloys

  **Answer.**

  **(a)** A type of chemical cell in which the flow of electric energy from an external source causes a redox reaction to occur.

  **(b)** A homogeneous mixture of two or more metals or one metal and one non-metal.

(iii) **(a)** Which particles are responsible for the conduction of electricity through                [3]

  i. Metals, and

  ii. Electrolytes?

  **Answer.** i Electrons

ii Ions

**(b)** Electroplating with Silver:

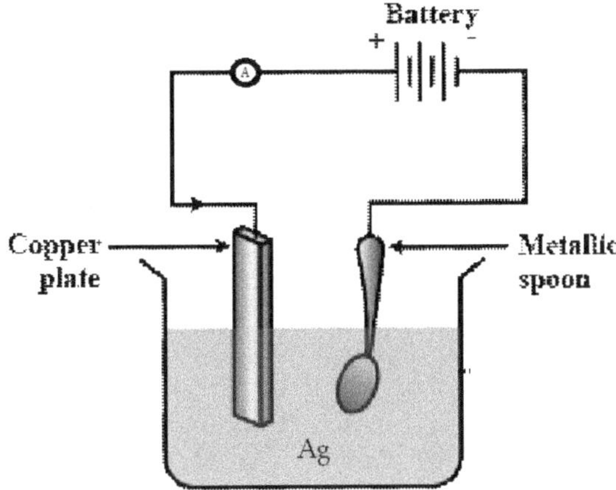


The following questions relate to the electroplating of an article with silver:

Complete the table given below for the electrolytic reactions:

i. ________________ $\rightleftharpoons Na^+ +$ ________________ .

ii. ________________ $\rightleftharpoons Ag^+ +$ ________________ .

**Answer.**

   i. $Na[Ag(CN)_2]$, $[Ag(CN)_2]^-$

   ii. $[Ag(CN)_2]^-$, $2CN^-$

(iv) $200\ cm^3$ of hydrogen and $150\ cm^3$ of oxygen are mixed and ignited, as per following reaction

   $2H_2 + O_2 \rightarrow 2H_2O$           **[3]**

What volume of oxygen remains unreacted, and amount of water vapour formed?

**Answer:**

**Equation**

$2H_2 + O_2 \rightarrow 2H_2O$

    2 vol. 1vol.$\rightarrow$ 2 vol.

    To calculate the amount of unreacted $O_2$

    $H_2 : O_2$

    $2 : 1$

    $200 : X$

    $X = 100\ cm^3$

    Amount of unused of oxygen $= 150 - 100$

                        $= 50\ cm^3$

    To calculate the amount of water formed

    $H_2 : H_2O$

    $2 : 2$

    $200 : X_1$

    $X_1 = 200\ cm^3$

    Amount of water vapors formed $= 200\ cm^3$

**Question : 7**

(i) Give two differences between Electroplating & electrorefining? [2]

**Answer.**

| **Electroplating** | **Electrorefining** |
| --- | --- |
| **(a)** It is an electrolytic process by which a film of one metal is coated over another metal. | **(a)** It is an electrolytic process by which metals (extracted by chemical methods) are freed from impurities present in them. |
| **(b)** The anode consists of the pure metal, whereas the cathode consists of the article to be electroplated. | **(b)** The anode consists of the impure block of the metal, whereas the cathode consists of a thin strip of the pure metal. |

(ii) On adding dilute ammonia Answer. to a colorless Answer. of a salt, a white gelatinous precipitate appears. This precipitate however dissolves on addition of excess of ammonia Answer.. Identify (choose from Na, Al, Zn, Pb, Fe ) [2]

(a) Which metal salt Answer. was used?

(b) What is the formula of the white gelatinous precipitate obtained?

**Answer.**

(a) Zn

(b) $Zn(OH)_2$

(iii) Write the general formula for the following: [3]

(a) Alcohol

(b) Aldehyde

(c) Carboxylic acid

**Answer.**

(a) $C_nH_{2n+1}OH$

(b) $C_nH_{2n}O$

(c) $C_nH_{2n}O_2$

(iv) Give reasons for the following: [3]

(a) Sulphury acid forms two types of salts with NaOH,

(b) A piece of wood becomes black when concentrated sulphuric acid is poured on it,

(c) Brisk effervescence is seen when oil of vitriol is added to sodium carbonate.

**Answer.**

(a) $NaOH + H_2SO_4 \rightarrow NaHSO_4 + H_2O$

$2NaOH + H_2SO_4 \rightarrow Na_2SO_4 + 2H_2O$

(b) A piece of wood becomes black when concentrated sulphuric acid is poured on it because black immediately gives a black spongy mass of carbon which rises. Steam is given off and the whole mass gets heated due to an exothermic reaction. They are said to get charred.

(c) Brisk effervescence is seen when oil of vitriol is added to sodium carbonate because of the evolution of carbon dioxide.
$$Na_2CO_3 + H_2SO_4 \rightarrow Na_2SO_4 + H_2O + CO_2 \uparrow$$

## Question : 8

(i) You are provided with two reagent bottles marked A and B. One contains $NH_4OH$ Answer. and the other contains NaOH Answer.. How will you identify them by a chemical test?     [2]

**Answer.**

| | | | | |
|---|---|---|---|---|
| $Zn^{2+}$ | $ZnSO_4$ [White] | $ZnSO_4 + 2NaOH \rightarrow Na_2SO_4 + Zn(OH)_2 \downarrow$ | Zinc hydroxide | Gelatinous white soluble |
| | | $[Zn(OH)_2 + 2NaOH[excess] \rightarrow 2H_2O + Na_2ZnO_2]$ | Sodium zincate | Colorless soln. |
| $Zn^{2+}$ | $ZnSO_4$ | $ZnSO_4 + 2NH_4OH \rightarrow (NH_4)_2SO_4 + Zn(OH)_2 \downarrow$ | Zinc hydroxide | White Gelatinous soluble |
| | | $[Zn(OH)_2 + 4NH_4OH \text{ [in excess]} \rightarrow 4H_2O + [Zn(NH_3)_2 ](OH)_2$ | Complex salt soln. Tetraamine zinc hydroxide | Colorless soln. |

(ii) Name the nitrate that     [2]
(a) Produces a colorless gas on heating.
(b) Produces a brown-colored and a colorless gas on heating.
Also, write the balanced chemical equations.
**Answer.**
(a) Sodium nitrate or potassium nitrate produces $O_2$ gas (colourless gas) on heating.
$$2NaNO_3(s) \xrightarrow{\Delta} 2NaNO_2(s) + O_2(g)$$
(b) Heavy metal nitrates, such as zinc nitrate, lead nitrate and copper (II) nitrate produce a brown-colored $NO_2$ gas and a colourless $O_2$ gas, on heating.
$$2Zn(NO_3)_2(s) \xrightarrow{\Delta} 2ZnO(s) + O_2(g) + 4NO_2(g)$$

(iii) Find the odd one out     [3]
(a) $C_3H_8, C_5H_{10}, C_2H_6, CH_4$
(b) Formic Acid, Nitric Acid, Acetic Acid, Propanoic Acid
(c) Ethanol, Methanal, Methanol, Propanol
**Answer.**
(a) $C_5H_{10}$
(b) Formic Acid
(c) Methanal

(iv) Draw the structural formula of a compound with two carbons in each of the following cases:     [3]

(a) An Alkane with carbon-to-Carbon single bond

**(b)** An Alcohol containing two carbon atoms

**(c)** An unsaturated hydrocarbon with a carbon - carbon triple bond.

**Answer.**

**(a)**

$$\begin{array}{c} \ \ \ \ H \ \ \ H \\ \ \ \ \ | \ \ \ \ | \\ H-C-C-H \\ \ \ \ \ | \ \ \ \ | \\ \ \ \ \ H \ \ \ H \end{array}$$

**(b)**
$$\begin{array}{c} \ \ H \ \ H \\ \ \ | \ \ \ | \\ H-C-C-O-H \\ \ \ | \ \ \ | \\ \ \ H \ \ H \end{array}$$

**(c)** $H - C \equiv C - H$

# UNSOLVED SAMPLE TEST PAPER

**Maximum Marks: 80**

Time allowed: Two hours

Answers to this Paper must be written on the paper provided separately.

You will not be allowed to write during first 15 minutes.

This time is to be spent in reading the question paper.

The time given at the head of this Paper is the time allowed for writing the answers.

**(Section A is compulsory. Attempt any four questions from Section B.**

**The intended marks for questions or parts of questions are given in brackets [ ].**

## SECTION A

### Answer all the questions from this section

**Question : 1**                                                                          [15]

Choose one correct answer to the question from the given option:

(i) With excess of chlorine, $NH_3$ forms:

    **(a)** HCl

    **(b)** $NH_4Cl$

    **(c)** $NCl_3$

    **(d)** NOCl

    **Answer.** (c) HCl

(ii) An alkaline earth metal is

    **(a)** Palladium

    **(b)** Calcium

    **(c)** Lead

    **(d)** Copper

    **Answer.** (b) Calcium

(iii) An organic weak acid is:

    **(a)** Formic acid.

    **(b)** Sulphuric acid.

    **(c)** Nitric acid.

    **(d)** Hydrochloric acid

    **Answer.** (a) Formic acid.

(iv) Ionization potential increases over a period from left to right because the :

    **(a)** Atomic radius increases and nuclear charge increases

    **(b)** Atomic radius decreases and nuclear charge decreases

    **(c)** Atomic radius increases and nuclear charge decreases

    **(d)** Atomic radius decreases and nuclear charge increases

**Answer.** (d) Atomic radius decreases and nuclear charge increases

(v) Bonding in this molecule can be understood to involve coordinate bonding :
  (a) Caron tetrachloride
  (b) Hydrogen
  (c) Hydrogen chloride
  (d) Ammonium chloride
  **Answer.** (d) Ammonium chloride

(vi) Which one of the following salt Answer.s on reaction with excess of ammonium hydroxide Answer. gives a deep blue Answer.?
  (a) $FeCl_3$ (aq)
  (b) $CuSO_4$ (aq)
  (c) $Al_2(SO_4)_3$(aq)
  (d) $ZnSO_4$(aq)
  **Answer.** (b) $CuSO_4$ (aq)

(vii) The type of bonding present in the nitrogen molecule:
  (a) Single Covalent Bond
  (b) Double Covalent Bond
  (c) Polar Covalent bond
  (d) Triple Covalent Bond
  **Answer.** (d) Triple Covalent Bond

(viii) The empirical formula of the compound is $CH_2O$, the possible molecular formula can be:
  (a) $C_3H_6O_3$
  (b) $C_2H_4O$
  (c) $C_4H_3O_2$
  (d) $C_4H_6O_2$
  **Answer.** (a) $C_3H_6O_3$

(ix) Persulphuric acid is the chemical name of :
  (a) Green vitriol
  (b) White vitriol
  (c) Oleum
  (d) Gypsum
  **Answer.** (c) Oleum

(x) Name the oxidizing agent used in Ostwald's process.
  (a) NO
  (b) $NO_2$
  (c) CO
  (d) $O_2$

**Answer.** (d) $O_2$

(xi) When fused lead bromide is electrolyzed, we observe:
    **(a)** A silver-grey deposit at anode and a reddish-brown deposit at cathode
    **(b)** A silver-grey deposit at cathode and a reddish-brown deposit at anode
    **(c)** A silver-grey deposit at cathode and reddish-brown fumes at anode
    **(d)** Silver grey fumes at anode and reddish-brown fumes at cathode
    **Answer.** (c) A silver-grey deposit at cathode and reddish-brown fumes at anode

(xii) A mineral from which the metal is extracted economically is known as:
    **(a)** Matrix
    **(b)** Gangue
    **(c)** Ore
    **(d)** None of these
    **Answer.** (c) Ore

(xiii) The number of $C - H$ bonds in ethane molecule are:
    **(a)** Four
    **(b)** Six
    **(c)** Eight
    **(d)** Ten
    **Answer.** (b) Six

(xiv) Twice of vapor density is:
    **(a)** Molecular Formula
    **(b)** Empirical formula
    **(c)** Chemical formula
    **(d)** Molecular weight
    **Answer.** (d) Molecular weight

(xv) The reaction at anode is:
    **(a)** Oxidation
    **(b)** Reduction
    **(c)** Redox
    **(d)** None of these
    **Answer.** (a) Oxidation

## Question : 2

(i) The corrects alphabet or word from the brackets to complete the following sentences. Write down only that as the answer. **[5]**
    **(a)** Element E has a low ionisation potential and low electronegativity. The element E is likely to be a (metal/non-metal).

**Answer.** Metal

**(b)** In the third period, element F is to the left of element G.

    i   The atom of element F would be expected to be (larger/smaller) than the atom of element G.

    ii  The element F would be (less/more) metallic in character than element G.

    iii  The element with greater electron affinity would be (F/G),

    iv  Element F would have a (greater/lesser) electron affinity than element G.

**Answer.**

    i  Larger

    ii  More

    iii  G

    iv  Lesser

(ii)  Match the following     **[5]**

| Column A | Column B |
|---|---|
| **(a)** $Pb^{2+}$ <br> **(b)** $Fe^{2+}$ <br> **(c)** $Zn^{2+}$ <br> **(d)** $Fe^{3+}$ <br> **(e)** $Cu^{2+}$ | i.   Reddish brown <br> ii.  White insoluble in excess <br> iii.  Dirty green <br> iv.  White soluble in excess <br> v.  Blue |

**Answer.**

**(a)** ii

**(b)** iii

**(c)** iv

**(d)** i

**(e)** v

(iii)  Complete the following by choosing a correct answer from the bracket.    **[5]**

**(a)** Salts of normal elements [1 (IA) to 17 (VIIA)] are generally........... [Colored/Colorless]

**(b)** Ferrous salts are...........in color.[Red/Green]

**(c)** An example of a weak alkali Answer.............[NaOH/ $NH_4OH$]

**(d)** Both ammonium and sodium hydroxide is used in analytical chemistry for identifying............ [Cations/Anions]

**(e)** The general formula for the homologous of alkynes series ...........[CnH2n+2/CnH2n-2]

**Answer.**

**(a)** Colorless

**(b)** Green

(c) $NH_4OH$

(d) Cations

(e) $CnH_{2n+2}/CnH_{2n-2}$

(iv) **(a)** Draw the structure of formula for the following. **[5]**

i Methanal

ii Acetylene

iii 2,2-Dichloropropane

**Answer.**

i.
```
        O
        ||
  H  –  C  –H
```

ii. $H - C \equiv C - H$

iii.
```
               Cl
               |
H₃C    –       C    –    CH₃
               |
               Cl
```

**(b)** Give IUPAC name of the following structure.

i 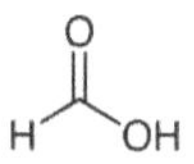


ii 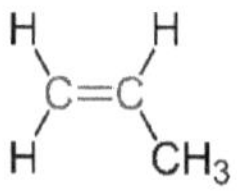


**Answer.**

i Methanoic acid

ii Propene

(v) Identify the following. **[5]**

**(a)** The property of concentrate $H_2SO_4$ by which it convert sulfur to $SO_2$

**(b)** The gas produced when sodium carbonate reacts with dilute nitric acid.

**(c)** The type of reaction when methane reacts with chlorine in presence of sunlight.

**(d)** The type of bond formed between water and H+ ion during formation of hydronium ion.

**(e)** A chemical formula which denotes simplest whole number ration of atoms of elements present in a compound.

**Answer.**

**(a)** Oxidizing

**(b)** $CO_2$

**(c)** Substitution

**(d)** CO-ordinate bond

**(e)** Empirical formula

**SECTION-B**

(Attempt any **four** questions)

## Question : 3

(i) An element Z has atomic number 16 Answer the following questions on Z  [2]

 **(a)** State the period and group to which Z belongs.

 **(b)** Is Z metal or a non-metal?

(ii) Write balanced equation for the following:  [2]

 **(a)** Action of heat on a mixture of copper and concentrated nitric acid.

 **(b)** Action of concentrated sulphuric acid on carbon.

(iii) Refer to the flow chart diagram below and give balanced equations with conditions, if any, for the following conversions A to C.  [3]

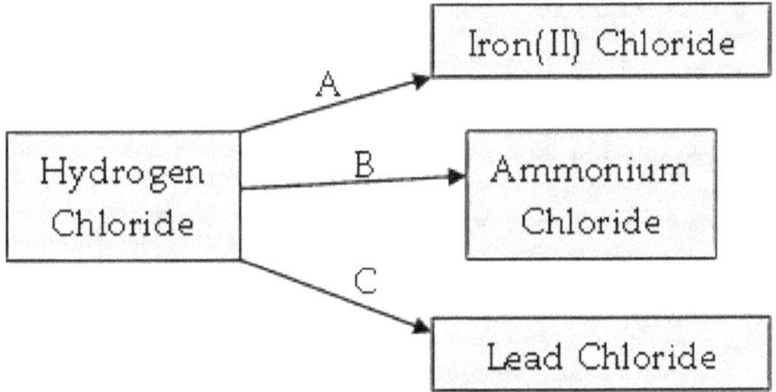


(iv) Fill in the blanks selecting the appropriate word from the given choices.  [3]

 **(d)** A compound having all the three types of bonds__________. [$CH_3COOH$/$NH_4Cl$]

 **(e)** In water molecule __________ atom has loan pair of electrons. [Oxygen/Hydrogen]

 **(f)** The molecule having single displaceable hydrogen__________. [ $CH_3COOH$ /$H_2CO_3$]

## Question : 4

(i) Find the percentage by mass of water of crystallization in Epsom salt [$MgSO_4.7H_2O$]  [2]

 Atomic masses ($Mg = 24, S = 32, O = 16, H = 1$)

(ii) The following table shows the test for Answer.s A and B. Write down the observation for the given test.  [2]

| Test | Observation | Conclusions |
| --- | --- | --- |
| 1. To the Answer., A sodium hydroxide Answer. was added. | | A contains $Fe^{3+}$ ions |
| 2 To Answer. B ammonium hydroxide was added slowly till in excess. | | B contains $Cu^{2+}$ ions |

(iii) Answer. A is a strong acid, Answer. B is a weak acid, and Answer. C is a strong alkali.  [3]

 **(a)** Which Answer. contains solute molecules in addition to water molecules.

 **(b)** Which Answer. could be a Answer. of glacial acetic acid?

 **(c)** Give an example of a Answer. which is a weak alkali.

{69}

(iv) Copper sulphate Answer. is electrolyzed using copper electrodes.  [3]

Study the diagram given alongside and answer the question that follows

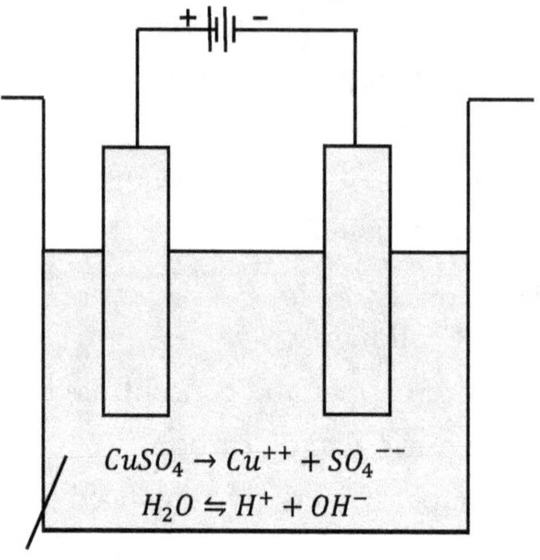


Aqueous Answer. of copper sulphate

**(a)** Which electrode to your left or right is known as the oxidizing electrode and why?

**(b)** Write the equation representing the reaction that occurs.

**(c)** State two appropriate observations for the above electrolysis.

## Question : 5

(i) Name the non-metal which  [2]

**(a)** Forms alloys.

**(b)** Is a liquid at room temperature.

(ii) **(a)** Identify the substance P.  [2]

The deliquescent salt P, turns yellow on dissolving in water and gives a reddish-brown precipitate with sodium hydroxide Answer..

**(b)** An ion gives white precipitate with which is insoluble in dilute acids.

(iii) Answer the following questions:  [3]

**(a)** Name the process used for the reduction of alumina.

**(b)** Name the anode, cathode and the electrolyte used in the process mentioned in (a)

**(c)** Why is cryolite used in the extraction of aluminum from aluminum oxide?

(iv) A metal M forms a volatile chloride containing 65.5% chlorine. If the density of the chloride relative to hydrogen is 162.5, find the molecular formula of the chloride. (Atomic mass: M = 56 and Cl = 35.5.)  [3]

## Question : 6

(i) Given reason.  [2]

**(a)** Why is hydrogen chloride gas not collected over water?

**(b)** Why concentrated sulphuric acid is not used for drying ammonia gas?

(ii) Define     **[2]**
   **(a)** Vapor density
   **(b)** Ionization energy

(iii) Name the following.     **[3]**
   **(a)** A gas which does not conduct electricity in the liquid state but conducts electricity when dissolved in water?
   **(b)** A catalyst used in the manufacture of nitric acid by Ostwald's process.
   **(c)** A compound formed when both sulfur trioxide and sulphury acid reacts.

(iv) Calculate the volume of methane gas that must be burnt completely to produce 100 lit of $CO_2$ at S. T. P.     **[3]**

## Question : 7

(i) Explain, why only glass apparatus should be used for the preparation of nitric acid by heating concentrated sulphuric acid and potassium nitrate?     **[2]**

(ii) The figure given below illustrates the apparatus used in the laboratory preparation of nitric acid.

    **[2]**

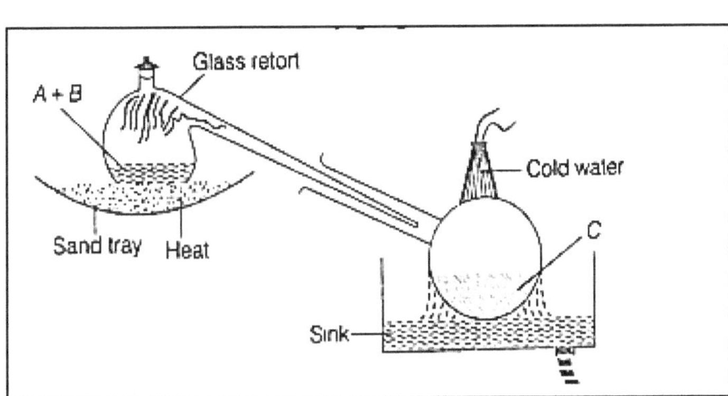


   **(d)** Name A (a liquid), B (a solid) and C (a liquid).
   (Do not give the formulae)
   **(e)** Write an equation to show how nitric acid undergoes decomposition.

(iii) Give the IUPAC names of the following compounds numbered (i) to (iii).     **[3]**

**(a)**
$$H-\overset{\overset{\displaystyle H}{|}}{\underset{\underset{\displaystyle H}{|}}{C}}-\overset{\overset{\displaystyle H}{|}}{\underset{\underset{\displaystyle H}{|}}{C}}-\overset{\overset{\displaystyle H}{|}}{\underset{\underset{\displaystyle H}{|}}{C}}-\overset{\overset{\displaystyle H}{|}}{\underset{\underset{\displaystyle OH}{|}}{C}}-\overset{\overset{\displaystyle H}{|}}{\underset{\underset{\displaystyle H}{|}}{C}}-H$$

**(b)**
$$H-\overset{\overset{\displaystyle H}{|}}{\underset{\underset{\displaystyle H}{|}}{C}}-\overset{\overset{\displaystyle H}{|}}{\underset{\underset{\displaystyle H}{|}}{C}}-\overset{\overset{\displaystyle O}{\|}}{C}-OH$$

(c)

$$H-\underset{\underset{Br}{|}}{\overset{\overset{H}{|}}{C}}-\underset{\underset{Br}{|}}{\overset{\overset{H}{|}}{C}}-H$$

(iv) Choose the role played by concentrated Sulphury acid as A, B which is responsible for the reactions 1 and 3.  **[3]**

   **(a)** Oxidizing agent

   **(b)** Non-Volatile Acid

   **(c)** A typical Acid

   i   $NaNO_3 + H_2SO_4 \xrightarrow{<200°C} NaHSO_4 + HNO_3$

   ii   $Zn + H_2SO_4 \xrightarrow{dil.} ZnSO_4 + H_2$

   iii   $S + 2H_2SO_4 \xrightarrow{Conc.} 3SO_2 + 2H_2O$

## Question : 8

(i) Give reasons for the following:  **[2]**

   **(a)** In the laboratory preparation of nitric acid, the mixture of concentrated sulphuric acid and sodium nitrate should not be heated very strongly above 200°C.

   **(b)** Though ammonium nitrite readily gives nitrogen gas on heating, a mixture of ammonium chloride and sodium nitrite in water is heated to prepare nitrogen gas in the laboratory.

(ii) For the preparation of hydrochloric acid in the laboratory  **[2]**

   **(a)** Why is direct absorption of hydrogen chloride gas in water not feasible?

   **(b)** What arrangement is done to dissolve hydrogen chloride gas in water?

(iii) Match the following columns.  **[3]**

| Column I (Types of isomerism) | Column II (Definition) |
| --- | --- |
| **(a)** Chain isomerism | (i) Same molecular formula but different functional group. |
| **(b)** Position isomerism | (ii) Same molecular formula but different carbon skeleton. |
| **(c)** Functional group isomerism | (iii) Difference in the position of substituent atom or functional group. |

(iv) Compound A is bubbled through bromine dissolved in carbon tetrachloride and the product is $CH_2Br - CH_2Br$.  **[3]**

$$A \xrightarrow{Br_2/CCl_4} CH_2Br - CH_2Br$$

   **(a)** What type of reaction has A undergone?

   **(b)** What is your observation?

**(c)** Name (not formula) the compound formed when steam reacts with A in the presence of an acid.

## SAMPLE TEST PAPER-4
### CHEMISTRY
(SCIENCE PAPER-2)

**Maximum Marks: 80**

Time allowed: Two hours

Answers to this Paper must be written on the paper provided separately.

You will not be allowed to write during first 15 minutes.

This time is to be spent in reading the question paper.

The time given at the head of this Paper is the time allowed for writing the answers.

**(Section A is compulsory. Attempt any four questions from Section B.**

**The intended marks for questions or parts of questions are given in brackets [ ].**

### SECTION A
**Answer all the questions from this section**

**Question : 1**                                                                 [15]

Choose one correct answer to the question from the given option:

(i) A compound which is thermally unstable:

    **(a)** NaCl

    **(b)** KCl

    **(c)** $NH_4Cl$

    **(d)** $ZnCl_2$

    **Answer.** (c) $NH_4Cl$


(ii) An amphoteric metal oxide is

    **(a)** $Na_2O$

    **(b)** $Al_2O_3$

    **(c)** CuO

    **(d)** $P_2O_5$

    **Answer.** (b) $Al_2O_3$


(iii) An aqueous Answer. having molecules and ions both

    **(a)** $KNO_3$

    **(b)** $H_2SO_4$

    **(c)** dil. HCl

    **(d)** $NH_4OH$

    **Answer.** (d) $NH_4OH$


(iv) Variation of the ionization energy of elements down the group

    **(a)** Increases

    **(b)** Remains constant

    **(c)** Decrease

    **(d)** First Increases then decrease

**Answer.** (c) Decrease

(v) Basicity of aq. Answer. of $H_3PO_3$ is
    **(a)** Three
    **(b)** Two
    **(c)** One
    **(d)** Four
    **Answer.** (b) Two

(vi) The salt which is soluble in excess of $NH_4OH$ is:
    **(a)** Zinc sulphate
    **(b)** Lead nitrate
    **(c)** Ferrous sulphate
    **(d)** Ferric chloride
    **Answer.** (a) Zinc sulphate

(vii) The empirical formula of the compound $CH_3COOH$ is:
    **(a)** $C_2H_4O_2$
    **(b)** $C_4H_8O_4$
    **(c)** $CH_2O$
    **(d)** $CH_4O_2$
    **Answer.** (c) $CH_2O$

(viii) The covalency of nitrogen in ammonium ions is:
    **(a)** Three
    **(b)** Two
    **(c)** Four
    **(d)** Five
    **Answer.** (c) Four

(ix) A large number of organic compounds exist in nature largely due to :
    **(a)** Catenation property of carbon
    **(b)** Isomerism of organic compounds
    **(c)** Both
    **(d)** The small size of carbon
    **Answer.** (c) Both

(x) The process by which concentration of bauxite is carried out:
    **(a)** Hall's Process
    **(b)** Haber's Process
    **(c)** Baeyer's Process
    **(d)** Oswald's Process

**Answer.** (c) Baeyer's Process

(xi) Ethene undergoes bromination in $CCl_4$ solvent this reaction is:
   **(a)** Elimination reaction
   **(b)** Addition reaction
   **(c)** Dehydration reaction
   **(d)** Substitution reaction
   **Answer.** (b) Addition reaction

(xii) Drying agent used to dry $NH_3$ Gas:
   **(a)** Concentrated sulphuric acid
   **(b)** Calcium oxide
   **(c)** Sulphurous acid
   **(d)** Calcium hydroxide
   **Answer.** (b) Calcium oxide

(xiii) During electrolysis the chemical process occurring at cathode:
   **(a)** Oxidation
   **(b)** Reduction
   **(c)** Redox
   **(d)** Displacement
   **Answer.** (b) Reduction

(xiv) Member of homologous series of organic compounds differs by:
   **(a)** $-CH_2$ group
   **(b)** $-CH_3$ group
   **(c)** $-C_2H_5$ group
   **(d)** None of these
   **Answer.** (a) $-CH_2$ group

(xv) A noble gas having duplet in valence shell:
   **(a)** Ne
   **(b)** Ar
   **(c)** He
   **(d)** Rn
   **Answer.** (c) He

## Question : 2

(i) Consider the section of periodic table given below [5]

| Group number | IA 1 | IIA 2 | IIIA 13 | IVA 14 | VA 15 | VIA 16 | VII A 17 | 0 18 |
|---|---|---|---|---|---|---|---|---|
| | LI | | D | | | O | J | Ne |

| | A | Mg | E | Si | | H | K | |
|---|---|---|---|---|---|---|---|---|
| | B | C | | F | G | | | L |

Note: in this table B doesn't represent boron

i. C doesn't represent carbon

ii. F doesn't represent fluorine

iii. K doesn't represent potassium

You must see the position of the elements in the periodic table

Some elements are given in their own symbol and position in the periodic table while others are shown with the letter. With reference to the table:

**(a)** Which is the most electronegative

**(b)** How many valence electrons are present in G

**(c)** Write the formula of the compound between B and H

**(d)** In the compound between F and J what type of bond will be formed?

**(e)** Draw the electron dot structure for the compound formed between C and K.

**Answer.**

**(a)** J

**(b)** 5

**(c)** $B_2H$

**(d)** Covalant

**(e)** $[C]^{++} 2\left[:\ddot{K}:\right]^{-}$

(ii) Match the following [5]

| Column A | Column B |
|---|---|
| **(a)** Basic salt | i. Reddish brown |
| **(b)** Ferric hydroxide | ii. NaCl |
| **(c)** Zinc hydroxide | iii. HCl |
| **(d)** Electrovalent compound | iv. Ca[OH]Cl |
| **(e)** Polar compound | v. Soluble in excess sodium hydroxide |

**Answer.**

**(a)** iv

**(b)** i

**(c)** v

**(d)** ii

**(e)** iii

(iii) Complete the following by choosing a correct answer from the bracket. [5]

    **(a)** An aqueous Answer. of HCl is ..........electrolyte. [Weak/strong]

**(b)** The atomic number of an element is the number of........... Present in an atom.[protons/electrons]

**(c)** evolution of bromine vapours occurs from........... During electrolysis of molten $PbBr_2$. [Anode /cathode]

**(d)** The molecular formula of the 3rd member of the alkenes series is............ $[C_3H_6/C_4H_8]$

**(e)** Funnel arrangement is used to prepare aqueous Answer. of...........$[HCl/HNO_3]$

**Answer.**

**(a)** Strong

**(b)** Protons

**(c)** Anode

**(d)** $C_4H_8$

**(e)** HCl

(iv) Identify the following: [5]
    **(a)** The catalyst is used to convert ethene into ethane.

    **(b)** A triatomic molecule having two lone pairs of electrons.

    **(c)** The gas evolved when dilute HCl reacts with zinc sulphide.

    **(d)** A metal having lowest ionisation energy.

    **(e)** An alkane having vapour density 15.

**Answer.**

**(a)** Ni or Pt

**(b)** $H_2O$

**(c)** $H_2S$

**(d)** Cs

**(e)** $C_2H_6$

(v) **(a)** Draw the structure for the following: [3]
    i   Pentachloro ethane

    ii   Methanolic acid

    iii   1,2-dichloro ethene

**Answer.**

    i

ii

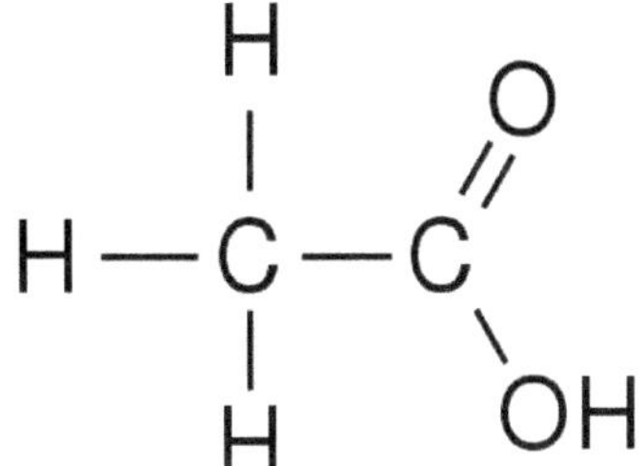

iii

$$H - \underset{\underset{Cl}{|}}{\overset{\overset{H}{|}}{C}} = \underset{\underset{Cl}{|}}{\overset{\overset{H}{|}}{C}} - H$$

**(b)** Name the following organic compounds in IUPAC system: [2]

i

ii    $Br - CH_2 - CH_2 - Br$

**Answer.**

   i    2-Methyl butane

   ii    1,2-dibromoethane

**SECTION-B**

(Attempt any **four** questions)

**Question : 3**

(i)   Identify the Anion represent in each of the following compounds [2]

   **(a)** When $AgNO_3$ Answer. is added to a Answer. of compound A, a white precipitate soluble in excess $NH_4OH$ Answer..

   **(b)** when dilute hydrochloride acid is added to compound B, a gas is produced which turns lime water milky but has no effect on acidified potassium dichromate Answer..

(ii) Write the product and balance the equation: [2]

**(a)** Cu + Conc. $HNO_3 \rightarrow$

**(b)** C + Conc. $H_2SO_4 \rightarrow$

(iii) From the diagram related with electroplating of an article with silver, answer the following questions:  **[3]**

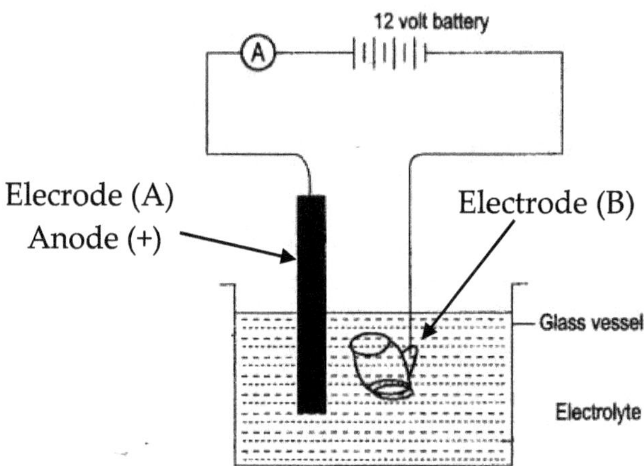


**Fig.** Silver electroplating

**(a)** Name the cathode used in this process
  - i    Highly cleaned article
  - ii   Impure dirty article
  - iii  Electrolyte
  - iv   None of these

**(b)** Name the electrolyte used
  - i    $AgNO_3$
  - ii   $Na[Ag(CN)_2]$
  - iii  HCN
  - iv   Both (i) and (ii)

**(c)** Name the anode used
  - i    HCN
  - ii   Silver plate
  - iii  Copper cup
  - iv   Platinum plate

(iv) Fill in the blanks selecting the appropriate word from the given choices.  **[3]**

**(a)** The main ore of Iron is __________. [Bauxite/Hematite]

**(b)** The functional group present in ethanol is __________. [alcoholic /Aldehydic]

**(c)** A non polar molecule having polar bonds __________. [$CH_4$/$CCl_4$]

**Question : 4**

(i)  Draw the electron dot structure of the following:                                    **[2]**

   (a) $NH_4^+$

   (b) $CaO$

(ii) Calculate:                                                                          **[2]**

   (a) Calculate the empirical formula of a compound whose molecular formulae is $C_4H_8O_2$ and empirical formula weight is 44.

   (b) Find out the mass percentage of carbon in $CO_3^{--}$ ion.  (C=12,O=16)

(iii) The following figure illustrates the apparatus used in the laboratory preparation of hydrogen chloride gas:                                                                     **[3]**

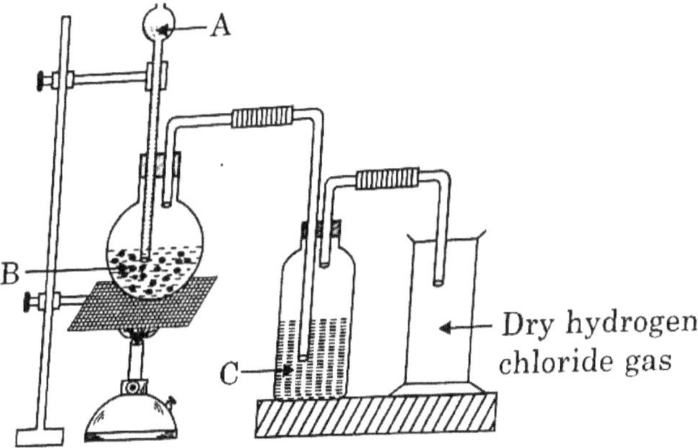


   (a)  Name A (a liquid), B (a solid), and C ( a liquid). (Do not give formulae.)

   (b) Write the balanced chemical equation for the reaction in which dilute hydrochloric acid acts

   as an acid.

   (c) Write the balanced chemical equation for the reaction between A and B when they are heated.

(iv) Give reason of following:                                                           **[3]**

   (a) Hydrochloric acid is considered as a strong acid whereas acetic acid is a weak acid. why?

   (b) During the extraction of aluminium cryolite and fluorspar are added to alumina. Why?

   (c) For the production of concentrated sulphuric acid, sulphur trioxide is not directly dissolved in water. Why?


**Question : 5**

(i)  Study the figure given below and answer the questions that follow:                  **[2]**

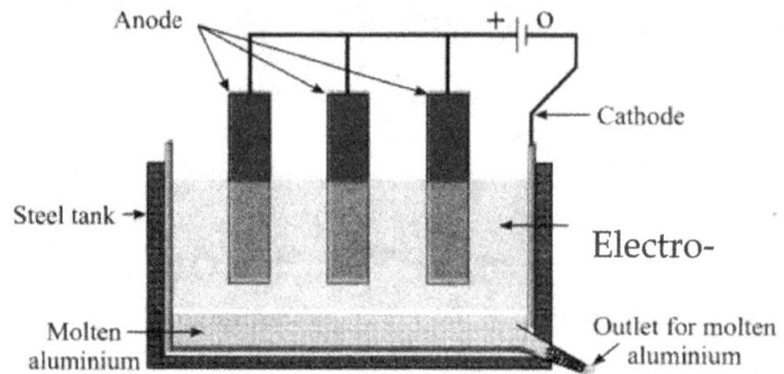


**(a)** Name the process used for the reduction of alumina.

**(b)** Name the anode, cathode and the electrolyte used in the process mentioned in (a)

(ii) Name a probable Cation present based on the following Observations:                                                    [2]

**(a)** Reddish brown precipitate insoluble in Ammonium hydroxide.

**(b)** Blue colored sulphate Answer..

(iii) Give balanced chemical equation for the following:                                                                      [3]

**(d)** $KCl + H_2SO_4 \xrightarrow[\text{Conc.}]{<200°c}$

**(e)** $CuO + 2HCl \rightarrow$

**(f)** $C_2H_2 + Cl_2 \xrightarrow{CCl_4}$

(iv) State one relevant observation for each of the following reaction                                                       [3]

**(a)** When $NH_3$ gas reacts with heated Litharge

**(b)** Dil. $H_2SO_4$ reacts with $BaCl_2$ Answer..

**(c)** Ferric chloride Answer. reacts with excess of NaOH Answer..

## Question : 6

(i) Define:                                                                                                                  [2]

**(a)** Electron affinity

**(b)** Dative bond

(ii) Ammonia may be oxidised to nitrogen monoxide in the presence of a catalyst according to the following equation.                                                                                                                [2]

$$4NH_3 + 5O_2 \rightarrow 4NO + 6H_2O$$

If 27 litre of reactants are consumed, what volume of nitrogen monoxide is produced at the same

temperature and pressure?

(iii) State the conditions required for the following reactions:                                                             [3]

**(a)** Conversion of NH₃ to nitric oxide

**(b)** Sulphur dioxide to sulphur trioxide

**(c)** Conversion of potassium nitrate to nitric acid.

(iv) Complete the following:                                              [3]

(a) $C + 4HNO_3 \xrightarrow[\phantom{xx}]{\text{(Conc)}\ \Delta}$ _______ + _______ + $2H_2O$

(b) $3Cu + 8\ HNO_3 \xrightarrow{\text{(Cold,dil.)}}$ _______ + _______ + $4H_2O$

(c) $S + 6HNO_3 \xrightarrow{\Delta} 2H_2O +$ _______ + _______

## Question : 7

(v) The equation for the burning of octane is:                            [2]

$$2C_8H_{18} + 25O_2 \rightarrow 16CO_2 + 18H_2O$$

Find out the volume of air needed for complete burning 50 C.C. octane if air has 20% oxygen by volume

(vi) A gas cylinder of capacity of 20 dm³ is filled with a gas X, the mass of which is 10 g when the same cylinder is filled with hydrogen gas at the same temperature and pressure the mass of the hydrogen is 2g, hence the relative molecular mass for the gas is           [2]

(a) 5

(b) 16

(c) 10

(d) 20

(vii) Give balanced equation for the electrode reaction involved in the following conversion at respective                                              [3]

(a) Aluminium oxide $\longrightarrow$ Oxygen gas $\longleftarrow$ Copper [II] sulphate

(b) Copper metal $\longrightarrow$ Copper ions $\longrightarrow$ Copper metal

(c) Hydrogen gas $\longleftarrow$ Acidified water $\longrightarrow$ Oxygen gas

(viii) Study the phenomena and answer the questions given below          [3]

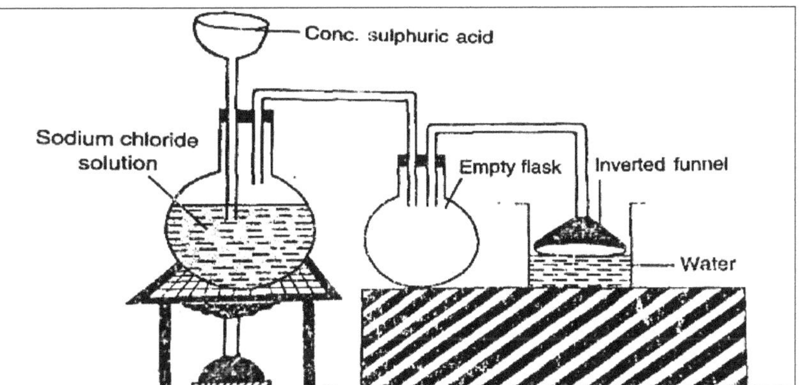


(a) Name the process whose remedy is shown in the figure and why this process take place

(b) What are the advantage of inverted funnel arrangement

**(c)** Name two gases which shows this phenomenon

**Question : 8**

(i) Draw the electron dot structure for the following [2]

    **(a)** $OH^-$ (Hydroxyl ion)

    **(b)** $MgCl_2$ (Magnesium chloride

(ii) Distinguish between the following [2]

    **(a)** $NaCl$ & $NaNO_3$

    **(b)** $Zn(NO_3)_2$ & $Pb(NO_3)_2$

(iii) Name the type of organic reaction: [3]

    **(a)** $C + 2H_2SO_4 \xrightarrow{\text{(Conc)}} CO_2 + 2H_2O + 2SO_2$

    **(b)** $CuSO_4.5H_2O \xrightarrow[H_2SO_4]{\text{Conc.}} CuSO_4 + 5H_2O$

    **(c)** $CH_3 - CH_2 - Br + \overset{\text{(Alcoholic)}}{KOH} \rightarrow KBr + H_2O + C_2H_4$

(iv) The atomic number of 4 elements W X Y and Z are 7, 8, 9, and 11 respectively. write the formula of compounds that are expected to be formed between the following pairs of elements: [3]

    **(a)** W and X

    **(b)** X and X

    **(c)** W and Z

    **(d)** Y and Y

**Maximum Marks: 80**
Time allowed: Two hours
Answers to this Paper must be written on the paper provided separately.
You will not be allowed to write during first 15 minutes.
This time is to be spent in reading the question paper.
The time given at the head of this Paper is the time allowed for writing the answers.

**(Section A is compulsory. Attempt any four questions from Section B.**
**The intended marks for questions or parts of questions are given in brackets [ ].**

## SECTION A
### Answer all the questions from this section

**Question : 1**                                                                    **[15]**

Choose one correct answer to the question from the given option:

(i)  To increase pH value of a neutral Answer. we should add

    **(a)** $HCl_{(aq.)}$

    **(b)** $NaOH_{(aq.)}$

    **(c)** $CH_3COONH_{4(aq.)}$

    **(d)** $NaCl_{(aq.)}$

    **Answer.** (b) $NaOH_{(aq.)}$

(ii)  Which of the following is not a typical property of an ionic compound

    **(a)** High mp

    **(b)** Conducts electricity in molten or aqueous Answer. state

    **(c)** They are insoluble in water

    **(d)** They exist as oppositely change ions even in the solid state

    **Answer.** (c) They are insoluble in water

(iii)  Saturated hydrocarbons have characteristics reaction of the type.

    **(a)** Addition

    **(b)** Substitution

    **(c)** Elimination

    **(d)** Oxidation

    **Answer.** (b) Substitution

(iv)  Which of the following does not conduct electricity

    **(a)** Molten sodium chloride

    **(b)** Aqueous sodium chloride

    **(c)** Solid sodium chloride

**(d)** None

**Answer.** (c) Solid sodium chloride

(v) The alloy which is used for making aircraft and light tools
   **(a)** Brass
   **(b)** Bronze
   **(c)** Solder
   **(d)** Duralumin
   **Answer.** (d) Duralumin

(vi) An elements in period 3 whose electron affinity is zero
   **(a)** Neon
   **(b)** Sodium
   **(c)** Argon
   **(d)** Sulfur
   **Answer.** (c) Argon

(vii) Which of the following precipitate is soluble in excess of NaOH Answer.
   **(a)** Lead hydroxide
   **(b)** Iron [ II] hydroxide
   **(c)** Iron [III] hydroxide
   **(d)** Copper hydroxide
   **Answer.** (a) Lead hydroxide

(viii) The vapour density of propane is $C = 12, H = 1$
   **(a)** 11
   **(b)** 22
   **(c)** 44
   **(d)** 88
   **Answer.** (b) 22

(ix) Commercial preparation of sulphuric acid is carried out by
   **(a)** Haber's process
   **(b)** Ostwald's process
   **(c)** Contact process
   **(d)** None
   **Answer.** (c) Contact process

(x) The metallic electrode which does not take part is an electrolytic reaction
   **(a)** Cu
   **(b)** Ni
   **(c)** Pt
   **(d)** Ag
   **Answer.** (c) Pt

(xi) The yellow explosive liquid formed when ammonia reacts with excess of chlorine gas
   (a) HCl
   (b) $N_2$
   (c) $NCl_3$
   (d) NOCl
   **Answer.** (c) $NCl_3$

(xii) Chemical formula of nitre is:
   (a) $NH_4Cl$
   (b) $KNO_3$
   (c) $NaNO_3$
   (d) NaCl
   **Answer.** (b) $KNO_3$

(xiii) The preferred catalyst for the conversion of $SO_2$ in $SO_3$ its contact process is
   (a) Platinised asbestos
   (b) Granulated iron
   (c) Vanadium pentoxide
   (d) Nickel
   **Answer.** (c) Vanadium pentoxide

(xiv) A dilute acid reacts with a metallic salt, evolves a rotten egg smell gas, which turns most lead acetate paper silvery black, the anion present in metallic salt is:
   (a) $CO_3^{--}$
   (b) $SO_3^{--}$
   (c) $S^{--}$
   (d) $SO_4^{--}$
   **Answer.** (c) $S^-$

(xv) The mass percentage of carbon in calcium carbide is ($ca = 40, c = 12$)
   (a) 18.75
   (b) 37.5
   (c) 75
   (d) 40
   **Answer.** (b) 37.5

## Question : 2

(i) The elements of one short period of the periodic table are given below in order from left to right

Li, Be, B, C, O, F and Ne.

[5]

   (a) To which period, do these elements belong?

**(b)** one element of this period is missing. Which is the missing element and where should it be placed?

**(c)** Which one of the elements in this period shows the property of catenation.

**(d)** Place the three elements, fluorine, beryllium and nitrogen. In the order of increasing Electronegativity.

**(e)** Which one of the above elements belongs to the halogen group?

**Answer.**

**(a)** Second

**(b)** Nitrogen, between carbon and oxygen

**(c)** Carbon

**(d)** Be < N < F

**(e)** F

(ii) Match the following [5]

| Column A | | Column B |
| --- | --- | --- |
| **(a)** Corban tetrachloride | i | hydrogen chloride |
| **(b)** Oxidation | ii | Covalent bonding. |
| **(c)** Reduction | iii | Loss of electrons. |
| **(d)** A polar Molecule | iv | Covalent and coordinate bond |

**Answer.**

**(a)** ii

**(b)** iii

**(c)** iv

**(d)** i

(iii) Fill in the blanks. [5]

**(a)** The insoluble base obtained when sodium hydroxide reacts with Iron (III) chloride is. ____________.[ Iron(II) hydroxide/ Iron(III) hydroxide]

**(b)** The negative logarithm [To the base 10] Of the hydrogen ion concentration expressed in moles/litre is known as__________.[pH/pOH]

**(c)** $FeCl_3$ is stored in airtight bottles because it is a __________substance. [Deliquescent/Efflorescent]

**(d)** __________ salts give a dirty green precipitate. Which turns brown on warming. [Ferrous/Zinc]

**(e)** Oxide of zinc and aluminium are ____________ in nature. [Acidic /Amphoteric]

**Answer.**

**(a)** Iron(III) hydroxide

**(b)** pH

**(c)** Deliquescent

**(d)** Ferrous

**(e)** Amphoteric

(iv) Identify the following. [5]

    **(a)** A molecule with one loan pair and 3 bond pair.

    **(b)** The gaseous organic products formed when $C_2H_5OH$ reacts with Conc. $H_2SO_4$.

    **(c)** Washing soda crystals are exposed to the atmosphere.

    **(d)** A nitrate salt which on thermal decomposition give buffy yellow residue.

    **(e)** The salt Answer. reacts with $AgNO_3$ Answer. to give a white ppt insoluble in dilute $HNO_3$.

**Answer.**

**(a)** $NH_3$

**(b)** $C_2H_4$

**(c)** $PbNO_3$

**(d)** $HCl$

**(e)** KCl or NaCl

(v) **(a)** Draw the structural formula for the following. [5]

    i   2-bromopropane.

    ii  Propanaldehyde.

    iii  Pentyne-2

    **Answer.**

i

$$H_3C - \underset{\underset{\displaystyle Br}{|}}{C}H - CH_3$$

ii

$$H-\underset{\underset{\displaystyle H}{|}}{\overset{\overset{\displaystyle H}{|}}{C}}-\underset{\underset{\displaystyle H}{|}}{\overset{\overset{\displaystyle H}{|}}{C}}-\overset{\displaystyle O}{C}\diagdown H$$

iii

$$H-\underset{\underset{\displaystyle H}{|}}{\overset{\overset{\displaystyle H}{|}}{C}}-\underset{\underset{\displaystyle H}{|}}{\overset{\overset{\displaystyle H}{|}}{C}}-C\equiv C-\underset{\underset{\displaystyle H}{|}}{\overset{\overset{\displaystyle H}{|}}{C}}-H$$

**(b)** Name the following organic compounds in IUPAC system.

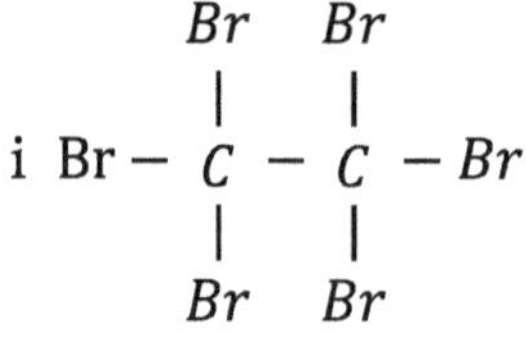

i

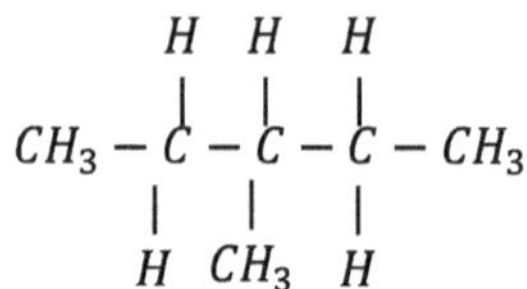

ii

**Answer.**

   i    1,1,2,2- tetra bromoethane

   ii    3-methyl pentane

## SECTION-B

(Attempt any four questions)

## Question : 3

(i)  Identify the Anion present in each of the following compounds.　　　　　　　　**[2]**

   **(a)** The salt reacts with dil. $H_2SO_4$ on reacting involving a gas. Which turns $KMnO_4$ Answer. pink to colourless?

   **(b)** The salt reacts with conc. $H_2SO_4$ evolving a coloured gas. Which turns KI paper brown?

(ii)  Write the products and balance the equation.　　　　　　　　**[2]**

   **(a)** $\underset{\text{(Excess)}}{NH_3} + O_2 \xrightarrow[\text{Heated}]{\text{Pt}}$

   **(b)** $NH_3 + Cl_2 \rightarrow$

(iii)  Arrange the following in increasing order as per the instruction given in the brackets　　**[3]**

   **(a)** Na, K, Cl, Si, S.　　　　　(Electro-positive character)

   **(b)** Be, Li, F, C, B, N, O　　　(Non-metallic character)

   **(c)** Br, F, I, Cl　　　　　　　(No. of Shells)

(iv)  Fill in the blanks selecting the appropriate word from the given choices:　　　　**[3]**

   **(a)** The compound doesn't have a loan pair of electrons is＿＿＿＿＿＿＿＿＿. [ammonia / carbon Tetrachloride.]

   **(b)** The atoms which provides the electrons pair for the formation of coordinate bond is known as the ＿＿＿＿＿＿＿. [donor/accepter]

   **(c)** Electrovalent compounds have a ＿＿＿＿＿ boiling point. [Low/High]

## Question : 4

(i) Name the principle ores from which following metals are extracted. **[2]**

   **(a)** Iron

   **(b)** Aluminum

(ii) 6 litre of nitrogen reacts with 20 litre of hydrogen to form ammonia under specific conditions as **[2]**

$$N_{2(g)} + 3H_{2(g)} \rightarrow 2NH_{3g}$$

Calculate the voumn of $NH_3$ produced, what is the other substance, if any, that remains in the resultant mixture?

(iii) Study the figure given below and answer the following questions. **[3]**

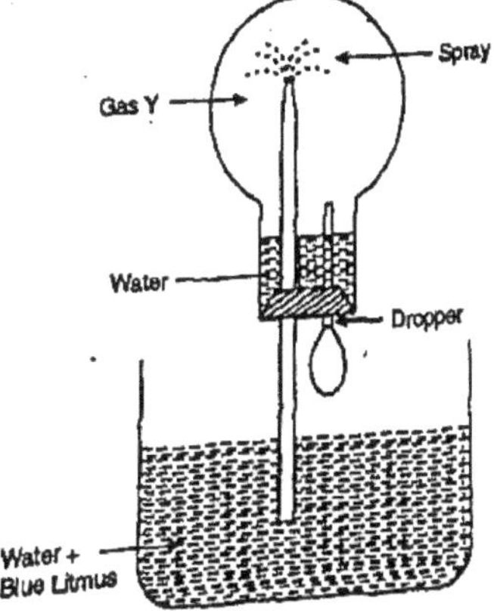


   **(a)** Identify the gas Y.

   **(b)** What Property of gas Y does this experiment demonstrate?

   **(c)** Name another gas which has the same property and can be demonstrated through this experiment.

(iv) Give one example to the each of the following properties of $H_2SO_4$. **[3]**

   **(a)** Dehydrating property

   **(b)** As a non-volatile acid

   **(c)** Oxidizing Nature

## Question : 5

(i) Name the followings: **[2]**

   **(a)** A solid oxidizing agent which will oxidize ammonia to nitrogen and itself gets reduced to metal.

   **(b)** A gaseous reducing agent which will reduce Chlorine to $NH_4Cl$

(ii) Name a probable ion present based on the following Observations: **[2]**

   **(a)** The salt Answer. reacts with $Ba(NO_3)_2$ Answer. to give a white precipitate insoluble in dilute $HNO_3$.

**(b)** The pink metal which is deposited at cathode during the electrolytes of the Answer. of its salt.

(iii) Give balanced chemical equation for the following: [3]

**(a)** Chloroform to carbon tetrachloride

**(b)** Methane to carbon dioxide.

**(c)** Ethene to ethylene dibromide.

(iv) **(a)** State two methods by which ammonia is generally prepared in laboratory. [3]

**(b)** Give a balanced chemical equation to illustrate each of the above-mentioned methods.

**(c)** Name the drying agent used for drying ammonia. State the reason for selecting the dying agent.

## Question : 6

(i)  Define: [2]

**(a)** Empirical formula

**(b)** Atomic radius

(ii)  Solve [2]

Calculate the percentage of nitrogen in aluminium nitride.[Al=27, N=14]

(iii)  Complete the following charts to obtain nitrogen from air: [3]

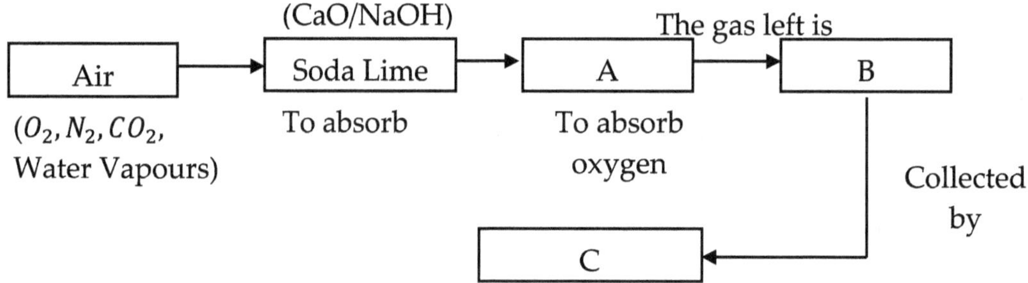


(iv) Complete the following reaction [3]

**(a)** $NH_4OH + H_2SO_{4_2} \xrightarrow{\text{dil.}}$

**(b)** $KNO_3 + H_2SO_4 \xrightarrow[\text{Conc.}]{<200°C}$

**(c)** $Mg + HNO_3 \xrightarrow{\text{dil.}}$

## Question : 7

(i) **(a)** An organic compound, on analysis, was found to contain 54.54% of carbon, 9.09% of hydrogen and 36.36% of oxygen. Determine the empirical formula of the compound. [2]

**(b)** What is the molecular formula of the compound if its vapour density is 44 ?

(ii) Identify the functional group in the following organic compounds: [2]

**(a)** $C_2H_5OH$

**(b)** $CH_3 - CH_2 - CH = CH_2$

(iii) Complete the following table of the process written on the left of the table given below.  **[3]**

| Process | Anode | Electrolyte | Cathode |
|---|---|---|---|
| Silver plating a spoon | | | |
| Purification of copper | | | |

(iv) The question i to iii refer to the following salt Answer.s listed (a) to (f).  **[3]**

    **(a)** Copper nitrate

    **(b)** Iron (II) sulphate

    **(c)** Iron (III) chloride

    **(d)** Lead nitrate

    **(e)** Magnesium sulphate

    **(f)** Zinc chloride

    i Which two Answer.s will give a white precipitate when treated with dilute hydrochloric acid followed by barium chloride Answer.?

    ii Which two Answer.s will give a white precipitate when treated with dilute nitric acid followed by silver nitrate Answer.?

    iii Which Answer. will give a white precipitate when either dilute hydrochloric acid or dilute sulphuric acid is added to it?

**Question : 8**

(v) Draw the electron dot structure for the following.  **[2]**

    **(a)** $NH_4^+$

    **(b)** $CO_2$

(vi) Identify a blue metal Answer. that turns deep blue on addition of an excess of $NH_4OH$ and $(NH_4)_2SO_4$ Give the balanced chemical equation for the reaction involved.  **[2]**

**(vii)** Study the flow chart and give the balanced equation with conditions for conversion A, B, and C.  **[3]**

$$FeCl_2 \xleftarrow{C} HCl \overset{A}{\underset{B}{\rightleftharpoons}} NaCl$$

(viii)**(a)** Why are the elements sodium and chlorine placed in the same period of the Periodic Table?

    **(b)** In the Periodic Table, how many periods consist of elements having atomic numbers 1 to 18?  **[3]**

    **(c)** Why do the elements placed in the same group of the Periodic Table have similar chemical properties?

**Maximum Marks: 80**

Time allowed: Two hours

Answers to this Paper must be written on the paper provided separately.

You will not be allowed to write during first 15 minutes.

This time is to be spent in reading the question paper.

The time given at the head of this Paper is the time allowed for writing the answers.

**(Section A is compulsory. Attempt any four questions from Section B.**

**The intended marks for questions or parts of questions are given in brackets [ ].**

## SECTION A

### Answer all the questions from this section

**Question : 1** [15]

Choose one correct answer to the question from the given option:

(i)  Which of the following compounds shows dissociation when dissolve in water?

**(a)** HCl

**(b)** $NH_3$

**(c)** NaCl

**(d)** $CCl_4$

**Answer.** (c) NaCl

(ii)  Which of the following metal chloride is soluble in hot water but insoluble in cold water?

**(a)** KCl

**(b)** AgCl

**(c)** $PbCl_2$

**(d)** NaCl

**Answer.** (c) $PbCl_2$

(iii)  HCl gas fumes in most air due to :

**(a)** HCl gas is heavier than air.

**(b)** HCl gas is diatomic gas.

**(c)** HCl gas is highly soluble in water.

**(d)** HCl gase is non-combustible

**Answer.** (c) HCl gas is highly soluble in water.

(iv)  Which property of metal favours formation of ionic bond

**(a)** The hardness of metal.

**(b)** Low E.N.

**(c)** Low I.E.

**(d)** Low electron affinity.

**Answer.** (c) Low I.E.

(v) The elements having highest value of ionization energy in period three:
   **(a)** Na
   **(b)** Si
   **(c)** Ar
   **(d)** P
   **Answer.** (c) Ar

(vi) The empirical formula of benzene ($C_6H_6$) is.
   **(a)** $C_6H_6$
   **(b)** $C_3H_3$
   **(c)** $C_2H_2$
   **(d)** CH
   **Answer.** (d) CH

(vii) A chloride which is thermally unstable
   **(a)** AgCl
   **(b)** $PbCl_2$
   **(c)** HCl
   **(d)** KCl
   **Answer.** (c) HCl

(viii) A chemical agent used for the concentration of bauxite ore by Baeyer's process:
   **(a)** $Na_2CO_3$
   **(b)** NaOH
   **(c)** $Ca(OH)_2$
   **(d)** $NH_4OH$
   **Answer.** (b) NaOH

(ix) Homologous series of organic compounds having functional group hydroxyl and carbonyl at the same position.
   **(a)** Alcohol
   **(b)** Ketone
   **(c)** Aldehyde
   **(d)** Carboxylic acid
   **Answer.** (d) Carboxylic acid

(x) $Fe + 2HCl \rightarrow A \xrightarrow{\text{NaOH}} B$, the color of B is:
   **(a)** Reddish brown
   **(b)** Gelatinous white
   **(c)** Dirty green
   **(d)** Milky white

**Answer.** (c) Dirty green

(xi) Dilution of $H_2SO_4$ is carried out by adding conc. $H_2SO_4$ to water and not water to conc. $H_2SO_4$.because:
  **(a)** Reaction is endothermic.
  **(b)** Reaction is exothermic
  **(c)** Expansion of volume occurs
  **(d)** $H_2SO_4$ & $H_2O$ are immiscible
  **Answer.** (b) Reaction is exothermic

(xii) The property of concentrated $H_2SO_4$ by which it is used to prepare $HNO_3$ from $KNO_3$.
  **(a)** Strong acid
  **(b)** Weak acid
  **(c)** Non- Volatile acid
  **(d)** Volatile acid
  **Answer.** (c) Non- Volatile acid

(xiii) An element X is in group 2 of the periodic table what will be the formula of its chloride
  **(a)** XCl
  **(b)** $XCl_2$
  **(c)** $XCl_3$
  **(d)** $XCl_4$
  **Answer.** (b) $XCl_2$

(xiv) Which of the following does not conduct electricity
  **(a)** Aqueous Answer. of $NH_3$
  **(b)** Aqueous Answer. of HI
  **(c)** HCl dissolved in Toluene
  **(d)** Aqueous Answer. of HCl
  **Answer.** (c) HCl dissolved in Toluene

(xv) Cold, dilute nitric acid reacts with copper to form
  **(a)** Hydrogen
  **(b)** Nitrogen oxide
  **(c)** Nitric oxide
  **(d)** Di- nitrogen oxide
  **Answer.** (c) Nitric oxide

**Question : 2**
(i) Elements X, Y, and Z belong to the third period of the Periodic Table. Their ionisation potential varies as Y > X > Z. [5]

**(a)** The atomic number of X is _________(more / less) than that of Y but______ (more / less) than that of Z.

**(b)** X is likely to be more electronegative than _________. (Y/Z)

**(c)** The atom of element Z would be expected to be_________than the atom of the element Y. (larger/smaller)

**(d)** The atom of elements X, Y and Z have _________ number of valence electrons. (same/different)

**Answer.**

**(a)** Less & More

**(b)** Z

**(c)** Larger

**(d)** Different


(ii) Match the following [5]

| Column A | Column B |
|---|---|

**(a)** $CuSO_4 \leftrightharpoons$ ____(cation) + ______ (anions)

**(b)** $H_2O \leftrightharpoons$ _____ (cation) +______ (anions)

**(c)** At cathode ___________+2e $\rightarrow$ ____

**(d)** At anode _______ $-2e^-$ $\rightarrow$ ____

**(e)** $Cu^{2+}$

i   $Cu^{2+}_{(aq.)} + 2e^-$

ii   $Cu^{2+} + SO_4^{2-}$

iii   $Cu_s - 2e^- \rightarrow Cu^{2+}_{(aq.)}$

iv   $H^+ + OH^-$

v   Pink

**Answer.**

**(a)** ii

**(b)** iv

**(c)** i

**(d)** iii

**(e)** v


(iii) Complete the following by choosing the correct answers from the bracket: [5]

**(a)** A Answer. whose pH is above 7 is........... [Vinegar/ liquour ammonia]

**(b)** $Ni^{2+}$ salts are...........in colour.[Red/Green]

**(c)** An example of strong alkali Answer.............[ $NaOH/NH_4OH$ ]

**(d)** To distinguish soluble salt of zinc and lead.............can be used. [$NaOH/NH_4OH$]

**(e)** Atomicity of the $NH_3$ molecule is...................[ 3/4]

**Answer.**

**(a)** Liquour ammonia

**(b)** Green

**(c)** NaOH

**(d)** $NH_4OH$

**(e)** 4


(iv) **(a)** Draw the structural formula for the following. [5]

    i  Butyne-2

    ii  Pentanol-2

    iii  Isobutane

**Ans**

i

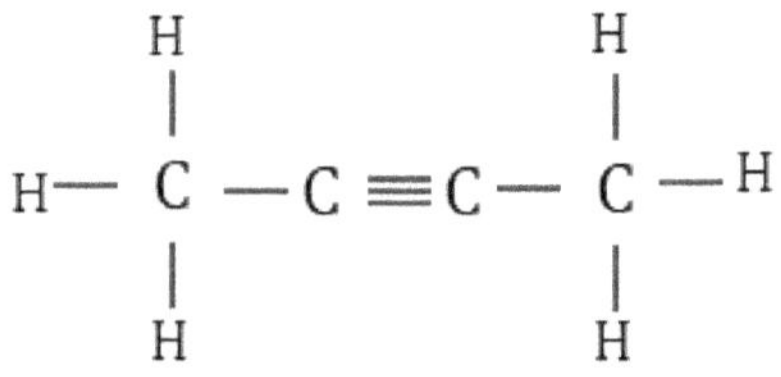

$$H- \overset{\displaystyle H}{\underset{\displaystyle H}{C}} -C \equiv C- \overset{\displaystyle H}{\underset{\displaystyle H}{C}} -H$$

ii

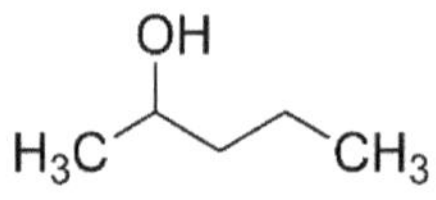

$$H_3C \overset{OH}{\diagup\!\diagdown}\!\diagup\!\diagdown CH_3$$

iii

$$\overset{3}{CH_3}-\overset{2}{\underset{\displaystyle CH_3}{CH}}-\overset{1}{CH_3}$$

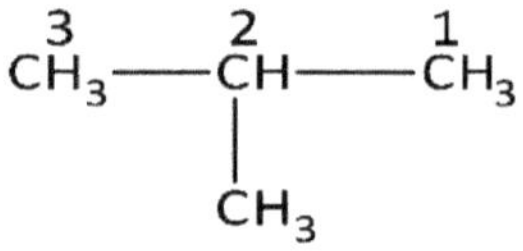

**(c)** Give IUPAC name of the following structure.

    i. $CH_3COOH$

    ii.     $(CH_3)_2CHCH_2CH_3$

**Answer.**

    i    Ethanoic Acid

    ii    2 Methyl butane


(v) Identify the following. [5]

    **(a)**  A greenish-yellow gas with pungent smell.

    **(b)**  An oxide which is yellow When hots and colourless when cold.

    **(c)**  A crystalline salt without water of crystallization.

    **(d)**  Gas involved when Zn reacts with dil. $H_2SO_4$.

    **(e)**  Bond between 2 non-metals.

**Answer.**

    **(a)**  Chlorine

    **(b)**  PbO

(c) NaCl

(d) Hydrogen

(e) Non-polar covalent bond

## SECTION B
### (Attempt any four questions.)

## Question : 3

(i) There are three elements E, F,G with atomic number 19, 8, and 17 respectively. Classify the elements as metal and nonmetal. **[2]**

(ii) What is the difference between the chemical nature of an aqueous Answer. of hydrogen chloride and aqueous Answer. of ammonia? **[2]**

(iii) Refer to the flow chart diagram below and give balanced equations with conditions, if any, for the following conversions A to C. **[3]**

$$Zn \xrightarrow{A} ZnSO_4 \xrightarrow{B} Zn(OH)_2 \xrightarrow{C} [Zn(NH_3)_4]SO_4$$

(iv) Fill in the blanks selecting the appropriate word from the given choices. **[3]**

(a) Solid NaCl is _____________ conductor of electricity. [Good/Bad]

(b) Ionic compounds are _____________.[Directional/non-directional ]

(c) The polarity of $CCl_4$ is __________. [Zero/One]

## Question : 4

(i) (a) Name the non-metal which is good conductor of electricity? **[2]**

(b) An aqueous Answer. of this compound is used as an electrolyte during the electrolytic Refining of copper. Name the compound.

(ii) Find percentage of oxygen in washing soda [$Na_2CO_3. 10H_2O$]. **[2]**

[Na=23, C=12, O=16]

(iii) Electrolysis of Acidified water or dilute sulphury acid: **[3]**

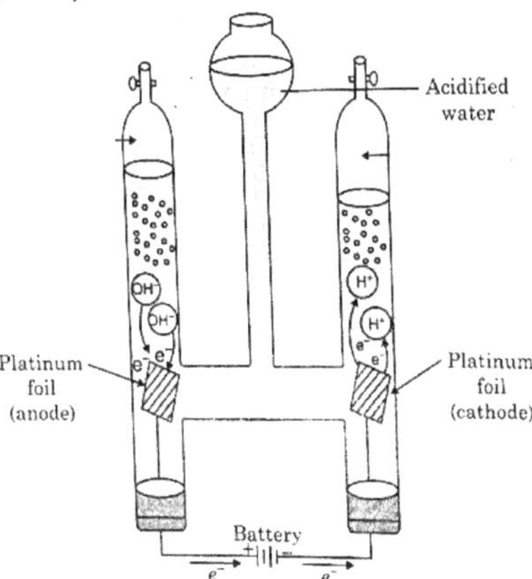


With reference to the electrolysis of acidulated water, answer the following:

(a) Explain why distilled water a non-electrolyte is.

{99}

**(b)** Name the gas released at the (i) cathode (ii) anode, write the electrode reactions and their volume ratio during the electrolysis of acidulated water.

(iv) Copy and complete the following table-column 3 has the names of gases to be prepared using the substances to be filled in column 1 along with dil. $H_2SO_4$ or conc. $H_2SO_4$ as to be indicated in column 2: **[3]**

| Column 1 | Column 2 | Column 3 |
| --- | --- | --- |
| Substance reacted with acid | Dil. $H_2SO_4$ or conc. $H_2SO_4$ | Gas |
| _____________ | _____________ | $CO_2$ |
| _____________ | _____________ | $SO_2$ |
| _____________ | _____________ | $H_2$ |

## Question : 5

(i) An aqueous Answer. contains the ions $Na^+, K^+, H^+, Cu^{2+}, SO_4^{2-}, Cl^-$, and $OH^-$, platinum electrode are used for electrolysis. Name the ions that would be the first to be discharged at the. **[2]**

**(d)** Anode

**(e)** Cathode

(ii) Calculate the volume of carbon dioxide formed when 80 c.c. of methane gas burns completely at same condition of temperature and pressure, as represented by the equation: **[2]**
$$CH_{4(g)} + 2O_{2(g)} \rightarrow CO_{2(g)} + 2H_2O_{(l)}$$

(iii) Name the kind of particle present in. **[3]**

**(a)** Sodium hydroxide Answer..

**(b)** Carbonic acid

**(c)** Sugar Answer.

(iv) The following questions relate to the electroplating of an article with nickel: **[3]**

**(a)** Name the electrode formed by the article to be electroplated.

**(b)** Which ions must be present in an electrolyte?

**(c)** Which substance must be taken as the anode?

## Question : 6

(i) Acetylene$C_2H_2$ burns in air, which contains 20% oxygen according to the equation. **[2]**
$$5C_2H_2 + 5O_2 \rightarrow 4CO_2 + 2H_2O$$

Determine the volume of air required for the complete combustion of 50cm³ of $C_2H_2$.

(ii) Define: **[2]**

(a) Normal salt

(b) Ores

(iii) (a) Ammonia can be obtained by adding water to: [3]

select the correct option

    i    Ammonium chloride.

    ii    Ammonium nitrite.

    iii    Magnesium nitride.

    iv    Manganese nitrate.

(b) Why ammonia gas is collected in water jars by the down ward displacement of air?

(c) Copy and compare the following table relating to an important industrial process .
Output refer to the product of the process, not the intermediate steps.

| Name of process | Inputs | Catalyst | Equation for catalyzed reaction | Output |
|---|---|---|---|---|
| Haber process | Hydrogen + | | | $NH_3$ |

(iv) A compound (molecular mass 246) has following data: [3]

| Element | Percentage | Relative no. of atoms |
|---|---|---|
| A | 9.76 | 0.406 |
| B | 13.01 | 0.406 |
| C | 26.01 | 1.625 |
| D | 51.22 | 2.846 |

From the data find out:

(a) Atomic weight of element A, B, C and D,

(b) Simple ratio and

(c) Molecular formula of the compound.


## Question : 7

(i) State the significant observation when: [2]

(a) HCl is bubbled through a Answer. of silver nitrate.

(b) Manganese (IV) oxides treated with concentrate HCl.

(ii) Name and write the nitrates which gives following on heating [2]

(a) Metal nitrite and oxygen

(b) No residue

(iii) The diagram show the laboratory preparation of hydrogen chloride. [3]

(a) Identify A and B.

(b) Write the equation for the reaction between A and B.

(c) How do you check whether or not the gas jar is filled with hydrogen chloride?

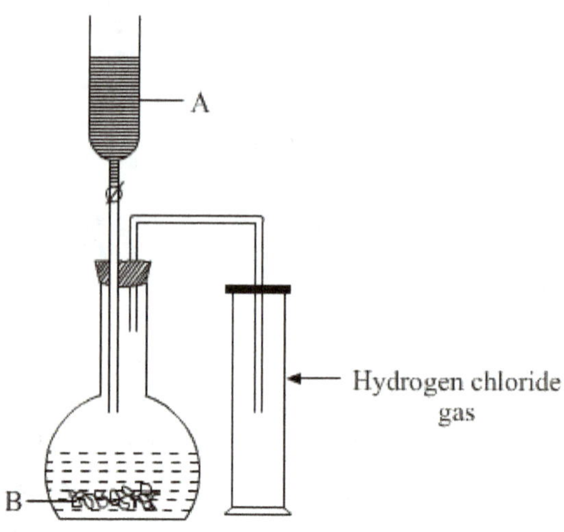


(iv) Give the IUPAC name of the following compounds numbered(i) to (iii). **[3]**

   **(a)**   $H_3C - CH - CH - CH_3$
   $\qquad\qquad\quad | \qquad |$
   $\qquad\qquad C_2H_5 \ CH_3$

   **(b)**   $CH_3 - CHO$

   **(c)**

$$
\begin{array}{c}
OH \\
| \\
H_3C - C - CH_3 \\
| \\
H
\end{array}
$$

## Question : 8

(i) **(a)** Name the salt used for the preparation of $NH_3$ gas in the laboratory by using $Ca(OH)_2$.   **[2]**

   **(b)** Name one catalyst used industrially, which speeds-up the conversion of $SO_2$ to $SO_3$ .

(ii) **(a)** What compounds are required for laboratory preparation of nitric acid?   **[2]**

   **(b)**  Why does pure nitric acid take yellowish-brown colour when exposed to the light.

(iii) Match the following columns.   **[3]**

| Column I | Column II |
|---|---|
| Hydrogenation | $C_2H_5OH \xrightarrow[300°C]{Al_2O_3} C_2H_4 + H_2O$ |
| Dehydration | $C_2H_4 + H_2 \xrightarrow[200°C]{Ni} C_2H_6$ |
| Dehydrohalogenation | $C_2H_5X + KOH \rightarrow C_2H_4 + KX + H_2O$ |

(iv) Name the reagents used for the following conversion:   **[3]**

**(a)**

$$CH_3 - CH_2 - \overset{\displaystyle O}{\overset{\displaystyle ||}{C}} - ONa \rightarrow C_2H_6$$

**(b)** $CH_2BrCH_2Br \rightarrow C_2H_2$

**(c)** $C_2H_5Br \rightarrow C_2H_4$

**Maximum Marks: 80**
Time allowed: Two hours
Answers to this Paper must be written on the paper provided separately.
You will not be allowed to write during first 15 minutes.
This time is to be spent in reading the question paper.
The time given at the head of this Paper is the time allowed for writing the answers.

**(Section A is compulsory. Attempt any four questions from Section B.**
**The intended marks for questions or parts of questions are given in brackets [ ].**

## SECTION A
### Answer all the questions from this section

**Question : 1** [15]

Choose one correct answer to the question from the given option:

(i) Concentric acid reacts with copper to form:
  **(a)** Nitrogen dioxide
  **(b)** Dinitrogen oxide
  **(c)** Hydrogen
  **(d)** Nitric oxide
  **Answer.** (b) Dinitrogen oxide

(ii) A nonmetal in the period three having a valency 1:
  **(a)** F
  **(b)** P
  **(c)** S
  **(d)** Cl
  **Answer.** (d) Cl

(iii) Fuse metal is an alloy of Sn and Pb .The role played by Tin (Sn) is:
  **(a)** Increase the m.p. of alloy
  **(b)** Decrease the m.p. of alloy
  **(c)** Provide lightness
  **(d)** None
  **Answer.** (b) Decrease the m.p. of alloy

(iv) A compound which is non electrolyte in gaseous phase , but behave as strong electrolytes in aq. State:
  **(a)** $NH_3$
  **(b)** HCl
  **(c)** $CH_4$

**(d)** $C_2H_4$
**Answer.** (b) HCl

(v) Type of salt which is found by partial displacement of displaceable hydrogen of acid by basic
   Radical is:
   **(a)** Normal salt
   **(b)** Acidic salt
   **(c)** Basic salt
   **(d)** Complex salt
   **Answer.** (b) Acidic Salt

(vi) non metal oxide which is neutral in nature:
   **(a)** $NO_2$
   **(b)** $CO_2$
   **(c)** CO
   **(d)** $SO_3$
   **Answer.** (c) CO

(vii) mass percentage of calcium in calcium carbonate is
   **(a)** 18
   **(b)** 20
   **(c)** 40
   **(d)** 60
   **Answer.** (c) 40

(viii) The molecule having two double bonds in its structure.
   **(a)** Oxygen
   **(b)** Carbon dioxide
   **(c)** Ethylene
   **(d)** Nitrogen
   **Answer.** **(b)** Carbon dioxide

(ix) Ammonia gas is collected by
   **(a)** Downward displacement of water
   **(b)** Upward displacement of air
   **(c)** Downward displacement of air
   **(d)** Upward displacement of water
   **Answer.** (c) Downward displacement of air

(x) In the reaction $Cu + 2H_2SO_4 \rightarrow CuSO_4 + SO_2 + H_2O$ the reduced product is
   **(a)** $CuSO_4$
   **(b)** $SO_2$
   **(c)** $H_2O$

**(d)** Cu

**Answer.** (b) $SO_2$

(xi) The compound element which reacts with hot conc. KOH Answer. and undergoes neutralization reaction

**(a)** Al

**(b)** FeO

**(c)** $Al_2O_3$

**(d)** MgO

**Answer.** (c) $Al_2O_3$

(xii) The gas produced when steam reacts with calcium carbide is

**(a)** $CH_4$

**(b)** $NH_3$

**(c)** $C_2H_2$

**(d)** $C_2H_4$

**Answer.** (c) $C_2H_2$

(xiii) For the electroplating of an article by silver the preferred electrolyte is

**(a)** $AgNO_3$

**(b)** AgCl

**(c)** $Na[Ag(CN)_2]$

**(d)** $Ag_2O$

**Answer.** (c) $Na[Ag(CN)_2]$

(xiv) General formula of the saturated organic compounds having hydroxy functional group

**(a)** $C_nH_{2n}OH$

**(b)** $C_nH_{2n+2}OH$

**(c)** $C_nH_{2n-2}OH$

**(d)** $C_nH_nOH$

**Answer.** (b) $C_nH_{2n+2}OH$

(xv) The electronic configuration of the elements belonging to group number 14 and period two is.

**(a)** 2,2

**(b)** 2,8,4

**(c)** 2,4

**(d)** 2,6

**Answer.** (c) 2,4

## Question : 2

(i) Write: [5]

    **(a)** A black metallic oxide which reacts with HCl to give a colour Answer..

    **(b)** Two colouless gases, which when mixed produced a white solid.

**(c)** A chloride which is soluble in excess of ammonium hydroxide.

**(d)** The experiment which demons trates that HCl is highly soluble in water.

**(e)** Acid used for the preparation of HCl gas.

**Answer.**

**(a)** CuO

**(b)** HCl nad $NH_3$

**(c)** AgCl

**(d)** Fountain Experiment

**(e)** Conc. $H_2SO_4$

(ii) Match the following [5]

| Column I | | Column II |
|---|---|---|
| **(a)** NaCl | i. | Homologous series |
| **(b)** $NH_4^+$ | ii. | $K_2SO_4Al_2(SO_4)_3.24H_2O$ |
| **(c)** Hydrocarbon | iii. | $KHSO_4$ |
| **(d)** Double salt | iv. | Electrovalent |
| **(e)** Acidic salt | v. | Dative bond |

**Answer.**

**(a)** iv

**(b)** v

**(c)** i

**(d)** ii

**(e)** iii

(iii) Complete the following by choosing the correct answers from the bracket: [5]

**(a)** Coke is used in extraction of metal _________________. [Oxidation/Reduction]

**(b)** Covalent compounds are formed by________of electron pair between non-metal. [Sharing/Donating]

**(c)** The molecule of water combines with a ____________to form hydronium ion. [Hydrogen atom/ Hydrogen ion]

**(d)** $CCl_4$ is soluble in __________. [ Water / Organic solvent]

**(e)** Salts ionize in aqueous Answer. on passage of electric current to give _________ions other than $H^+$ion. [Negative/Positive]

**Answer.**

**(a)** Reduction

**(b)** Sharing

**(c)** Hydrogen ion

**(d)** Organic solvent

**(e)** Positive

(iv) Complete the table given below: [5]

|  | Nature of anode | Nature of Cathode | Ions present in Electrolyte |
|---|---|---|---|
| **(a)** Electroplating an iron rod with silver |  |  |  |
| **(b)** Electroplating a copper sheet with nickel |  |  |  |
| **(c)** Electrorefining of silver |  |  |  |
| **(d)** Extraction of potassium from KCl |  |  |  |
| **(e)** Extraction of aluminium from $Al_2O_3$ |  |  |  |

**Answer.**

|  | Nature of anode | Nature of Cathode | Ions present in Electrolyte |
|---|---|---|---|
| **(a)** Electroplating an iron rod with silver | Silver | Iron rod | $Na[Ag(CN)_2]_{aq}$ |
| **(b)** Electroplating a copper sheet with nickel | Nickel | Copper sheet | Aq. Sol. $Ni(SO)_4$ |
| **(c)** Electrorefining of silver | Impure Silver | Pure Silver | $Na[Ag(CN)_2]$ |
| **(d)** Extraction of potassium from KCl | Graphite | Iron | Molten KBr |
| **(e)** Extraction of aluminium from $Al_2O_3$ | Thick Graphite rod | Gas Corbon lining | Molten mixture of $Al_2O_3\ Na_3AlF_6\ CaF_2$ |

(v) **(a)** Complete the following table which relates to the homologous series of hydrocarbons.  **[5]**

| General Formula | IUPAC name of the homologous sereis | Characteristic bond type | IUPAC name of the second member of the series |
|---|---|---|---|
| $C_nH_{2n-1}$ | i | ii | iii |
| $C_nH_{2n+2}$ | iv | v | iv |

**Answer.**

    i. Alkyne

    ii. $-C \equiv C -$

    iii. Propyne

    iv. Alkane

    v. $-C - C -$

    vi. Ethane

**(b)** Give IUPAC names of the following:

   i.   Formic acid

   ii.  Neo-pentane

**Answer.**

   i.   Methanoic acid

   ii.  2,2-dimethyl propane

**SECTION-B**

**(Attempt any four questions.)**

## Question : 3

(i)   In the brown ring test answer the following questions.                    [2]

   **(a)** Which ion is determined by brown ring test.

   **(b)** Why is freshly prepared iron [II] sulphate is used in the test?

(ii)  Write the products and balance the equation.                              [2]

   **(c)** $C + HNO_3 \xrightarrow{\text{Conc.}}$

   **(d)** $Cu + HNO_3 \xrightarrow{\text{Conc.}}$

(iii) Give appropriate scientific reason for the following statements:          [3]

   **(c)** During electrolysis of molten lead bromide, graphite, anode is preferred to other electrodes.

   **(d)** $CCl_4$ does not conduct electricity.

   **(e)** Why $SO_3$ obtain during the contact process is not directly absorbed in water.

(iv)  The pH value of 3 Answer.s A, B, and C are given as follows. (A=12, B=2,C=7) answer the following questions.                                              [3]

   **(d)** Which Answer. will have no effect on litmus Answer.?

   **(e)** Which Answer. will liberate carbon dioxide when reacted with sodium carbonate?

   **(f)** Which Answer. will turn red litmus Answer. blue?

## Question : 4

(i)   Give the chemical formula for the following ores:                         [2]

   **(d)** Bauxite

   **(e)** Calamine

(ii)  Draw the electron dot structure of                                        [2]

   **(d)** $H_3O^+$

   **(e)** $NH_3$

(iii) Answer the following with reference to HCl.                               [3]

   **(a)** What will you see if dil. HCl reacts with Mg.

   **(b)** Name the gas evolved when dil. HCl reacts with sodium thiosulphate

   **(c)** Write a balanced chemical equation for the reaction involved in (b) above.

{109}

(iv) Electrons are been added to Cl element: [3]

    **(a)** Is chlorine getting oxidized or reduced.

    **(b)** What charge will chlorine have after addition of one electron.

    **(c)** Which electrode will chlorine migrate to during the process of electrolysis.


## Question : 5

(i) State two relevant observation for the reaction. [2]

    Ammonium hydroxide Answer. is added to the coper (II) Nitrate Answer.:

    **(d)** In small quantities.

    **(e)** In excess quantities.

(ii) Name the compound [2]

    **(a)** Which Answer. becomes a deep inky blue colour when excess of ammonium hydroxide is added to it.

    **(b)** Which Answer. gives a white ppt. with excess of $NH_4OH$.

(iii) Give balanced chemical equation for the following: [3]

    **(a)** Laboratory Preparation of Ethane from Sodium Ethanoate.

    **(b)** Preparation of Ethyne from calcium carbide.

    **(c)** Ethene reacting with Bromine water.

(iv) Give reason: [3]

    **(a)** Lead is not used for welding purposes, but its alloy solder is used:

    **(b)** In the electrolysis of acidified water, dilute sulfuric Acid is preferred in dilute Nitric Acid.

    **(c)** Extraction of aluminum from its ore is based on its position in the activity series.


## Question : 6

(i) 67.2 ltr of $H_2$ combines with 44.8 litre of $N_2$ gas to $NH_3$ : [2]

$$N_{2(g)} + H_{2(g)} \rightarrow 2NH_{3(g)}$$

Calculate the volume of $NH_3$ produced. What is substance if any, that remains in the resultant mix.

(ii) Answer The following regarding lab preparation of nitric acid. [2]

    **(a)** The precaution taken during the preparation of nitric acid.

    **(b)** The method of identification of product i.e. acid formed.

(iii) Identify the following reaction as either oxidation or reduction. [3]

    **(a)** $O + 2e^- \rightarrow O^{2-}$

    **(b)** $K \rightarrow K^+ + e^-$

    **(c)** $Fe^{3+} + e^- \rightarrow Fe^{2+}$

(iv) Convert dil. $H_2SO_4$ to: [3]

    **(a)** Hydrogen

**(b)** Carbon dioxide

**(c)** Sulphur dioxide

## Question : 7

(i) A compound gave the following data. C=57.82%, O=38.58% & the rest hydrogen. Its vapour density is 83. Find its empirical formula and molecular formula. [C=12, O=16 ,H =1 ] **[2]**

(ii) Identify the functional group in the following organic compounds: **[2]**

    **(a)** $CH_3 - CH_2 - CH_2 - OH$

    **(b)** $CH_3 - CH_2 - CH_2 - CH_3$

(iii) A copperware is to be electroplated with silver. Answer the following questions: **[3]**

    **(a)** Which ions must be present in the electrolyte?

    **(b)** Which substance must be taken as the anode?

    **(c)** Which substance must be taken as the cathode?

(iv) Distinguish between the following **[3]**

    **(a)** Strong & weak electrolyte

    **(b)** Dissociation & ionisation

    **(c)** Elecroplating & electrorefinig

## Question : 8

(i) Name the elements from: **[2]**

    **(a)** Alkali metals

    **(b)** Alkalin earth metals

(ii) An aqueous Answer. contains the ions $Na^+, K^+, H^+, Cu^{2+}, SO_4^{2-}, Cl^-$ and OH. If platinum electrodes are used for the electrolysis, name the ions that would be the first to be discharged at the **[2]**

    **(a)** Anode.

    **(b)** Cathode.

(iii) Match all the equations pertaining to chemical reactions of acetic acid in Column I with the correct products from column II. **[3]**

| Column I | Column II |
|---|---|
| **(a)** $CH_2 = CH_2 + HBr \rightarrow CH_3 - CH_2Br$ | **(c)** $C_2H_4 + 3O_2 \rightarrow 2CO_2 + 2H_2O$ |

$$\begin{array}{cc} CH_2Br & CH \\ \textbf{(b)} \quad | \quad + 2KOH \rightarrow ||| + 2KBr + 2H_2O \\ CH_2Br & CH \end{array}$$

**Column II**

    i.   Oxidation

    ii.  Addition

    iii.  Dehydro halogenation

(iv) **(a)** The elements present in the outer most shell of an atom. **[3]**

    **(b)** The elements present in the first period.

    **(c)** Most active non-metal.

# PREVIOUS YEAR QUESTION PAPER

**Maximum Marks: 80**
Time allowed: Two hours
Answers to this Paper must be written on the paper provided separately.
You will not be allowed to write during first 15 minutes.
This time is to be spent in reading the question paper.
The time given at the head of this Paper is the time allowed for writing the answers.

**(Section A is compulsory. Attempt any four questions from Section B.**
**The intended marks for questions or parts of questions are given in brackets [ ].**

## SECTION A
### Answer all the questions from this section

**Question 1.**

A. Choose the correct answer from the options given below:                    [5]

(i) An electrolyte that completely dissociates into ions is :
   **(a)** Alcohol
   **(b)** Carbonic acid
   **(c)** Sucrose
   **(d)** Sodium hydroxide
   **Answer:** (a) Sodium hydroxide


(ii) The most electronegative element from the following elements is :
   **(a)** Magnesium
   **(b)** Chlorine
   **(c)** Aluminum
   **(d)** Sulfur
   **Answer:** (b) Chlorine


(iii) The reason for using Aluminum in the alloy duralumin is:
   **(a)** Aluminum is brittle
   **(b)** Aluminum gives strength
   **(c)** Aluminum brings lightness
   **(d)** Aluminum lowers the melting point
   **Answer:** (c) Aluminum brings lightness


(iv) The drying agent used to dry HCl gas is:
   **(a)** Cone. $H_2SO_4$
   **(b)** $ZnO$
   **(c)** $Al_2O_3$
   **(d)** $CaO$

**Answer:** (a) Cone. H₂SO₄

(v) A hydrocarbon which is a greenhouse gas is:
   **(a)** Acetylene
   **(b)** Ethylene
   **(c)** Ethane
   **(d)** Methane
   **Answer:** (d) Methane


B. Fill in the blanks with the choices given in brackets: **[5]**
   (i) Conversion of ethanol to ethene by the action of concentrated sulphuric acid is an example of ______________
   (dehydration / dehydrogenation / dehydrohalogenation)
   (ii) When sodium chloride is heated with concentrated sulphuric acid below 200°C, one of the products formed is______________
   (Sodium hydrogen sulphate / sodium sulphate / chlorine)
   (iii) Ammonia reacts with excess chlorine to form ______________.
   (nitrogen / nitrogen trichloride / ammonium chloride)
   (iv) Substitution reactions are characteristic reactions of ______________.
   (alkynes / alkenes / alkanes)
   (v) In Period 3, the most metallic element is ______________.
   (sodium / magnesium / aluminum)
   **Answer:**
   (i)   Dehydration
   (ii)  Sodium hydrogen sulfate
   (iii) Nitrogen trichloride
   (iv)  Alkanes
   (v)   Sodium


C. Write a balanced chemical equation for each of the following reactions: **[5]**
   (i) Reduction of copper (II) oxide by hydrogen.
   (ii) The action of dilute sulphury acid on sodium hydroxide.
   (iii) The action of dilute sulphuric acid on zinc sulfide.
   (iv) Ammonium hydroxide is added to the ferrous sulfate Answer..
   (v) Chlorine gas is reacted with ethene.
   **Answer:**
   (i)   $CuO + H_2 \longrightarrow Cu + H_2O$
   (ii)  $2NaOH + H_2SO_4 \longrightarrow Na_2SO_4 + 2H_2O$
   (iii) $ZnS + H_2SO_4 \longrightarrow ZnSO_4 + H_2S$
   (iv)  $FeSO_4 + 2NH_4OH \longrightarrow (NH4)_2SO_4 + Fe(OH)_2\downarrow$

(v)

$$CH_2\!\!=\!\!CH_2 + Cl_2 \longrightarrow \underset{\underset{Cl}{|}}{CH_2}\!\!-\!\!\underset{\underset{Cl}{|}}{CH_2}$$

D. State one observation for each of the following: **[5]**
   (i) Concentrated nitric acid is reacted with sulfur.
      Dense brown fumes of nitrogen dioxide gas will be released
  (ii) Ammonia gas is passed over heated copper (II) oxide.
      The black color of copper oxide will change to reddish pink copper.
 (iii) Copper sulfate Answer. is electrolyzed using copper electrodes.
 (iv) A small piece of zinc is added to dilute hydrochloric acid.
  (v) Lead nitrate is heated strongly in a test tube.

**Answer:**

(i)   $S + 6HNO_3\ (Conc.) \xrightarrow{\Delta} H_2SO_4 + 6NO_2 + 2H_2O$

(ii)  $3CuO + 2NH_3 \xrightarrow{\Delta} 3Cu + N_2 + 3H_2O$
     (Black)         (Reddish Pink)

(iii) When copper sulfate Answer. is electrolyzed using copper electrodes, the reddish pink
     deposit of copper metal takes place on the cathode.

(iv)  $Zn + 2HCl \rightarrow ZnCl_2 + H_2\uparrow$
     Zinc metal dissolves forming a Answer. with the liberation of hydrogen gas
     which bums with a blue flame and gets extinguished with a pop sound.

(v)   $2\,Pb(NO_3)_2 \quad \longrightarrow \quad 2PbO + \quad 4NO_2 + O_2$
    (White powder)    (Yellow)  (Reddish brown gas)
    The white powder of lead nitrate decomposes to form yellow-colored lead oxide and
    liberates dense brown fumes of nitrogen dioxide gas.

E. (i) Calculate: **[5]**
    The number of moles in 12 g of oxygen gas. [O = 16]
    The weight of 1022 atoms of carbon.
    [C = 12, Avogadro's No. = $6 \times 10^{23}$

    **Answer:**

    Oxygen gas $(O_2)$
    Molecular mass = 16 × 2 = 32 g
    32 g of oxygen gas → 1 mole
    1 g of oxygen gas → $\dfrac{1}{32}$ mole
    12 g of oxygen gas → $\dfrac{1}{32}\times 12$ mole = 0.375 mole
    $2.6.022 \times 10^{23}$ atoms of carbon weigh → 12 g
    1 atom of carbon weighs → $\dfrac{12}{6\times 10^{23}}$
    $10^{22}$ atoms of carbon will weigh → $\dfrac{12}{6\times 10^{23}}\times 10^{22} = \dfrac{12}{60} = \dfrac{1}{5} = 0.2$ g

(ii) Molecular formula of a compound is $C_6H_{18}O_3$. Find its empirical formula.

**Answer:**

Molecular formula = $C_6H_{18}O_3$

Take the common multiple

Molecular formula = $(C_2H_6O)_{33}$

Molecular formula = (Empirical formula)$_{,,}$

Thus, empirical formula = $C_2H_6O$

F. (i) Give the IUPAC name of the following organic compounds: [5]

    1. $HC \equiv C - CH_3$

    2. $CH_3 - \overset{O}{\underset{C}{||}} - H$

**Answer:**

    1. Prop – 1– yne or propyne

    2. Ethanal

(ii) What is the special feature of the structure of ethyne?

**Answer:**

    Ethanal

    $H - C \equiv C - H$

    A special feature of the structure of ethyne is the presence of triple bond.

(iii) Name the saturated hydrocarbon containing two carbon atoms.

**Answer:**

    Ethane

(iv) Give the structural formula of Acetic acid.

**Answer:**

    Acetic acid ($CH_3COOH$)

G. Give the appropriate term defined by the statements given below: [5]

   (i) The formula represents the simplest ratio of the various elements present in one molecule of the compound.

**Answer:**

    Empirical formula

   (ii) The substance that releases hydronium ion as the only positive ion when dissolved in water.

**Answer:**

    Acid

   (iii) The tendency of an atom to attract electrons towards itself when combined in a covalent compound.

**Answer:**

    Electronegativity

(iv) The process by which certain ores, especially carbonates, are converted to oxides in the absence of air.

**Answer:**

Calcination

(v) The covalent bond is in which the electrons are shared equally between the combining atoms.

**Answer:**

Non-polar covalent bond

H. Arrange the following according to the instructions given in brackets : **[5]**

(i) K, Pb, Ca, Zn. (In the increasing order of the reactivity)

**Answer:**

$Pb < Zn < Ca < K$

(According to the position in the reactivity series)

(ii) $Mg^{2+}, Cu^{2+}, Na^{1+}, H^{1+}$ (In the order of preferential discharge at the cathode)

**Answer:**

$Na^{1+} < Mg^{2+} < H^{1+} < Cu^{2+}$

(According to electrochemical series of metals)

(iii) Li, K, Na, H (In the decreasing order of their ionization potential)

**Answer:**

$H > Li > Na > K$

(Smaller the size greater the ionization potential)

(iv) F, B, N, O (In the increasing order of electron affinity)

**Answer:**

$B < N < O < F$

(Smaller the size more the electron affinity)

(v) Ethane, methane, ethene, ethyne. (In the increasing order of the molecular weight)
[H = 1, C = 12]

**Answer:**

| Ethane | Methane | Ethene | Ethyne |
|---|---|---|---|
| $(C_2H_6)$, | $CH_4$, | $C_2H_4$, | $C_2H_2$ |
| 30 | 16 | 28 | 26 |

Methane  <  Ethyne  <  Ethene  <  Ethane

**Section II [40 Marks]**

**(Attempt any four questions.)**

**Question 2.**

Draw the electron dot structure of: **[3]**

(i) Nitrogen molecule [N = 7]

**Answer:**

Nitrogen molecule

$$N = 7 \Rightarrow 2,\ 5$$
$$\qquad\qquad K\quad L$$
$$N = 7 \Rightarrow 2,\ 5$$
$$\qquad\qquad K\quad L$$

N :: N

The nitrogen atom shares three electrons forming a triple covalent bond.

(ii) Sodium chloride [Na = 11, Cl = 17]

**Answer:**

Sodium chloride'

$$Na(11) \Rightarrow 2, 8, 1$$
$$\qquad\qquad K\,L\,M$$
$$Cl(17) \Rightarrow 2, 8, 7$$
$$\qquad\qquad K\,L\,M$$

$[Na]^+ \equiv [:cl:]^+$

Sodium loses one electron to chlorine forming a positive ion and chlorine gains one electron forming a negative ion. These ions form an electrovalent bond and are held strongly by electrostatic forces of attraction.

(iii) Ammonium ion [N = 7, H = 1]

**Answer:**

Ammonium ion

$N\,(7) \rightarrow$

$H\,(1) \rightarrow H^X$

Formation of ammonia

Formation of proton

$H - 1e^- \ H^+$

Formation of ammonium ion

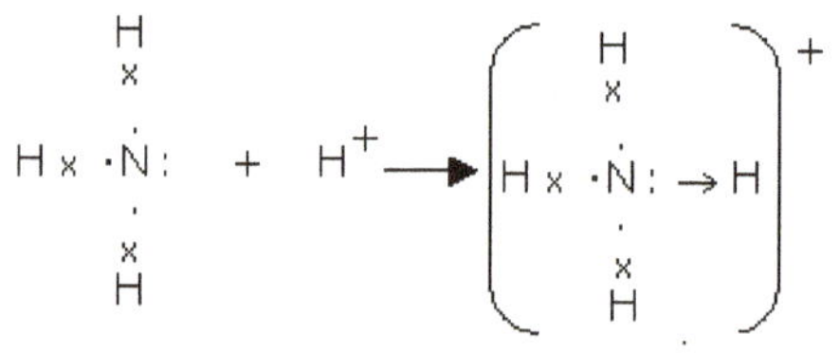

$$
\begin{array}{c}
\overset{\displaystyle H}{\underset{\displaystyle H}{H\text{x} \cdot \dot{N}:}} \quad + \quad H^+ \longrightarrow
\left[\ \overset{\displaystyle H}{\underset{\displaystyle H}{H\text{x} \cdot \dot{N}: \rightarrow H}}\ \right]^+
\end{array}
$$

Ammonia donates its lone pair to proton forming ammonium ion.

**(b)** The pH values of three Answer.s A, B, and C are given in the table. Answer the following questions: **[3]**

| Answer. | pH value |
| --- | --- |
| A | 12 |
| B | 2 |
| C | 7 |

(i) Which Answer. will have no effect on the litmus Answer.?

(ii) Which Answer. will liberate $CO_2$ when reacted with sodium carbonate?

(iii) Which Answer. will turn red litmus Answer. blue?

**Answer:**

(i)  C (Because pH 7 is neutral).

(ii)  B (Because acids liberate $CO_2$ gas when treated with carbonates and acids have pH less than 7)

(iii)  A (Bases turn red litmus blue and they have pH of more than 7)

(c)  Study the extract of the Periodic Table given below and answer the questions that follow. Give the alphabet corresponding to the element in question. DO NOT repeat an element. **[4]**

(i)  Which element forms an electrovalent compound with G?

(ii)  The ion of which element will migrate towards the cathode during electrolysis?

(iii)  Which non-metallic element has the valency of 2?

(iv)  Which is an inert gas?

**Answer:**

(i)

$$B\begin{bmatrix} B^{+2} \quad G^{-1} \\ \times \\ BG_2 \end{bmatrix}$$

(ii)  A [Positive ions migrate towards the cathode; hence A will form A+ and migrate towards cathode]

(iii)  E

(iv)  F

## Question 3.

(a) Name the particles present in:

(i)  Strong electrolyte

(ii)  Non-electrolyte

(iii)  Weak electrolyte

**Answer:**

(i)  Only ions

(ii)  Molecules

(iii)  Ions as well as molecules

(b) Distinguish between the following pairs of compounds using the reagent given in the bracket.

**[3]**

(i)  Manganese dioxide and copper (II) oxide, (using concentrated HCl)

**Answer:**

$$MnO_2 \ + \ 4HCl \ \rightarrow \ MnCl_2 + \ 2H_2O + Cl_2 \uparrow$$
$$\text{(black)} \qquad \text{(colorless)} \qquad \text{(greenish-yellow gas)}$$

(ii)  Ferrous sulfate Answer.-and ferric sulfate Answer., (using sodium hydroxide Answer.)

**Answer:**

$$FeSO_4 + 2NaOH \rightarrow Fe(OH)_2 \downarrow + Na_2SO_4$$
$$\text{dirty green}$$
$$Fe_2(SO_4)_3 + 6NaOH \rightarrow 2Fe(OH)_3 + 3Na_2SO_4$$
$$\text{reddish brown}$$

(iii)  Dilute hydrochloric acid and dilute sulphury acid, (using lead nitrate Answer.)

**Answer:**

$$Pb(NO_3)_2 + 2HCl \rightarrow PbCl_2 \downarrow + 2HNO_3$$
(white ppt.)
(Insoluble in cold water but dissolves in warm water)
$$Pb(NO_3)_2 + H_2SO_4 \rightarrow PbSO_4 + 2HNO_3$$
(white ppt.)
(Insoluble both in cold and warm water)

**(c)** Choose the method of preparation of the following salts, from the methods given in the list:**[4]**

[List: A. Neutralization B. Precipitation C. Direct combination D. Substitution]

(i)  Lead chloride

(ii)  Iron (II) sulfate

(iii)  Sodium nitrate

(iv)  Iron (III) chloride

**Answer:**

(i)  Lead chloride $\rightarrow$ Precipitation(B)

(ii)  Iron (II) sulfate $\rightarrow$ Substitution (D)

(iii)  (in) Sodium nitrate$\rightarrow$Neutralisation (A)

(iv)  Iron (III) chloride $\rightarrow$ (Direct combination) (C)

## Question 4.

**(a)** Complete the following equations :  [3]

(i)  S + cone. HNO₃ →

(ii)  C + cone. H₂SO₄ →

(iii)  Cu + dil. HNO₃ →

**Answer:**

(i)  S + 6HNO₃ ât' H₂ SO₄ + 6NO₂ + 2H₂O

(ii)  C + 2H₂ SO₄ ât' 2H₂O + CO₂ + 2S0₂

(iii)  3Cu + 8HNO₃ ât' 3Cu (NO₃ )₂ + 2NO + 4H₂O

**(b)** Write a balanced chemical equation for the preparation of  [3]

(i)  Ethene from bromoethane

**Answer:**

+ KOHf (alc.) CH₂ = CH₂ + KBr+H₂O

$$\begin{array}{ccc} & H & Br \\ & | & | \\ H- & C - C & -H \\ & | & | \\ & H & H \end{array}$$

(ii)  Ethyne using calcium carbide

**Answer:**

$$CaC_2 + 2H_2O \rightarrow Ca(OH)_2 + C_2H_2 \uparrow$$
calcium carbide                    acetylene

(iii)  Methane from sodium acetate.

**Answer:**

$$CH_3COONa + NaOH \xrightarrow{CaO} CH_4 + Na_2CO_3$$
$$\text{sodium acetate}$$

(c)  Name the following organic compounds : **[4]**
   (i)   The compound with 3 carbon atoms whose functional group is carboxyl.
   (ii)  The first homolog whose general formula is $C_nH_{2n}$.
   (iii) The compound reacts with acetic acid to form ethyl ethanoate.
   (iv)  The compound is formed by the complete chlorination of ethyne.

**Answer:**
   (i)   Propanone
   (ii)  Ethene
   (iii) Ethanol
   (iv)  1,1,2,2 tetrachloro ethane

## Question 5.

(a) Give the chemical formula of **[3]**
   (i)   Bauxite
   (ii)  Cryolite
   (iii) Sodium aluminate

**Answer:**
   (i)   $Al_2O_3. 2H_2O$
   (ii)  $Na_3AlF_6$
   (iii) $NaAlO_2$

(b) Answer the following questions based on the extraction of aluminum from alumina by the Hall Heroult's$\rightarrow$ Process: **[3]**
   (i)   What is the function of cryolite used along with alumina as the electrolyte?
   (ii)  Why is powdered coke sprinkled on top of the electrolyte?
   (iii) Name the electrode, from which aluminum is collected.

**Answer:**
   (i)   Cryolite acts as a solvent and lowers the fusion temperature from 2050Â°C to 950Â°C.
   (ii)  A layer of powdered coke is sprinkled over the surface of the electrolyte to reduce the heat loss by radiation and prevent the carbon rod from binning in the air.
   (iii) Cathode

(c) Match the alloys given in column I to the uses given in column II:

| Column I | Column II |
|---|---|
| (i)   Duralumin | (a) Electrical fuse |
| (ii)  Solder | (b) Surgical instruments |
| (iii) Brass | (c) Aircraft body |
| (iv)  Stainless Steel | (d) Decorative articles |

**Answer:**
   (i)   Duralumin $\rightarrow$ Aircraft body
   (ii)  Solder $\rightarrow$ Electrical fuse
   (iii) Brass $\rightarrow$ Decorative articles

(iv) Stainless steel $\rightarrow$ Surgical instruments

## Question 6.

(a) Identify the substances underlined: [3]

(i) The catalyst is used to oxidize ammonia.

(ii) The organic compound when solidified- forms an ice-like mass.

(iii) The dilute acid is an oxidizing agent.

**Answer:**

(i) Platinum

(ii) Acetic acid

(iii) Nitric acid

(b) Copper sulfate Answer. reacts with sodium hydroxide Answer. to form a precipitate of copper hydroxide according to the equation: [3]

$$2NaOH + CuSO_4 \rightarrow Na_2SO_4 + Cu(OH)_2 \downarrow$$

(i) What mass of copper hydroxide is precipitated by using 200 gm of sodium hydroxide? [H = 1, O = 16, Na = 23, S = 32, Cu = 64]

**Answer:**

$$2NaOH_2 + CuSO_4 \rightarrow Na_2SO_4 + Cu(OH)_2$$
$$2[23 + 16 + 1] \qquad\qquad [64 + 32 + 2]$$
$$80 \qquad\qquad\qquad 98$$

98 g of $Cu(OH)_2$ is precipitated by using 80 g of NaOH

1 g of $Cu(OH)_2$ is precipitated by using $\dfrac{80}{98}$ g of NaOH

200 g of Cu(OH)2 is precipitated by using $\dfrac{80}{98}$ g $\times$ 200g = 163.26 g of NaOH

(ii) What is the color of the precipitate formed?

**Answer:**

Pale blue precipitates

(c) Find the empirical formula and the molecular formula of an organic compound from the data given below:

C = 75.92%, H = 6.32% and N = 17.76%

The vapor density of the compound is 39.5.

[C= 12, H= 1,N= 14] [4]

**Answer:**

| Symbol | Percentage | At. Weight | Relative ratio | Simplest ratio |
|---|---|---|---|---|
| C | 75.92% | 12 | $\dfrac{75.92}{12} = 6.32$ | $\dfrac{6.32}{1.26} = 5$ |
| H | 6.32% | 1 | $\dfrac{6.32}{1} = 6.32$ | $\dfrac{6.32}{1.26} = 5$ |
| N | 17.76% | 14 | $\dfrac{17.76}{14} = 1.26$ | $\dfrac{1.26}{1.26} = 1$ |

Empirical Formula $\Rightarrow C_5H_5 N$

Vapour density = 39.5

Molecular Mass = 2 $\times$ V.D.

= 2 $\times$ 39.5 = 79

Empirical formula Mass = 12 $\times$ 5 + 5 $\times$ 1 + 1 $\times$ 14

$= 60 + 5 + 14$

$= 79$

n = Molecular formula mass Empirical formula mass$= \dfrac{79}{79}$

Thus, both the Empirical formula and Molecular formula are $C_3H_5N$.

## Question 7.

(a) Name the gas that evolved in each of the following cases :                    [3]

    (i) Alumininum undergoes electrolytic reduction.

    (ii) Ethene undergoes a hydrogenation reaction

    (iii) Ammonia reacts with heated copper oxide

**Answer:**

    (i) Oxygen

    (ii) Ethane

    (iii) Nitrogen

(b) Study the flow chart given and give balanced equations to represent the reactions A, B, and C

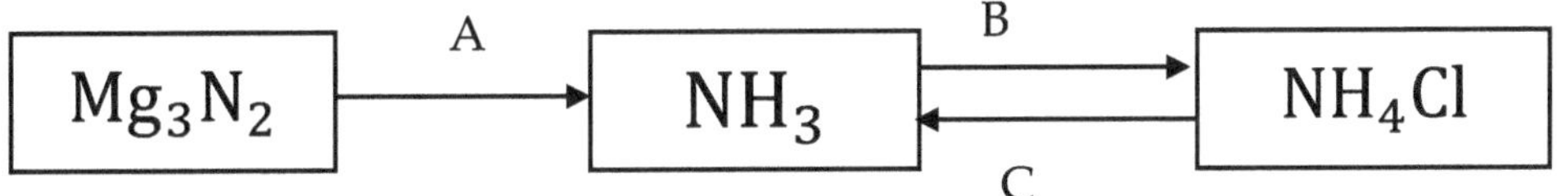


**Answer:**

    (i)   $Mg_3N_2 + 6H_2O \rightarrow 3Mg(OH)_2 + 2NH_3$

    (ii)  $NH_3 + HCl \rightarrow NH_4Cl$

    (iii) $NH_4Cl + NaOH \xrightarrow{\Delta} NaCl + H_2O + NH_3 \uparrow$

(c) Copy and complete the following table which refers to the industrial method for the prepara on of ammonia and sulphuric acid :                    [4]

| Name of the compound | Name of the process | Catalytic equations (with the catalyst) |
|---|---|---|
| Ammonia | ( i )________ | ( ii )________ |
| Sulphuric acid | ( iii )________ | (iv)________ |

**Answer:**

    (i) Haber's process

    (ii) $N_2 + 3H_2 \xrightarrow[\substack{\text{200-900 atm} \\ \text{catalyst} \rightarrow Fe \\ \text{promotor} \rightarrow Mo}]{450°-500°C} 2NH_3 \uparrow$

    (iii) Contact process

    (iv) $2SO_2 + O_2 \underset{V_2O_5/K_2O}{\overset{450°-500°C}{\rightleftharpoons}} 2SO_3 \uparrow$

**CHEMISTRY**
(SCIENCE PAPER-2)

**Maximum Marks: 80**

Time allowed: Two hours

Answers to this Paper must be written on the paper provided separately.

You will not be allowed to write during first 15 minutes.

This time is to be spent in reading the question paper.

The time given at the head of this Paper is the time allowed for writing the answers.

**(Section A is compulsory. Attempt any four questions from Section B.**

**The intended marks for questions or parts of questions are given in brackets [ ].**

## SECTION A

**Answer all the questions from this section**

**Question 1.**

In the periodic Table, elements of period 3 are arranged in the increasing order of ionization potential as:　　　　　　　　　　　　　　　　　　　　　　　　[1]

(a)  B, N, Cl, Ar

(b)  Mg, Si, S, Ar

(c)  Ar, Si, S, Mg

(d)  Si, Ar, Cl, Mg

**Answer. 1-(b)** Ionization potential increases from left to right in a periodic table.

**Question 2.**

If Relative Molecular Mass of Butane ($C_4H_{10}$) is 58 then its vapour density will be:　　　　[1]

(a)  58

(b)  29

(c)  32

(d)  16

**Answer. 2-(b)** Vapour Density $= \dfrac{\text{Molar mass}}{2} = \dfrac{58}{2} = 29$

**Question 3.**

Identify one statement that holds true for electrolysis of molten lead bromide:　　　　[1]

(a)　Silver grey metal deposits at the anode

(b)　Temperature is not maintained during the electrolysis

(c)　Brown vapours of bromine are obtained at the anode.

(d)　Electrolyte contains $H^+$ ions along with $Pb^{2+}$ ions

**Answer. 3-(c)** In electrolysis of molten lead bromide, brown vapours of bromine are obtained at
　　　　　　anode.

## Question 4.
The tendency of an atom to attract shared pair of electrons to itself when forming a chemical bond is known as: [1]

(a) Electron affinity
(b) Electronegativity
(c) Ionization potential
(d) Nuclear charge

**Answer. 4-(b)** The tendency of an atom to attract shared pair of electrons to itself when forming a chemical bond is known as electronegativity.

## Question 5.
Solid sodium chloride **does not** conduct electricity as:

(a) The strength of the bond is weak
(b) It contains free ions
(c) It does not contain any free ions
(d) It contains free ions as well as molecules

**Answer. 5-(c)** Solid NaCl does not contain electricity it does not contain electricity.

## Question 6.
Elements A and B have electronic configurations 8 and 13 respectively. The chemical formula formed between A and B will be: [1]

(a) AB
(b) $B_3A_3$
(c) $A_2B_3$
(d) $B_2A_3$

**Answer. 6-(d)** Electronic configuration of A- 2, 6

Electronic configuration of B- 2, 8, 3

A required to gain 2 electrons to complete its octet so valency of A=-2 B required to donate 3 electrons to complete its octet so valency of B=+3 B is cation and A is anion so by using crisscross method in ionic compounds.

Chemical formula will be $B_2A_3$.

## Question 7.
The percentage of hydrogen present in NaOH is: (Relative Molecular Mass of NaOH = 40) (At. Wt. of H = 1) [1]

(a) 2.5
(b) 25
(c) 0.25
(d) 0.025

Answer. 7-(a)

$$\% \text{ of H} = \frac{\text{Atomic mass of H}}{\text{Molar mass of NaOH}} = \frac{1}{23 + 16 + 1} \times 100 = \frac{100}{40} = 2.5\%$$

## Question 8.

A salt formed by incomplete neutralization of an acid by a base: [1]

**(a)** Basic salt

**(b)** Acid salt

**(c)** Normal salt

**(d)** Complex salt

**Answer. 8-(b)** A salt that is formed by incomplete neutralization of acid is acidic salt.

## Question 9.

The colour of the precipitate formed after the addition of a small amount of sodium hydroxide Answer. to an aqueous Answer. of ferric chloride is: [1]

**(a)** Gelatinous white

**(b)** Pale blue

**(c)** Reddish brown

**(d)** Dirty green

**Answer. 9-(c)** $Fe(OH)_3$ precipitate formed after the addition of a small amount of sodium hydroxide Answer. to an aqueous Answer. of ferric chloride. $Fe(OH)_3$ is Reddish brown in colour.

## Question 10.

Alkaline earth metals have the same: [1]

**(a)** Number of valence electrons

**(b)** Number of shells

**(c)** Metallic property

**(d)** Ionization potential

**Answer. 10-(a)** Alkaine earth metals are present in same group so they have same number of valence electrons.

## Question 11.

Which of the following compounds neither dissociate not ionise in water?

**(a)** Hydrochloric acid

**(b)** Sodium hydroxide

**(c)** Potassium Nitrate

**(d)** Carbon tetrachloride

**Answer. 11-(d)** Carbon tetrachloride is non-polar covalent compound. So it neither dissociate nor ionise in water

## Question 12.

The table shows the electronic configuration of four elements. [1]

| element | electronic configuration |
|---|---|
| W | 2, 6 |
| X | 2, 8 |
| Y | 2, 8, 1 |

| Z | 2, 8, 7 |
|---|---|

Which pair of atoms will form a covalent compound?

(a) Two atoms of W

(b) Two atoms of X

(c) An atom of W and an atom of X

(d) An atom of Y and an atom of Z

**Answer. 12-(a)** Two atoms of W will share 2-2 electrons to form covalent compound and become stable.

## Question 13.

Element with an atomic number 19 will: [1]

(a) Accept an electron and get oxidized

(b) Accept an electron and get reduced

(c) Lose an electron and get oxidized

(d) Lose an electron and get reduced

**Answer. 13-(C)** After loosing one electron, it will have electronic configuration of inert gas. So it will loose one electron and loosing electron is oxidation process.

## Question 14.

Which of the following has two sets of lone pair of electrons in them? [1]

(a) Ammonia

(b) Methane

(c) Water

(d) Ammonium ion

**Answer. 14-(c)** Water molecule is having two lone pairs in molecule.

## Question 15.

If the empirical mass of the formula $PQ_2$ is 10 and the Relative Molecular Mass is 30, then the molecular formula will be: [1]

(a) $PQ_2$

(b) $P_3Q_2$

(c) $P_6Q_2$

(d) $P_3Q_6$

Answer. 15-(d)

## Question 16.

Which of the following is a tribasic acid?

(a) $H_2SO_4$

(b) $Al(OH)_3$

(c) $H_3PO_4$

(d) $Ca(OH)_2$

**Answer.:** (c) $H_3PO_4$ has three displaceable hydrogens.

**Question 17.**

If a Answer. of an electrolyte mixture has calcium ions, cupric ions, zinc ions and magnesium ions, which of these ions would you see preferentially discharged at the cathode? [1]

(a) Calcium ions

(b) Zinc ions

(c) Cupric ions

(d) Magnesium ions

**Answer. 17-(C)** Cupric ion preferentially discharged at the cathode due to its high mobility.

**Question 18.**

Which of the following ions will readily discharge at the anode during the electrolysis of acidulated water? [1]

(a) OH

(b) $SO_4^{2-}$

(c) $Cl^-$

(d) $H^+$

**Answer. 18-(a)** OH ions will readily discharge at the anode during the electrolysis of acidulated water.

**Question 19.**

If the imperial formula of a compound is CH and its vapour density is 13, then its molecular formula will be: [1]

(At. Wt. C=12, H=1)

(a) CH

(b) $C_2H_2$

(c) $C_4H_4$

(d) $C_3H_3$

Answer. 19-(b)

Empirical formula= CH

Empirical formula mass = 12+1=13

Molecular formula=(empirical formula $)_n$

$$n = \frac{V.D \times 2}{\text{empirical formula mass}} = \frac{13 \times 2}{13} = 2$$

$$\therefore \text{molecular formula} = (CH_2)$$

$$= C_2H_2$$

**Question 20.**

Aqueous Answer. of Cupric chloride forms a deep blue Answer. on addition of: [1]

(a) Dropwise sodium hydroxide

(b) Excess sodium hydroxide

(c) Dropwise ammonium hydroxide

(d) Excess ammonium hydroxide

**Answer. 20-(d)** Aqueous Answer. of Cupric chloride forms a deep blue Answer. on addition of excess ammonium hydroxide

## Question 21.

Which statement about conduction of electricity is correct?  [1]
  **(a)**  Electricity is conducted in aqueous Answer. by electrons
  **(b)**  Electricity is conducted in a metal wire by ions
  **(c)**  Electricity is conducted in a molten electrolyte by electrons
  **(d)**  Electricity is conducted in an acid Answer. by ions
  **Answer. 21-(d)** Electricity is conducted in an acid Answer. by ions

## Question 22.

If an element has low ionization potential, then it is likely to be a:
  **(a)**  Metal
  **(b)**  Metalloid
  **(c)**  Non metal
  **(d)**  Inert gas
  **Answer. 22-(a)** Metals have low ionization potential.

## Question 23.

Which electron arrangement for the outer shell electrons in a covalent compound is correct?  [1]

  **(a)**  $H \overset{XX}{\underset{\bullet\bullet}{\overset{X}{\bullet}}} Cl$

  **(b)**  $\overset{X}{\underset{XX}{H}} Cl$

  **(c)**  $H \overset{X}{\bullet} N \overset{\bullet\bullet}{\underset{X\bullet}{}} H$  with H below

  **(d)**  $H \overset{X}{\bullet} N \overset{X}{\bullet} H$  with H below

**Answer. 23-(c)** Following structure is following octet and duplet rule.

$$H \overset{X}{\bullet} \overset{\bullet\bullet}{N} \overset{X}{\bullet} H$$
$$H$$

## Question 24.

The products formed when an acid reacts with a base is:
  **(a)**  Salt and hydrogen
  **(b)**  Salt and oxygen

(c)   Salt and water
(d)   Salt and carbon dioxide
**Answer. 24-(c)** When acid reacts with base, Salt and water is formed.

## Question 25.

In the circuit below, the lamp lights up.                                    [1]

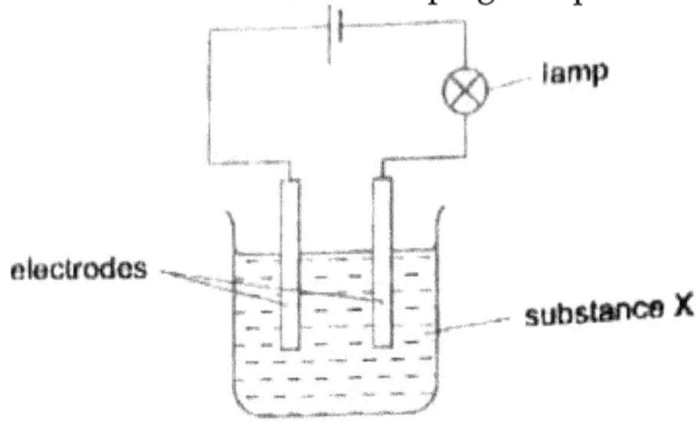


What could X be?
(a)   A Answer. of alcohol in water
(b)   A Answer. of sodium chloride in water
(c)   Sugar Answer.
(d)   Solid potassium chloride
**Answer. 25-(b)**
In the circuit below, the lamp lights up than X should be an Ionic compound.

## Question 26.

Which one of the following is a non-metallic cation?
(a)   $K^+$
(b)   $NH_4^+$
(c)   $Cu^{2+}$
(d)   $Na^+$
**Answer. 26-(b)** Ammonium ion is non-metallic.

## Question 27.

Type of bonding present in hydrogen chloride:                                 [1]
(a)   Metallic
(b)   Ionic
(c)   Covalent
(d)   Coordinate
**Answer. 27-(c)** Bonding present in non-metal and non-metal is covalent.

## Question 28.

The non-metallic properties of elements from left to right in a Periodic Table:   [1]
(a)   Increases

**(b)** Decreases

**(c)** Remains same

**(d)** First increases and then decreases

**Answer. 28-(a)** The non-metallic properties of elements from left to right in a Periodic Table increase.

## Question 29.

The aqueous Answer. that contains both ions and molecules:                    [1]

**(a)** Sulphuric acid

**(b)** Nitric acid

**(c)** Acetic acid

**(d)** Hydrochloric acid

**Answer. 29-(c)** Acetic acid contains both ions and molecules because it is a weak electrolyte.

## Question 30.

The basic oxide which is an alkali:                    [1]

**(a)** Copper oxide

**(b)** Sodium oxide

**(c)** Ferric oxide

**(d)** Zinc oxide

**Answer. 30-(b)** Metallic oxides are alkaline in nature.

## Question 31.

If the pH of a Answer. is '2', then Answer. is a:                    [1]

**(a)** Strong acid

**(b)** Strong alkali

**(c)** Weak acid

**(d)** Weak alkali

**Answer. 31-(a)** pH=2, that means Answer. is strong acid.

## Question 32.

The acidity of aluminium hydroxide is:

**(a)** 3

**(b)** 1

**(c)** 4

**(d)** 2

**Answer. 32-(a)** Aluminium hydroxide can donate 3 OH ions , hence  acidity is 3.

## Question 33.

Hydracids are those acids which contain:

**(a)** Hydrogen with any metal

**(b)** Hydrogen, a non-metal and oxygen

**(c)** Hydrogen and a non-metal other than oxygen

**(d)** Hydrogen and oxygen only

**Answer. 33-(c)** Hydracids are those acids which contain Hydrogen and a nonmetal other than oxygen.

## Question 34.                                                                                    [1]

The oxidation reaction among the following is:

**(a)** $Fe^{3+} + 3e^- \rightarrow Fe$

**(b)** $Fe^{2+} - 1e^- \rightarrow Fe^{3+}$

**(c)** $Cl_2 + 2e^- \rightarrow 2Cl^{1-}$

**(d)** $Cu^{2+} + 2e^- \rightarrow Cu$

**Answer. 34-(b)** Loss of electrons is oxidation.

## Question 35.

A student added excess of sodium hydroxide Answer. to each of the salt Answer..

An insoluble precipitate formed was observed in:

**(a)** Calcium nitrate

**(b)** Zinc nitrate

**(c)** Lead nitrate

**(d)** Sodium nitrate

**Answer. 35-(a)** An insoluble precipitate formed was observed in Calcium nitrate because it forms Ca (OH)$_2$.

## Question 36.

Which apparatus could be used to electroplate an iron nail with copper?

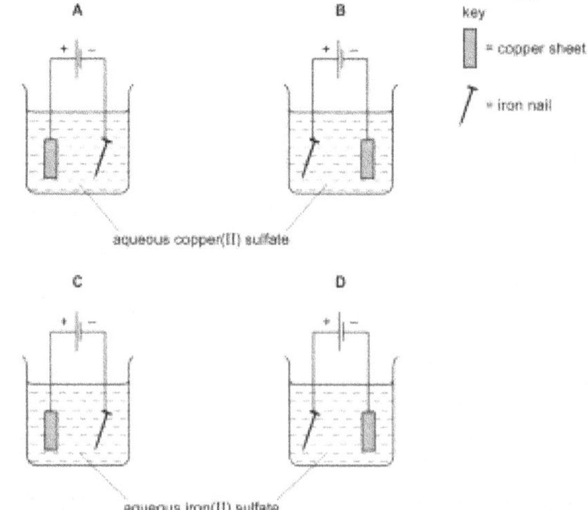


**Answer. 36-(a)** First apparatus is having correct combination of anode-cathode with battery.

**Question 37.**

The table below shows the electronic arrangements of six atoms, A to F.

| Atom | A | B | C | D | E | F |
|---|---|---|---|---|---|---|
| Electronic configuration | 2, 5 | 2 | 2, 6 | 2, 8, 6 | 2, 8, 8 | 2, 8, 3 |

With respect to the table select the following:

(i) Two atoms from the same group of the periodic table: [1]
    **(a)** D and E
    **(b)** C and D
    **(c)** E and F
    **(d)** C and E
    **Answer:** (b) C and D

(ii) Two noble gases: [1]
    **(a)** A and B
    **(b)** E and F
    **(c)** B and E
    **(d)** D and E
    **Answer:** (c) B and E

(iii) The atom which is the most electronegative: [1]
    **(a)** A
    **(b)** B
    **(c)** C
    **(d)** F
    **Answer:** (c) C

(iv) The atom which has the highest ionization potential: [1]
    **(a)** A
    **(b)** B
    **(c)** E
    **(d)** F
    **Answer:** (b) B

Answer..37
(i) **(b)** Elements which have same number of outermost electrons are present in same group.
(ii) **(c)** Element which have complete duplet or octet are inert gases.
(iii) **(c)** Valency of C is -2. (It can accept 2 electrons to complete its octet).
(iv) **(b)** B is He which is inert gas so it will have highest ionization potential.

# CHEMISTRY
## (SCIENCE PAPER-2)

**Maximum Marks: 80**
Time allowed: Two hours
Answers to this Paper must be written on the paper provided separately.
You will not be allowed to write during first 15 minutes.
This time is to be spent in reading the question paper.
The time given at the head of this Paper is the time allowed for writing the answers.

**(Section A is compulsory. Attempt any four questions from Section B.**
**The intended marks for questions or parts of questions are given in brackets [ ].**

## SECTION A
### Answer all the questions from this section

**Question 1.**

Choose the correct answers to the questions from the given options. (Do not copy the question. Write the correct answer only.) [10]

(i)  The ore of Aluminum is:
   **(a)** Calamine
   **(b)** Hematite
   **(c)** Magnetite
   **(d)** Cryolite
   **Answer.** (d) Cryolite

(ii)  Hydrogen chloride gas is not collected over water, as:
   **(a)** It is highly soluble in water.
   **(b)** It is less soluble in water.
   **(c)** It is lighter than air.
   **(d)** It is heavier than air.
   **Answer.** (a) It is highly soluble in water

(iii)  An aqueous Answer. of ammonia is:
   **(a)** Neutral
   **(b)** Acidic
   **(c)** Basic
   **(d)** Amphoteric
   **Answer.** (c) Basic

(iv)  The acid which is least volatile is:
   **(a)** Hydrochloric acid
   **(b)** Nitric acid

**(c)** Dilute sulphuric acid

**(d)** Concentrated sulphuric acid

**Answer.** (d) Concentrated sulphuric acid

(v) The gas formed, when calcium bisulphite reacts with dilute HNO:

**(a)** Sulphur trioxide

**(b)** Hydrogen

**(c)** Sulphur dioxide

**(d)** Hydrogen sulphide

**Answer.** (c) Sulphur Dioxide

(vi) The IUPAC name of formic acid:

**(a)** Propanoic acid

**(b)** Methanoic acid

**(c)** Ethanoie acid

**(d)** Butanoīe acid

**Answer.** (b) Methanoic acid

(vii) The metallic oxide when reacts with HCl forms salt and water:

**(a)** Carbon monoxide

**(b)** Nitrous oxide

**(c)** Ammonium hydroxide

**(d)** Sodium Oxide

**Answer.** (d) Sodium Oxide

(viii) Vanadium pentoxide is used as a catalyst in the preparation of:

**(a)** Nitrogen gas

**(b)** Nitrogen dioxide gas

**(c)** Sulphur trioxide gas

**(d)** Carbon dioxide gas

**Answer.** (c) Sulphur trioxide gas

(ix) The Catalyst used for the conversion of Ethene to Ethane:

**(a)** Iron

**(b)** Nickel

**(c)** Cobalt

**(d)** Molybdenum

**Answer.** (b) Nickel

(x) The substance which helps to lower the fusion point of the mixture in the Hall Heroult Process:

**(a)** Coke

**(b)** Concentrated sodium hydroxide

**(c)** Fluorspar

**(d)** Concentrated potassium hydroxide

**Answer.** (c) Fluorspar

### SECTION B

**(Attempt any three questions from this Section.)**

**Question 2.**

  (i)  Define: [2]

    **(a)** Isomerism

    **(b)** Ores

    **Answer:**

    **(a)** Compound having the same molecular formula, but different properties are known as isomers and this phenomenon are known as isomerism.

    **(b)** The naturally occurring minerals from which metals- can be extracted profitably and conveniently are called – ores.

  (ii)  Name the following: [2]

    **(a)** The property by which carbon links with itself to form a long chain.

    **(b)** The saturated hydrocarbons have a general formula $C_nH_{2n-2}$

    **Answer:**

    **(a)** Catenation

    **(b)** $C_nH_{2n+2} \rightarrow$ Alkane

  (iii)  Draw the structural diagram of: [3]

    **(a)** pentanal

    **(b)** propanol

    **(c)** 2-butene

    **Answer: (a)**

$$
\begin{array}{ccccccccc}
 & H & & H & & H & & H & & O \\
 & | & & | & & | & & | & & \| \\
H- & C & - & C & - & C & - & C & - & C-H \\
 & | & & | & & | & & | & & \\
 & H & & H & & H & & H & &
\end{array}
$$

    **(b)**

$$
\begin{array}{ccccccc}
 & H & & H & & OH \\
 & | & & | & & | \\
H- & C & - & C & - & C & -H \\
 & | & & | & & | \\
 & H & & H & & H
\end{array}
$$

(c)

$$H_3C-CH_2-\overset{\displaystyle H}{\underset{\displaystyle H}{C}}=\overset{\displaystyle H}{\underset{\displaystyle H}{C}}-CH_3$$

(iv) Complete and balance the following chemical equations: [3]

(a) $H_2C = CH_2 + Cl_2 \xrightarrow[\text{interstate}]{CCl_4}$

(b) $C_2H_6 + O_2$ [excess] $\rightarrow$

(c) $CH_4 + O_2$ [excess] $\rightarrow$

**Answer:**

(a)
$$\begin{array}{ccc} Cl & & Cl \\ | & & | \\ H_2C & - & CH_2 \end{array}$$

(d) $2C_2H_6\ 7O_2 \rightarrow 4CO_2 + 6H_2O$

(e) $CH_4 + 2O_2 \rightarrow CO_2 + 2H_2O$

## Question 3.

(i) State the following: [2]

(a) A compound formed when excess ammonia gas reacts with chlorine.

(b) A substance is added to water, to manufacture sulphuric acid in the Contact process.

**Answer:**

(a) $NH_4Cl$

(b) $SO_3$

(ii) Identify the gas **P** and **Q** in the reactions given below: [2]

(a) A compound reacts with an acid to form gas **P** which has no effect on acidified $K_3Cr_2O$ r
Answer. but turns lime water milky.

(b) A metallic nitrate reacts on heating and gives oxygen gas along with a coloured gas Q.

**Answer:**

(a) Metallic carbonate salt

(b) $Pb\ (NO_3)_2$

(iii) State the observation for the following: [3]

(a) Dry ammonia gas reacts with oxygen in the presence of a catalyst.

(b) Excess chlorine gas reacts with ammonia gas.

(c) Carbon reacts with hot concentrated nitric acid.

**Answer.**

(a) $4NH_3 + 5O_2 \xrightarrow[800°C]{Pt} 4NO + 6H_2O$

No further combines with oxygen to form reddish-brown acidic gas $NO_2$

$$2NO + O_2 \rightarrow \underset{\text{reddish brown gas}}{2NO_2}$$

(b) $NH_3 + \underset{(\text{ExCeNR})}{3Cl_2} \rightarrow 3HCl + NCl_3$

[Nitrogen trichloride
yellow liquid]

A yellow-colored liquid which is explosive in nature is obtained.

**(c)** $c + 4HNO_3 \longrightarrow \underset{\text{colourless acidic gas}}{CO_2} + \underset{\text{reddish brown acidic gas}}{4NO_2} + 2H_2O$

(iv) Write balanced equation for the following conversions: [3]
    **(a)** Carbon from cane sugar and concentrated sulphuric acid.
    **(b)** Ferric nitrate from ferric hydroxide and nitric acid.
    **(c)** Ammonium sulphate from ammonium hydroxide and sulphuric acid.

**Answer:**

**(a)** $C_{12}H_{22}O_{11} \xrightarrow{\text{cmc.}H_2SO_4} 12C + 11H_2O$
    Cane Sugar

**(b)** $Fe(OH)_3 + 3HNO_3 \longrightarrow Fe(NO_3)_2 + 3H_2O$

**(c)** $2NH_4OH + H_2SO_4 \rightarrow (NH_4)_2SO_4 + 2H_2O$

## Question 4.

(i) State the relevant reason for the following: [2]
    **(a)** Concentrated alkali is used for the concentration of bauxite ore.
    **(b)** Fused alumina is reduced to aluminium by electrolysis.

**Answer:**

**(a)** Bauxite ore is $Al_2O_3 \cdot 2H_2O$ which is a hydrated amphoteric metal oxide f reacts with cone NaOH forming a soluble salt $NaAlO_2$, and impurities like $Fe_2O_3$ and $Sio_2$ remains unaffected (Exists in solid form) & can be separated easily.

**(b)** $Al_2O_3$ is a- highly stable oxide and aluminium has- a strong affinity for oxygen.

(ii) State one use of the given alloys: [2]
    **(a)** Magnalium
    **(b)** Duralumin

**Answer:**

**(a)** Aircraft
**(b)** Ships

(iii) Complete the table given below which refers to the Laboratory preparation of Ammonia gas: [3]

| Laboratory preparation | Reactants used | Products formed | Drying agent | Method of collection |
| --- | --- | --- | --- | --- |
| Ammonia gas | (a) | Calcium chloride + water + ammonia | (b) | (c) |

**Answer.**
**(a)** Calcium hydroxide and ammonium chloride
**(b)** Quicklime
**(c)** Downward displacement of air

(iv)  Identify the terms for the following: **[3]**
    **(a)** The process used to purify Alumina by electrolytic reduction.
    **(b)** The experiment was used to demonstrate the high solubility of HCl gas.
    **(c)** The chemical property of sulphuric acid forms two types of salts with an alkali.
    **Answer:**
    **(a)** Electrolytic reduction
    **(b)** Fountain experiment
    **(c)** Dibasic nature of sulphuric acid

## Question 5.

(i)  Write the balanced chemical equation for the following: **[2]**
    **(a)** The action of heat on manganese dioxide and concentrated hydrochloric acid.
    **(b)** Zine reacts with dilute hydrochloric acid to form zine chloride.
    **Answer:**
    **(a)** $MnO_2 + \underset{4HCl}{\overset{conc.}{}} \longrightarrow MnCl_2 + 2H_2O + Cl_2 \uparrow$
    **(b)** $Zn + 2HCl \longrightarrow ZnCl_2 + H_2(g) \uparrow$

(ii)  Select the right answer from the brackets and complete the statements: **[2]**
In electrolysis of fused Alumina, the anode is made of (a) [gas carbon/ graphite] and the product formed at cathode is (b) [oxygen/aluminium].
**Answer: (a)** Graphite
       **(b)** Aluminium

(iii)  Give the IUPAC name for the following: **[3]**
**(a)**                                        **(c)**

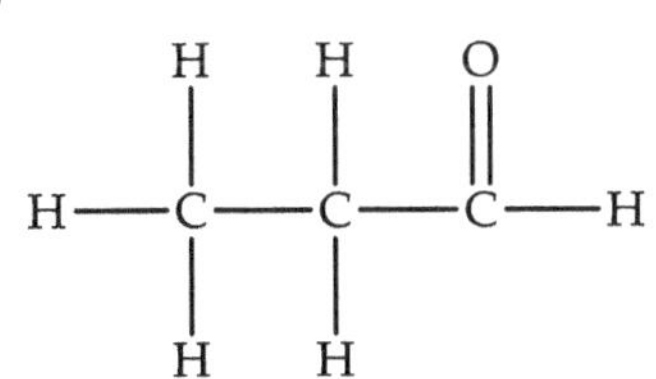

**(b)**

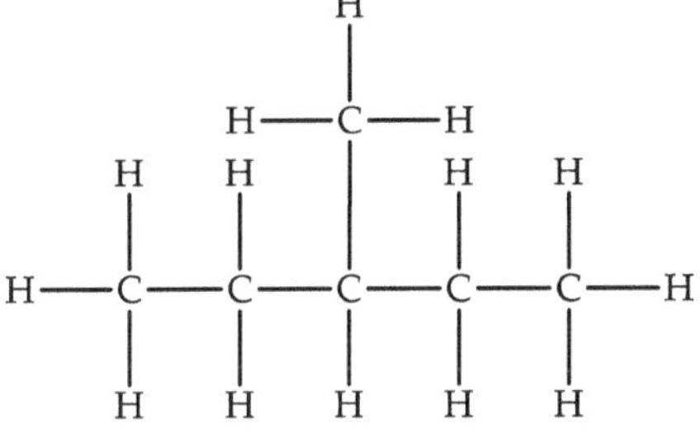

{139}

**Answer: (a)** Ethene

   **(b)** Propanal

   **(c)** 3- Methyl pentane

(iv) Study the diagram, which shows the Brown Ring Test and answer the questions given below: **[3]**

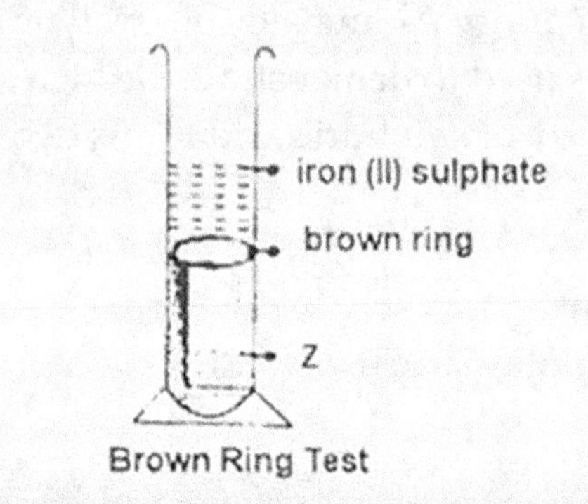



Brown Ring Test

**(a)** Which ion is determined by Brown Ring Test?

**(b)** Why is freshly prepared iron[II] sulphate used in the test?

**(c)** Name the substance Z.

**Answer:**

**(a)** Nitrate ion ($NO_3$)

**(b)** Because on standing ferrous sulphate is oxidized by atmospheric oxygen to ferric sulphate which will not give the test.

**(c)** Conc. $H_2SO_4$

## Question 6.

(i) Distinguish between the following as directed: **[2]**

   **(a)** Sodium sulphite Answer. and sodium sulphate Answer.. [using dilute $H_2SO_4$ ]

   **(b)** Lead salt Answer. and zinc salt Answer..

   [Using $NH_4OH$ Answer. in excess]

**Answer:**

**(a)** Sodium sulphatic Answer. reacts with dil. $H_2SO_4$, evolving $CO_2$ gas which turns lime water

milky white, while dil $H_2SO_4$ does not react with sodium sulphate Answer..

**(b)** $NH_4OH$ reacts with zine salt to give gelatinous white ppt. of $Zn(OH)_2$, which gets dissolved in excess of $NH_4OH$ som, while Lead salt on reacting with NH4OH sim. give chalky white ppt. of $Pb(OH)_2$, which reminding insoluble in excess of NH4 OH som.

(ii) Give one word for the following statements: **[2]**

   **(a)** The compounds of various metals found in nature with earthly impurities.

   **(b)** A homogeneous mixture of two or more metals of a metal and a non-metal in specific ratios.

**Answer:**

**(a)** Minerals

**(b)** Alloy

(iii) Identify the acid in each case: [3]

    **(a)** The acid is formed when Sulphur reacts with concentrated nitric acid.

    **(b)** An acid, which on adding to lead nitrate Answer. produces a white precipitate which is soluble on heating.

    **(c)** The acid formed when potassium nitrate reacts with the least volatile acid.

**Answer:**

**(a)** Sulphuric acid ($H_2SO_4$)

**(b)** Hydrochloric acid (dil HCl)

**(c)** Nitric acid

(iv) Match column A with column B: [3]

| Name (A) | The functional group (B) |
| --- | --- |
| 1. Aldehyde | **(a)** $-OH$ |
| 2. Carboxylic acids | **(b)** $-CHO$ |
| 3. Alcohol | **(c)** $-COOH$ |

**Answer:**

| Name (A) | The functional group (B) |
| --- | --- |
| 1. Aldehyde | **(b)** $-CHO$ |
| 2. Carboxylic acids | **(c)** $-COOH$ |
| 3. Alcohol | **(a)** $-OH$ |

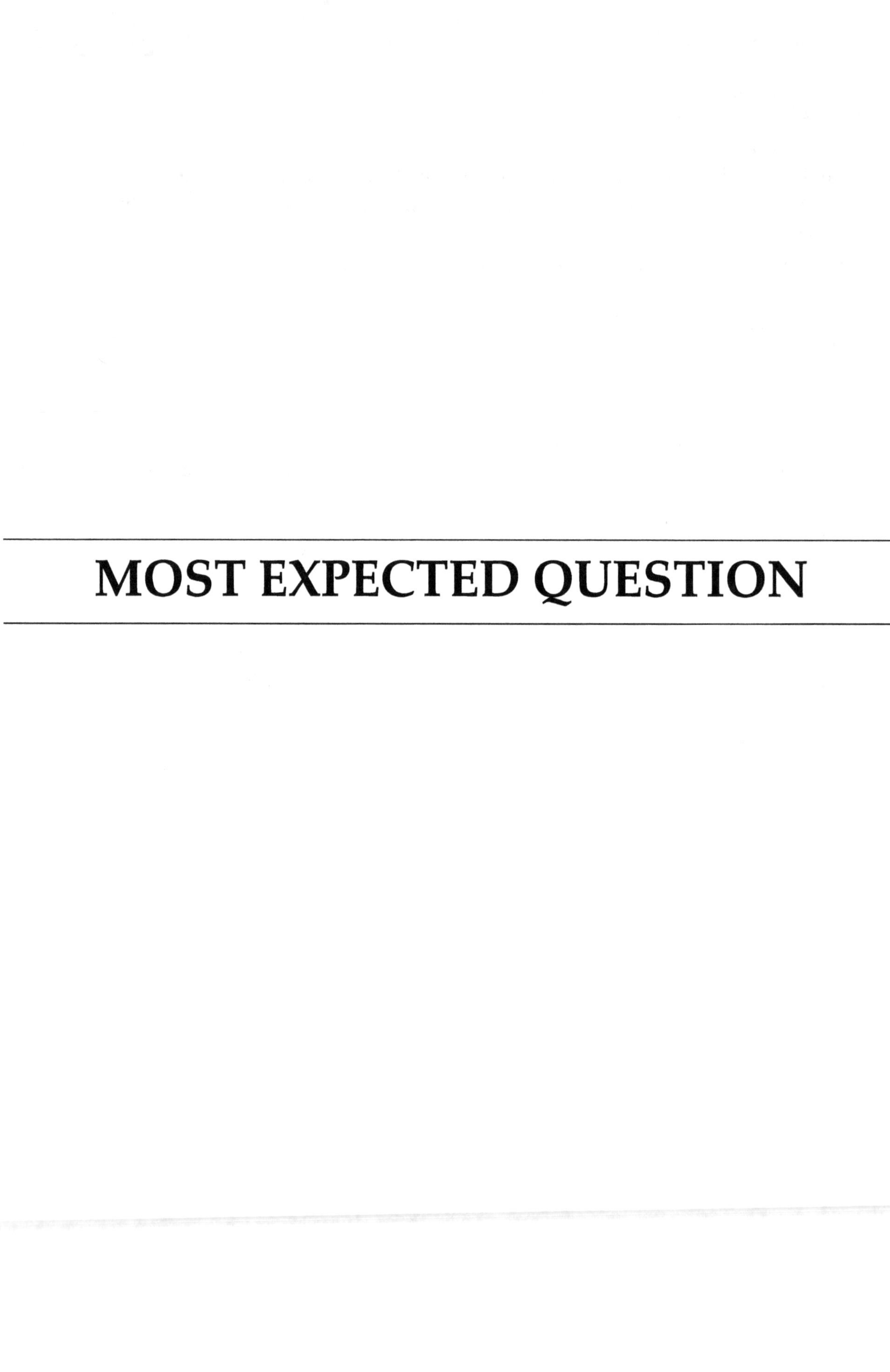

MOST EXPECTED QUESTION

**Maximum Marks: 80**

Time allowed: Two hours

Answers to this Paper must be written on the paper provided separately.

You will not be allowed to write during first 15 minutes.

This time is to be spent in reading the question paper.

The time given at the head of this Paper is the time allowed for writing the answers.

**(Section A is compulsory. Attempt any four questions from Section B.**

**The intended marks for questions or parts of questions are given in brackets [ ].**

## SECTION A

### Answer all the questions from this section

**Question : 1** [15]

Choose one correct answer to the question from the given option:

(i)  The chemical name of corundum is.

    **(a)** Iron Sulphide,

    **(b)** Zinc oxide.

    **(c)** Hydrated aluminium oxide.

    **(d)** Anhydrous aluminium oxide?

    **Answer.** (d) Anhydrous aluminium oxide


(ii)  An active metal which can not displace hydrogen from dilute acid.

    **(a)** Iron

    **(b)** Zinc.

    **(c)** Lead

    **(d)** Aluminium.

    **Answer.** (c) Lead


(iii) Liquor ammonia is.

    **(a)** $NH_3$ gas

    **(b)** Liquid $NH_3$

    **(c)** Aqueous Answer. of $NH_3$

    **(d)** Ammonia and alcohol mixture.

    **Answer.** (c) Aqueous Answer. of $NH_3$


(iv) Nitric acid oxidised sulphur in to:

    **(a)** $SO_2$

    **(b)** $H_2SO_4$

    **(c)** $NO_2$

**(d)** $H_2S$
**Answer.** (b) $H_2SO_4$

(v) Conc. $H_2SO_4$ Convert cane sugar to sugar charcoal, the property of $H_2SO_4$ Depicted is.
    **(a)** Typical acid
    **(b)** Oxidizing agent
    **(c)** Drying agent
    **(d)** Dehydrating agent
    **Answer.** (d) Dehydrating agent

(vi) The first organic compound synthesised in laboratory from inorganic compound:
    **(a)** $CH_4$
    **(b)** $C_2H_6$
    **(c)** $(NH_2)_2CO$
    **(d)** $C_2H_5OH$
    **Answer.** (c) $(NH_2)_2CO$

(vii) The number of electrons in a cation is:
    **(a)** Equal to atomic number.
    **(b)** Greater than atomic number.
    **(c)** Less than atomic number.
    **(d)** None.
    **Answer.** (c) Less than atomic number.

(viii) The elements belonging to period 2 of periodic table, which gains 3 electrons to complete its octet.
    **(a)** B
    **(b)** N
    **(c)** C
    **(d)** F
    **Answer.** (b) N

(ix) Which of the following compound is expected to be insoluble in water?
    **(a)** NaCl
    **(b)** HCl
    **(c)** $NH_3$
    **(d)** $CH_4$
    **Answer.** (d) $CH_4$

(x) At 25°C an acidic Answer. of relation holds good is:
    **(a)** $[H^+] = 1.0 \times 10^{-7} \text{ mol L}^{-1}$
    **(b)** $[H^+] > 1.0 \times 10^{-7} \text{ mol L}^{-1}$
    **(c)** $[H^+] < 1.0 \times 10^{-7} \text{ mol L}^{-1}$
    **(d)** $[H^+] = 1.0 \times 10^{-14} \text{ mol L}^{-1}$

**Answer.** (a) $[H^+] = 1.0 \times 10^{-7}$ mol $L^{-1}$

(xi) The electrolyte used during the purification of copper during electrorefining.
   (a) Aqueous Answer. of $ZnSO_4$ .
   (b) Aqueous Answer. of $CuSO_4$ .
   (c) Molten $ZnSO_4$
   (d) Molten $CuSO_4$
   **Answer.** (b) Aqueous Answer. of $CuSO_4$ .

(xii) The number of covalent bonds between the atoms of element having 6 valence shell electrons.
   (a) One
   (b) Two
   (c) Three
   (d) Four
   **Answer.** (b) Two

(xiii) Empirical formula of compound $H_3C - C \equiv C - CH_3$ .
   (a) $C_4H_6$
   (b) $C_2H_2$
   (c) $C_2H_3$
   (d) $C_2H_4$
   **Answer.** (c) $C_2H_3$

(xiv) Mass percentage of nitrogen in urea $NH_2CONH_2$ (N=14,O=16,C=12,H=1
   (a) 53.4
   (b) 46.6
   (c) 23.3
   (d) 40
   **Answer.** (b) 46.6

(xv) Under the same condition of temperature and pressure, gases reacts in a definite volume ratio. This is in accordance with:
   (a) Boyle's law
   (b) Charle's law
   (c) Avogadro's law
   (d) Gay-lussac's law
   **Answer.** (d) Gay-lussac's law

## Question : 2
(i) **(a)** Answer The following questions with reference to group 2[IIA]:                   [3]
      i   The nature of oxide.
      ii  The formula of chloride of the element with electronic configuration 2,8,2.

iii  Change in its ionization enthalpy.

**Answer.**

i  Basic

ii  $MgCl_2$

iii  Decrease down the group

**(b)** Answer The following questions with reference to modern periodic table:  [2]
  i  Most metallic element.

  ii  The elements in period 3 which doesn't from oxide.

**Answer.**

i  Cs

ii  Ar

(ii)  Select the most probable substance from A, B, C, D & E which need to be added to distinguish:[5]

| | |
|---|---|
| **(a)** Ammonium sulphate and ammonium chloride | i  Cone, hydrochloric acid |
| **(b)** Potassium sulphate and ammonium sulphate | ii  Ammonia gas |
| **(c)** Liquor ammonia and liquid ammonia | iii  Barium chloride |
| **(d)** Ammonia and sulphur dioxide gas | iv  Phenolphthalein |
| **(e)** Copper [II] oxide and copper [II] chloride | v  Sodium hydroxide |

**Answer.**

**(a)** iii

**(b)** v

**(c)** iv

**(d)** i

**(e)** ii

(iii)  Complete the following by choosing the correct answers from the bracket:  [5]
  **(a)** To distinguish soluble salt of copper and lead ___________ can be used.[NaOH/NH$_4$OH]

  **(b)** The hydroxide which is insoluble in excess of NaOH is ________ [Zn(OH)/Fe(OH)$_3$]

  **(c)** Metals have ________ ionization potential. [High/Low ]

  **(d)** Group 18 elements have valance electron in valance shell. [ 4/8 ]

  **(e)** Group 2 elements are called ___________ metal. [ Alkali/ alkaline earth]

**Answer.**

(a) $[NH_4OH]$

(b) $[Fe(OH)_3]$

(c) Low

(d) 8

(e) Alkaline earth

(iv) **(a)** Draw the structural formula for the following: **[3]**

   i  N-butyl alcohol

   ii  Neo pentane

   iii  2-butyne

**Answer.**

i. 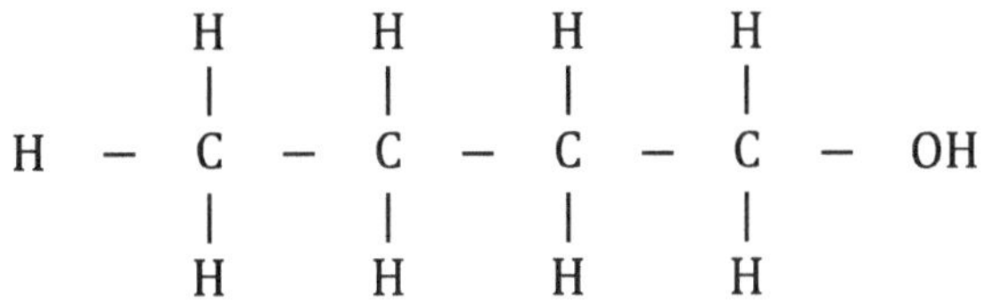
$$H-\overset{\displaystyle H}{\underset{\displaystyle H}{C}}-\overset{\displaystyle H}{\underset{\displaystyle H}{C}}-\overset{\displaystyle H}{\underset{\displaystyle H}{C}}-\overset{\displaystyle H}{\underset{\displaystyle H}{C}}-OH$$

ii. 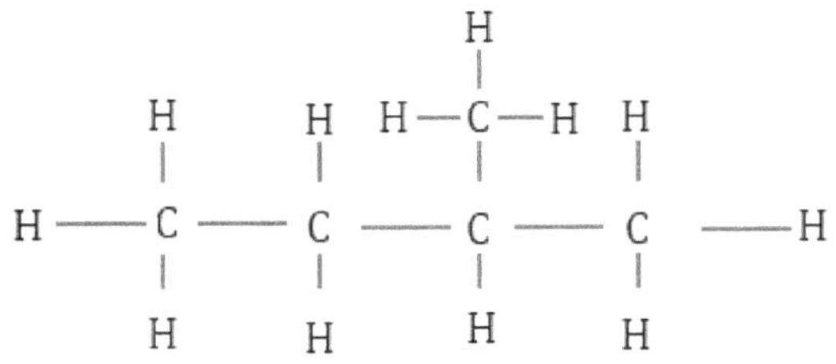
$$H-\overset{\displaystyle H}{\underset{\displaystyle H}{C}}-\overset{\displaystyle H}{\underset{\displaystyle H}{C}}-\overset{\displaystyle H-\overset{H}{\underset{}{C}}-H}{\underset{\displaystyle H}{C}}-\overset{\displaystyle H}{\underset{\displaystyle H}{C}}-H$$

iii. 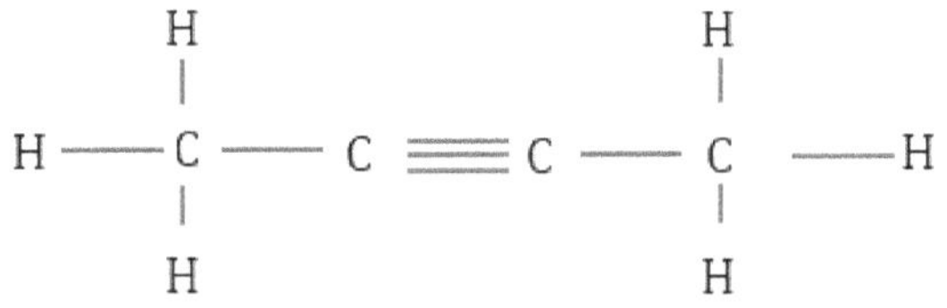
$$H-\overset{\displaystyle H}{\underset{\displaystyle H}{C}}-C\equiv C-\overset{\displaystyle H}{\underset{\displaystyle H}{C}}-H$$

**(d)** Name the following organic compounds in IUPAC common names: **[2]**

i  $(H_3C)(CH_3)C=C(H)(H)$

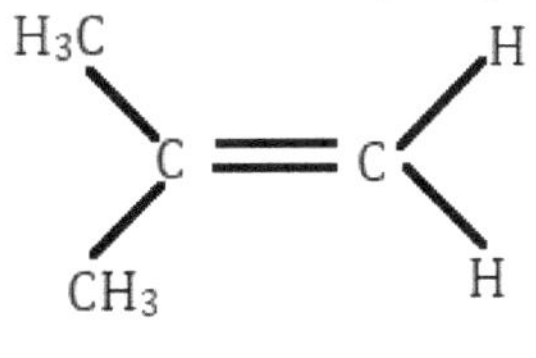

ii  $C_2Cl_6$

**Answer.**

   i  2-Methyl propene

   ii  Hexachloroethane

(v) Identify the following substances: **[5]**

   **(a)** An acidic gas which gives dense white fumes with $NH_3$.

(b) An alkane which can also be called a green house gas.

(c) A solid which when kept in the open, forms a Answer. after sometime.

(d) An alloy used in electrical fittings.

(e) A metal which gives hydrogen gas on reacting with both dilute acid and alkali.

**Answer.**

(a) $HCl$

(b) $CH_4$

(c) $FeCl_3$

(d) Brass

(e) $Al$

## SECTION-B
### (Attempt any four questions.)

**Question : 3**

(i) What is the common feature of the electronic configurations of the elements at the end of period 2 and period 3 ? [2]

(ii) Write the balanced equation for the following conversions: [2]

(a) Aluminium to Aluminate.

(b) Alumina to brown metal.

(iii) Refer to the flow chart diagram below and give balanced equations with conditions, if any, for the following conversions A to C. [3]

(a) $NH_3 + \underset{A}{\underline{\hspace{2cm}}} \rightarrow NH_4Cl$

(b) $AgNO_3 + A \rightarrow \underset{B}{\underline{\hspace{2cm}}} + HNO_3$

(c) $B + NH_4OH \rightarrow \underset{C}{\underline{\hspace{2cm}}} + 2H_2O$

(iv) Fill in the blanks selecting the appropriate word from the given choices. [3]

(a) The bond between two elements in group 17(VII A) of the periodic table is likely to be ______. [Ionic/ Covalent]

(b) In the reaction of $Cl_2 + 2KI \rightarrow 2KCl + I_2$ the conversion of 2I to $I_2$ is deemed as ___________. [Oxidation/ Reduction]

(c) NaCl an electrovalent compound is formed as a result of the transfer of _______ valence electrons. [One/ Two]

**Question : 4**

(i) Give reason: [2]

(a) An aqueous Answer. of $NH_3$ acts as a weak base.

(b) Ammonium salts are formed when ammonia reacts with dilute acids in the gaseous or aqueous medium.

(ii) Percentage of nitrogen in urea $(NH_2CONH_2)$ atomic masses [N=14 , C=12, O=16,H=1]    **[2]**

(iii) Answer the following questions pertaining to the brown ring test for nitric acid.    **[3]**

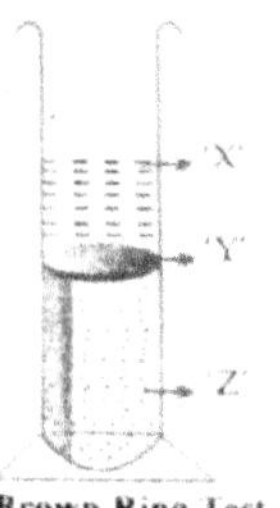



    **(a)** Name the chemical constituent of the brown ring ' Y

    **(b)** Which of the two Answer.s - iron [II] sulphate or conc sulphuric acid? do 'X ' and 'Z ' represent.

    **(c)** State why the unstable brown ring decomposes completely on disturbing the test tube.

(iv) Choose the answer from the given option:    **[3]**

    **(a)** $CH_3COOH,/Ca(OH)_2/Hcl$

      i    Monobasic acid

      ii    Weak base

      iii   Strong acid in aqueous Answer..

## Question : 5

(i) Name the following    **[2]**

    **(a)** Main components of duralumin

    **(b)** Name of an allotrope of a non-metal that allows electricity to pass through it.

(ii) Identify the oxidation/reduction in given equations    **[2]**

    **(a)** $Pb^{2+} + 2e^- \rightarrow Pb$

    **(b)** $Zn \rightarrow Zn^{2+} + 2e^-$

(iii) **(a)** Why the anode has to be replaced from time to time in electrolytic reduction of alumina.    **[3]**

    **(b)** Aluminium is a more active metal than iron but suffers less corrosion.

    **(c)** Name the alloy of Zn used in Naval ships.

(iv) **(a)** A compound has the following percentage composition by mass($C = 54.55\%, H = 9.09\%$, $O = 36.26\%$ ). Its vapour density is 44. Find the empirical and molecular formula of a compound. ($H = 1, C = 12, O = 16$)    **[2]**

    **(b)** Give the relation between empirical and molecular formulas.    **[1]**

## Question : 6

(i) How will you prove that Hydrogen acid contains:    **[2]**

    **(a)** Hydrogen

**(b)** Chlorine

Write the equation for the reaction

(ii) Define: [2]

    **(a)** Electronegativity.

    **(b)** Basic salt.

(iii) Give reaction only [3]

    **(a)** The action of heat on conc. $HNO_3$

    **(b)** The action of heat on lead nitrate.

    **(c)** The action of conc. $HNO_3$ on Cu metal

(iv) The equation $4NH_3 + 5O_2 \rightarrow 4NO + 6H_2O$, represents the catalytic oxidation of ammonia. If 100 cm³ of ammonia is used. Calculate the volume of oxygen required to oxidise ammonia completely & amount of NO formed. [3]

## Question : 7

(i) Correct the following statement: [2]

    **(a)** $HNO_3$ is a strong reducing agent.

    **(b)** Nitric acid remains colourless even when exposed to light.

(ii) Copy and complete the following table relating to an important industrial process and its final output. [2]

| Name of process | Inputs | Catalyst | Equation for catalyzed reaction output |
|---|---|---|---|
| Contact process | Sulphur dioxide + oxygen | | |

(iii) Identify the acid in each case. [3]

    **(a)** A dilute mineral acid which forms white ppt when treated with barium chloride Answer..

    **(b)** Which property of sulphuric acid accounts for its use as a dehydrating agent?

    **(c)** Conc. $H_2SO_4$ is both an oxidising agent and a non-volatile acid. Write one equation each to illustrate the above-mentioned properties of sulphuric acid.

(iv) Define: [3]

    **(a)** Chain isomerism

    **(b)** Position isomerism

    **(c)** Functional isomerism

## Question : 8

(i) **(a)** Select the correct answer [2]

    The aqueous Answer. of the compound which contains both ions and molecules is

    **(d)** $H_2SO_4$

**(e)** HCl

**(f)** $HNO_3$

**(g)** $CH_3COOH$

**(b)** Correct the following statement -

Lead bromide conducts electricity.

(ii) What is observed when hot concentrated caustic soda Answer. is added to [2]

**(a)** Zinc and

**(b)** Aluminium ?

Write balanced equations.

(iii) Complete the following equations. [3]

**(a)** $CH_4 \xrightarrow[-HCl]{Cl_2} A \xrightarrow[-HCl]{Cl_2} B \xrightarrow[-HCl]{Cl_2} C$

**(b)** $C_2H_2 \xrightarrow{H_2} A \xrightarrow{H_2} B \xrightarrow[-HBr]{Br_2} C$

**(iv)** Draw the 3 isomers of pentane and give their IUPAC names. [3]

**Maximum Marks: 80**
Time allowed: Two hours
Answers to this Paper must be written on the paper provided separately.
You will not be allowed to write during first 15 minutes.
This time is to be spent in reading the question paper.
The time given at the head of this Paper is the time allowed for writing the answers.

**(Section A is compulsory. Attempt any four questions from Section B.**
**The intended marks for questions or parts of questions are given in brackets [ ].**

## SECTION A
### Answer all the questions from this section

**Question : 1** [15]

Choose one correct answer to the question from the given option:

(i) If elements M belongs to period 3 and group II A then it will have.
   **(a)** 3 Shells and 2 valence electron.
   **(b)** 2 Shells and 2 valence electron.
   **(c)** 3 Shells and 3 valence electron.
   **(d)** 2 Shells and 3 valence electron.
   **Answer.** (a) 3 Shells and 2 valence electron.

(ii) Metal salt which can be used to distinguish between reagents NaOH and $NH_4OH$ .
   **(a)** Ferrous salt
   **(b)** Copper salt
   **(c)** Zinc salt
   **(d)** Ferric salt
   **Answer.** (b) Copper salt

(iii) The number of electron lost or gained by an atom refers to.
   **(a)** Donation.
   **(b)** Acceptance.
   **(c)** Covalency.
   **(d)** Electro valency.
   **Answer.** (d) Electro valency.

(iv) An acid which is not oxoacid.
   **(a)** $HNO_3$
   **(b)** $H_2SO_4$
   **(c)** HCl

**(d)** $HClO_4$
**Answer.** (c) $HCl$

(v) The empirical formula of butane is
    **(a)** $C_4H_8$
    **(b)** $C_4H_{10}$
    **(c)** $C_2H_5$
    **(d)** $CH_{2.5}$
    **Answer.** (c) $C_2H_5$

(vi) Stainless steel does not contain.
    **(a)** Cr
    **(b)** Al
    **(c)** C
    **(d)** Ni
    **Answer.** (b) Ni

(vii) The aim of fountain experiment is to prove that.
    **(a)** Gas is lighter than air.
    **(b)** Gas is heavier than air.
    **(c)** Gas is acidic or basic in nature
    **(d)** Gas is highly soluble in water.
    **Answer.** (d) Gas is highly soluble in water.

(viii) Nitrogen gas can be obtained by oxidation of
    **(a)** NO
    **(b)** $NH_3$
    **(c)** HCl
    **(d)** $H_2O$
    **Answer. (b)** $NH_3$

(ix) Dilute sulphuric acid will produce a white ppt when added to a Answer. of:
    **(a)** Copper nitrate
    **(b)** Lead nitrate
    **(c)** Ferric chloride
    **(d)** Potassium sulphate
    **Answer.** (d) Potassium sulphate

(x) The functional group present in acid is:

    **(a)** $-\overset{O}{\overset{||}{C}}-H$

$$
\textbf{(b)} \quad
\begin{array}{c}
\text{O} \\
\| \\
-\text{C} - \text{OH}
\end{array}
$$

$$
\textbf{(c)} \quad
\begin{array}{c}
\text{O} \\
\| \\
-\text{C} -
\end{array}
$$

$$
\textbf{(d)} \quad
\begin{array}{c}
\text{O} \\
\| \\
-\text{C} - \text{O} -
\end{array}
$$

**Answer.** (b)
$$
\begin{array}{c}
\text{O} \\
\| \\
-\text{C} - \text{OH}
\end{array}
$$

(xi) Vapor density and molecular mass of a compound are related to each other by:

(a) Molecular mass $=\dfrac{\text{V.D.}}{2}$

(b) Molecular mass $=2 \times$ V. D.

(c) Molecular mass $=$ V. D.

(d) Molecular mass $=\dfrac{\text{V.D.}}{5}$

**Answer.** (b) Molecular mass $=2 \times$ V. D.

(xii) The correct IUPAC name of oxalic acid is:

(a) Ethanoic acid

(b) Ethane dioic acid

(c) Methanolic acid

(d) Propanoic acid

**Answer.** (b) Ethane dioic acid

(xiii) A non -metallic allotrope which can conduct current:

(a) Red phosphorus

(b) White phosphorus

(c) Diamond

(d) Graphite

**Answer.** (d) Graphite

(xiv) The only gas which can evolve from cathode during electrolysis:

(a) $Br_2$

(b) $Cr_2$

(c) $O_2$

(d) $H_2$

**Answer.** (d) $H_2$

(xv) The type of bond present between the atoms of elements having atomic number 9.

(a) Non-polar covalent bond

**(b)** Polar covalent

**(c)** Co-ordinate covalent bond

**(d)** Ionic bond

**Answer.** (b) Non-polar covalent bond

## Question : 2

(i) **(a)** Which is greater in size?  [3]

  i  An atom or a cation

  ii  An atom or an anion

  iii  $Fe^{2+}$ or $Fe^{3+}$

**Answer.**

  i. Atom

  ii. Anion

  iii. $F^{2+}$

**(b)** Which has higher E.A., Fluorine or Neon.  [1]

**Answer.** Fluorine

**(c)** Which has maximum metallic character Na, Li or K.  [1]

**Answer.** K

(ii) Match the following in column A with the correc answer from the choices given in column B :  [5]

| Column A | Column B |
|---|---|
| **(a)** Ammonium hydroxide soln. | i.  Contains only ions |
| **(b)** Dilute hydrochloric acid | ii.  Contains only molecules |
| **(c)** Carbon tetrachloride | iii.  Contact process |
| **(d)** Manufacture of Nitric acid | iv.  Contains ions and molecules |
| **(e)** Manufacture of Sulphuric acid | v.  Ostwald process |

**Answer.**

**(a)** iv

**(b)** i

**(c)** ii

**(d)** v

**(e)** iii

(iii) Complete the blanks **(a)** to **(e)** in the passage given, using the following words.  [5]
[Ammonium, reddish brown, hydroxyl, nitrogen dioxide, ammonia, dirty green, alkaline, acidic].

In the presence of a catalyst nitrogen and hydrogen combine to give **(a)** ............ gas. When the same gas is passed through water it forms a Answer.. which will be **(b)** ............... in nature, and will contain the ions **(c)** ............... and **(d)** ............. A **(e)** ............... coloured precipitate of iron [II] hydroxide is formed when the above Answer. is added to iron [II] sulphate Answer..

**Answer.**

**(a)** $NH_3$

**(b)** Alkaline

**(c)** Ions

**(d)** Molecule

**(e)** Dirty green

(iv) Identify the following: [5]

    **(a)** An alkaline gas which produced dense white fumes when reacts with HCl gas.

    **(b)** General formula for carboxylic acid.

    **(c)** Ions formed by loss of electrons.

    **(d)** The acid which is prepared by catalytic oxidation of ammonia.

    **(e)** Acidity of sodium hydroxide.

**Answer.**

**(a)** $NH_3$

**(b)**
$$R - \overset{\overset{\displaystyle O}{\|}}{C} - OH$$

**(c)** Cations

**(d)** $HNO_3$

**(e)** One

(v) **(a)** Draw the structural formula for the following: [3]

    i    Sodium acetate

    ii   Chloroform

    iii  1,2,Di-Bromo ethane

**Answer.**

i.
$$H - \overset{\overset{\displaystyle H}{|}}{\underset{\underset{\displaystyle H}{|}}{C}} - \overset{\overset{\displaystyle O}{\|}}{C} - ONa$$

ii.
$$H - \overset{\overset{\displaystyle Cl}{|}}{\underset{\underset{\displaystyle Cl}{|}}{C}} - Cl$$

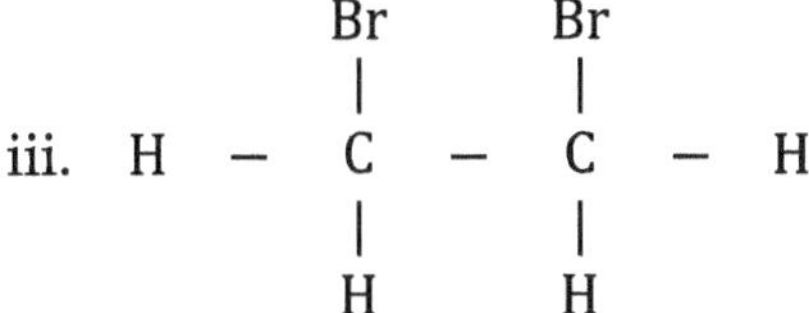

(b) Explain the following:                                                      [2]
   i   Catenation
   ii  Tetravalency of carbon

**Answer.**
   i.   Self interlinking property
   ii.  Valency of carbon is 4.


**SECTION -B**
**(Attempt any four questions.)**

## Question : 3

(i)  (a) Electrolysis of molten lead bromide is considered as a redox Reaction.   [1]

   (b) The blue color Answer. of aq. $CuSO_4$ does not change when it electrolysed using Cu electrode.                                                                          [1]

(ii) Give reason for the following                                              [2]

   (a) Fumes are seen evolving out when a bottle of hydrochloric acid is opened.

   (b) Liquified hydrogen chloride does not conduct an electric current.

(iii) (a) Name the elements which has the highest electron affinity.            [3]

   (b) Name the elements which has the highest electronegativity.

   (c) Name the elements which may be placed on group 1 but is not a metal.

(iv) (a) How many atoms of element of group 17 will combine with one atom of element group 14.

[1]

   (b) Compare the properties of covalent 4 electrovalent compound on the following points.   [2]
      i   Solubility
      ii  Structure


## Question : 4

(i)  Nitrogen reacts with hydrogen to give ammonia calculate the volumn of the ammonia gas formed when nitrogen reacts 6 liters of Hydrogen.                                  [2]

(ii) Give reason for the following:                                             [2]

   (a) Sulphuric Acid from two types of salt with an alkali.

   (b) Barium nitride Answer. can be used to distinguish between dil. $H_2SO_4$ and dilute $HNO_3$.

(iii) Answer the following related to the Ostwald process.                      [3]

{157}

(a) Chamber where Nitric acid is cooled.

(b) Chamber where Nitrogen dioxide gets oxidized to Nitric acid.

(c) Principles which governs the Ostwald's process.

(iv) A metal 'X' used to make calorimeters reacts with concentrated nitric acid to form a soluble salt Y. When few drops of ammonium hydroxide are added pale blue precipitates 'Z' are obtained. These precipitates dissolve in excess of ammonium hydroxide to form deep blue Answer. 'A'. Identify the metal X and give all the chemical equations.

[3]

## Question : 5

(i) Complete and balance the equations                                          [2]

(a) $Pb + \underset{\text{excess}}{KOH} \rightarrow$

(b) $Zn(OH)_2 + \underset{\text{excess}}{NaOH} \rightarrow$

(ii) Name the compounds on following observations:                              [2]

(a) Chalky white precipitate with NaOH

(b) No precipitate with $NH_4OH$

(iii) Explain. Why?                                                             [3]

(a) Cu, though a good conductor of electricity is a non-electrolyte.

(b) Solid sodium chloride doesn't allow electricity to pass through.

(c) Sugar Answer. is nonelectrolyte.

(iv) (a) Why aluminium utensils should not be cleaned with powders containing alkalis?   [3]

(b) What is red mud, how it is removed?

(c) Electrolytic reduction is done to obtain aluminum?

## Question : 6

(i) Define:                                                                     [2]

(a) Acid salt

(b) Metallic character

(ii) Acetylene burn in air according to the reaction.                           [2]

$$2C_2H_2 + 5O_2 \rightarrow 4CO_2 + 2H_2O$$

At 100°C calculate the volumn of air required to completely burn 500 c.c. of acetylene.

(iii) (a) Why is hydrogen kept in the metal activity series?                     [3]

(b) Name an ore of Zn.

(c) On what factors does purification of metals depends

(iv) Study the flow chart and give. Balanced equation with condition for the conversion A B and C.

[3]

$$\text{NaCl} \xrightarrow{A} \text{HCl} \xrightarrow{B} \text{ZnCl}_2$$
$$\downarrow C$$
$$\text{MnCl}_2$$

## Question : 7

(i) Calculate the percentage of sodium in sodium aluminium fluoride($Na_3AlF_6$). [2]

    [ $F = 19, Al = 27, Na = 23$]

(ii) Identify the functional group in the following organic compounds. [2]

    **(a)** HCOOH

    **(b)** $C_3H_7OH$

(iii) Define electroplating? [3]

    & state two important reason for electroplating.

(iv) **(a)** what do you understand by pH scale? [1]

    **(b)** Complete the following chart: [2]

$$cold, dil \; \xrightarrow{NaOH} A+B$$
$$HNo_3 \qquad \downarrow Heat$$
$$Gas^+$$

## Question : 8

(i) Give laboratory preparation of the following organic compound. [2]

    **(a)** Ethane

    **(b)** Acetylene

(ii) Identify A,B,C and D

$$CH_3I + 2[H] \rightarrow [A] \xrightarrow{Cl_2} [B]$$
$$\downarrow O_2$$
$$[C] + [D]$$

[2]

(iii) Give reason: [3]

    **(a)** During electrolytic reaction who the always deposits at the cathode?

    **(b)** During electrolytic reaction oxidation reaction occurs of which electrode ss?

    **(c)** The metal to be plated on the article is always made of anode and it has to be replaced periodically?

(iv) Demonstrate an experiment to show HCl is heavies than air? With diagram. [3]